The Search For Quality Love Relationships

Love Is Not A Game

(But You Should Know the Odds)

Randy Hurlburt
In collaboration with Harold Bessell, Ph. D.

Personhood Press

Copyright © 2004, Randy Hurlburt

All Rights Reserved.
Except for brief quotations in published book reviews, no portion of this book may be reproduced, transmitted, displayed, exhibited or otherwise used in any form or by any media or means, whether now known or hereafter invented, including but not limited to reproduction by means of photocopying or information storage and retrieval systems of any kind, without prior written permission from the author. For information, and to request permission for any contemplated use, please contact Randy Hurlburt, 5519 Clairemont Mesa Blvd. #140, San Diego, CA 92117, or visit www.loveisnotagame.com.

Printed in United States of America

For information address:
Personhood Press
"Books for ALL that you are!"
Post Office Box 1185
Torrance, California 90505
800.662.9662
email: personhoodpress@att.net
http://www.personhoodpress.com

Love Is Not A Game (But You Should Know the Odds)
by Randy Hurlburt

ISBN 1-932181-13-X

cover & illustrations by: www.reesecreative.com
interior design & layout by: www.madhof.com

Grateful acknowledgement is made for permission to reprint excerpts from THE LOVE TEST by Harold Bessell, Ph.D. Copyright 1984 by Harold Bessell, Ph.D. Used with the express permission of the estate of Harold Bessell.

Grateful acknowledgement is made for excerpts reprinted with the permission of the Simon & Schuster Adult Publishing Group from MY SECRET GARDEN, by Nancy Friday. Copyright © 1973 by Nancy Friday.

Grateful acknowledgement is made for permission to reprint excerpts from MEN IN LOVE by Nancy Friday, copyright © 1980 by Nancy Friday. Used by permission of Dell Publishing, a division of Random House, Inc.

Grateful acknowledgement is made for permission to reprint excerpts from NEUROSIS AND HUMAN GROWTH: The Struggle Toward Self-Realization by Karen Horney. Copyright 1950 by W. W. Norton & Company, Inc., renewed © 1978 by Renate Patterson, Brigitte Swarzenski, and Marianne VonEckardt. Used by permission of W. W. Norton & Company, Inc.

Grateful acknowledgement is made for permission to reprint submitted excerpts from throughout SOUL MATES by THOMAS MOORE. Copyright © 1994 by Thomas Moore. Reprinted by permission of HarperCollins Publishers, Inc.

Grateful acknowledgement is made for permission to reprint excerpts from THE TEACHINGS OF DON JUAN: A YAQUI WAY OF KNOWLEDGE, 30TH ANNIVERSARY EDITION, by Carlos Casteneda. Copyright © 1968 Regents of the University of California, © renewed 1996 Carlos Casteneda.

Grateful acknowledgement is made for excerpts reprinted with the permission of the Simon & Schuster Adult Publishing Group from THE ROAD LESS TRAVELED, by M. Scott Peck, M. D. Copyright © 1978 by M. Scott Peck, M. D.

Grateful acknowledgement is made for excerpts reprinted from THE POWER OF SEXUAL SURRENDER by Marie N. Robinson, copyright © 1959 by Marie N. Robinson. Used by permission of Doubleday, a division of Random House, Inc.

Grateful acknowledgement is made for permission to reprint lyrics from XANADU, Words and Music by Jeff Lynne, © 1980 EMI BLACKWOOD MUSIC INC. All Rights Reserved. International Copyright Secured. Used by Permission.

Grateful acknowledgement is made for permission to reprint lyrics from SOUTHERN CROSS, Words and Music by Michael Curtis, Richard Curtis and Stephen Stills, Copyright © 1974 (Renewed) Three Wise Boys Music LLC (BMI) and Gold Hill Music, Inc. (ASCAP). International Copyright Secured. All Rights Reserved. Reprinted by Permission.

Grateful acknowledgement is made for permission to reprint lyrics from SOUTHERN CROSS, Copyright 1982 Gold Hill Music and Three Wise Boys Music LLC. All rights on behalf of Gold Hill Music administered by Sony ATV Music Publishing 8 Music Square West, Nashville, TN 37203. All rights reserved. Used by Permission.

In Memoriam

Harold Bessell, Ph. D.
Husband, Father, Friend, Therapist, Author

The world is a better place
because of his creative mind.

The Good are attracted by Men's perceptions,
And think not for themselves;
Till Experience teaches them to catch
And to cage the Fairies & Elves

And then the Knave begins to snarl
And the Hypocrite to howl;
And all his good Friends show their private ends,
And the Eagle is known from the Owl.

William Blake

LOVE IS NOT A GAME
Table of Contents

Acknowledgements
Prequel
Prologue
Introduction

Secret 1 — Power and Magic 1
    (Romantic Chemistry)
    The Story of Mike and Lori
    What is Romantic Chemistry?
    Chemistry is Permanent
    Chemistry is Power
    Chemistry is Connection
    Chemistry is Measurable
    Chemistry Comes in Degrees
    Chemistry is Usually Unbalanced
    Thresholds of Romantic Chemistry
    Introducing the Love Dice
    Soulmates, Magic, and the Violin
    The Story of Tom and Mary
    Summary
    Assignment

Secret 2 — Gyro Stabilization 23
    (Emotional Maturity)
    What is Emotional Maturity and Why is it Important?
    Maturity is Stability
    Maturity is Measurable
    Maturity Comes in Degrees
    Maturity Can Increase (But Often Does Not)
    Maturity is Usually Unbalanced
    Maturity Thresholds
    The Story of Rick and Jackie

The Story of Dan and Barbara
Summary: Definition of "Quality Love Relationship"
Assignment

Secret 3 — Kissing Frogs 47
(Why Is It So Hard to Find a Lover?)
Reality, Probability, and the Love Dice
Love Types
The Story of Nate and Shari
The Story of Bruce and Karen
Summary
Assignment

Secret 4 — The Spaceship 75
(All Systems Go)
The Spaceship Model
Another Look at some Love Types
Summary: A Total System
Assignment

Secret 5 — Diamonds Take a Long Time to Grow 83
(Can People Change?)
The Story of Barry and Linda
Maturity Growth Rates
The Story of Mario and Elise
The Story of Bob and Janice
The Therapy Lover
The False Hope
Improving Your Odds
Compromises
Summary
Assignment

Secret 6 — Sex Is Like Water 115
(Emotional Closeness Is Like Food)
The Complexity of Sex
The Purpose of Sex
Sex in a Soulmate Relationship
Sex in Other Relationships
Deprivation in General
The War Between the Sexes
Deprivation in Women
The Story of Charlotte
The Story of April
Deprivation in Men
The Story of Jerry
The Story of Troy
The Sahara Desert
Solutions to Sexual and Emotional Deprivation
The Secret of Sexual Surrender
The Story of Steve and Rachel
Summary
Assignment

Secret 7 — Enjoy Sweet Distractions 173
(The Safety Net)
The Safety Net
Diversified Investments
The Story of Trevor and Melanie
The Story of Fred and Margie
Sources of Distractions
Summary
Assignment

Secret 8 — Look for the Rainbow of Values 195
(Friendship Plus)
Possible Values

The Story of Chad and Katie
Perfect Friends
A New Model for Dating
Summary
Assignment

Secret 9 — Without Fear There Would Be No Courage 215
(Fear Means It's Real)
Stories of Fear
Mike and Lori Revisited
Rick and Jackie Revisited
Nate and Shari Revisited
Bruce and Karen Revisited
Barry and Linda Revisited
Mario and Elise Revisited
Steve and Rachel Revisited
Other Fears
The Story of Pete and Inga
Summary
Assignment

Secret 10 — If You're Trying to Relax, Don't Ask Questions 239
(Let It Be)
Summary
Assignment

Secret 11 — Discover the True Meaning of Fantasies 247
(Genuine Acceptance)
Making Love Fun
Why are sexual fantasies important?
Where do sexual fantasies come from?
Why is it so hard to accept sexual fantasies?
What happens if we don't accept sexual fantasies?
Can sexual fantasies hurt you?

How well can different types of relationships accept sexual fantasies?
Can fantasies clash?
Are fantasies the triumph of love over rage?
Summary
Assignment

Secret 12 — Trust the River 269
(Spirituality)
Sex and Spirituality
The Spiritually Advanced Person
Stability
Freedom
Flexibility
Forgiveness
The Story of Jason and Keli
The Story of Ted and Paula
Faith
Summary
Assignment

Summary and Checklist
Appendix 1—Comparison Charts:
        Chemistry, Infatuation, Sex and Emotional Maturity
Appendix 2—Romantic Attraction Questionnaire
Appendix 3—Emotional Maturity Rating Form
Appendix 4—Sexually Transmitted Disease Information
Appendix 5—Sexual Fantasy Stories
References

An Important Caution to the Reader

The contents of this book represent the opinion and experience of the author and are not intended to give medical, legal, financial or other professional advice to the reader or to take the place of consultation with an attorney, psychologist, physician or other qualified professional advisor, counselor or practitioner. Readers are strongly cautioned to use their own judgment and discretion in assessing the risks and making the decision whether or not to use any of the advice, information or other contents of this book, including the "Assignments" and "Solutions" that are presented herein. If any doubt exists, readers should consult an appropriate professional.

This book is sold without warranties or guarantees of any kind, express or implied, and the author and publisher disclaim any responsibility or liability for any loss, damage or other consequences resulting from any use of this book, or the information, advice or other contents of this book.

The stories set forth in this book, while based on fact, have been modified so as not to reveal the identity of any real person. Any resemblance between persons depicted in this book and real persons, living or dead, is strictly coincidental.

Acknowledgments

*Once meek and in a perilous path
The just man kept his course
Along the vale of death.
Till the villain left the paths of ease
To walk in perilous paths, and drive
The just man into barren climes.
Now the sleeping serpent walks
In mild humility,
And the just man rages in the wilds
Where lions roam.*
William Blake

To my children, Mike and Christy: I am writing this book for you. I have enjoyed immensely our time together with soccer teams, Indian Guides, Indian Princesses, walks, talks, dinners, and family gatherings. But the enduring value of my life is in the "secrets" recorded here.

It will be sufficient for me if, in reading this book, you come to know your father better. If you gain some additional knowledge that benefits you, so much the better.

I also hope that others will gain insights from this book. But it is not for everyone. More than likely only those readers who want an especially high standard of relationship and are willing to think outside the box will find this book of value.

To my collaborating author, Dr. Harold Bessell: I feel very lucky to have had the benefit of your knowledge and guidance. Your unconventional approach to psychotherapy enabled me to discover the person inside me who was searching for meaning. You helped me understand what was possible and helped me deal with the frustrations and tensions of getting there so slowly. You gave me a deeper and more satisfying life—I will miss you terribly.

To author and pioneer Nancy Friday: A special thanks for permission to use excerpts from your books *My Secret Garden* and *Men In Love*. You opened the subject of sexual fantasies for the world to see, and thereby created new opportunities for human fulfillment. Inclusion of your material makes my book better.

To my friend Shelley: Thank you for being a steadfast friend and listening to my crazy ideas even though you didn't always agree with them. No one else ever tried to understand them or appreciate them like you did. Your help with editing has also been invaluable.

To John and Traci Soderberg: John, thank you for the artistic talent and love you put into the "Ascension of Io" sculpture. Io's beauty, her innocence, her grace—the feeling of freedom, the upward energy—every day she inspires me. Life is short, but bronze is forever! Traci, your friendship and your support for my writing have meant more than I can say.

To Gilbert Ortega and Gil Jr.: I will be eternally grateful to you for helping me purchase "Io" from your gallery. I know it was hard for you to part with her. However, in a very important way you enabled me to begin this book. Thank you. (P. S.—You are welcome to come visit her anytime!)

To Paul Reese (Reese Creative): Your artistic talents in cover design and illustrations are the best! The chapter icons make each secret memorable. I have appreciated your guidance as a friend and coworker.

To Christina Cicero (Words, Ink): Thank you for believing in the concept of my book and for your tireless hours in editing it to help me convey my message in the best way possible. Your insights have improved the book immensely.

To Madeline Hoefer: It has been a pleasure working with you in the typesetting of the book. Every author needs someone with your talent and diligence in making everything fit together and look good.

To Aew my love: You have touched my heart, and given me the opportunity to live the secrets in this book. I look forward to learning where the river of life is taking us.

To all the others who have been my teachers, friends, associates, and contributors: I wish I could name each of you and thank you personally. You have shown me the many ways relationships can be. The secrets in this book belong to you.

The Love Goddess

The Ascension of Io: Sculpture in Bronze
John M. Soderberg, 1979

PREQUEL

Short Flights of Fantasy

Once upon a time a young girl heard about love. She heard that love was heaven and all you needed was a skyrocket of a man to take you there.

So our brave girl, wanting to go to heaven, began checking out skyrockets. Like on the Fourth of July, she found they came in all colors and sounds. One day during her search she passed by a Saturn Spacecraft. She didn't know much about spaceships, and it was so tall she didn't even give it a second glance. She decided on a red skyrocket with a loud bang. It lit up the night and made the earth move under her feet.

A few years later our young lady began wondering why she hadn't yet reached heaven. It seemed that her skyrocket kept letting her down far short of where she really wanted to go. So she began looking for a better skyrocket, clearly understanding that she had picked the wrong one before. This time she would be a little more cautious, take a little more time, and not make the same mistake again.

During her wanderings, the young lady again passed by the Saturn Spacecraft. Being wiser than the first time, she stopped for a moment to give it some thought. But she concluded it wasn't moving fast enough to take her where she wanted to go. Meanwhile the skyrockets kept popping off all around. This time she chose a green one with no bang.

A few more years passed, and again our young woman found herself feeling let down, discouraged, and confused. It seemed that heaven was harder to reach than she had thought. But being a brave soul, she gathered all of her experience and wisdom together, vowing to be extremely cautious and careful this time.

One thing she had learned was that there's more to a skyrocket than initially meets the eye, so it's important to look inside as well as outside. She again came upon the Saturn Spacecraft. This time she noticed a sign that she had overlooked the two previous times reading "Destination—True Love." By now that seemed distant indeed! But always hopeful, and using her newfound wisdom, she looked inside. However, upon seeing the explosive mixture in there, she instantly turned and ran as fast and as far as she could. On her way out she ripped down the sign to protect her friends from being tricked into such a dangerous situation. She settled upon a yellow skyrocket with whirling curli-cues.

A few years later, and our woman is not so young anymore. She still has not reached heaven. But she has become very wise. She has learned that love is really hell, not heaven. She tells her friends and finds that they agree. Individually and collectively they decide to stay away from skyrockets, and spend their time on more valuable things such as work, children, and/or social activities. She hopes her daughter will enjoy the senior prom…

PROLOGUE

The Longer Flight Toward Truth

*Most gulls don't bother to learn more
than the simplest facts of flight—
how to get from shore to food
and back again.*
　　　　　　From *Jonathan Livingston Seagull*
　　　　　　By Richard Bach

The young lady in our "prequel" was disillusioned by repeated failures in her search for love. But hope springs eternal, and she valiantly remained optimistic that her daughter would succeed where she did not. Unfortunately the mother did not learn what she needed to know to be successful in love, and it is unlikely that her daughter will learn either. The cycle of hope and disillusionment is set to repeat itself once more.

The search for a quality love relationship will always fail when you latch onto a "skyrocket" of a man (or woman). Although such skyrockets are plentiful, they have neither the power nor the stability to take you to heaven. Skyrockets, like people, are not always what they seem. What you need (and what she passed up) is a "Saturn Spacecraft" with both power and stability.

Unfortunately this cycle of hope and disillusionment is all too common in today's world. Our culture provides us with only about half the knowledge we need. The other half is kept hidden behind strong beliefs and equally strong taboos. The relative absence of good information, and the abundance of misinformation serve to create a lot of skyrockets but not many Saturn Spacecraft. So those searching for a quality love relationship are often frustrated, all the more so after several unfruitful attempts.

I myself fell victim to the cultural pressures and ignorance. Searching for my path to heaven I fell in love with a green skyrocket. A few years, two children, and much confusion and discouragement later I found myself divorced and ready to try a red skyrocket with a loud bang.

Thankfully, while in the process of being let down (again) by the red skyrocket, but before getting married a second time, I met Harold Bessell. He said, "There is a lot you don't know about love." I was skeptical, of course, so he said, "You don't have to believe me (or anyone else), let the world teach you." And that's what I've done:

> *I have been around the world*
> *Looking for that woman-girl*
> *Who knows love can endure*
> *And you know it will.*
>
> From the song "Southern Cross"
> By M. Curtis, R. Curtis, and S. Stills

My search for the truth about quality love relationships has taken me to some faraway places – Europe, South America, Asia, Mars, Venus, Krypton, Xanadu, to name a few. Many people have shared their personal stories with me during this journey. I felt pain at their disillusionment and I felt frustration that I had come so far and not yet found fulfillment myself.

Nearly at my wits' end I went to visit the love goddess Io. She lives on one of the moons of Jupiter, having been exiled there during the invasion of Earth by the Martians and Venusians. I said, "I can't find the love I want, I don't know where else to look, and I don't know what to believe."

She said, "Randy, it is hard to find quality love on Earth because your society still has a lot to learn. But you have gained much knowledge in your travels. You can help Earth evolve toward a higher level of understanding if you speak openly about what you have seen."

I said, "I have seen so much. I am confused."

She continued, "I have been watching you and waiting for you. I knew you would come here sooner or later. I have a set of stone tablets that tell the secrets of love and sex. You will find in them a synthesis of what you already know but cannot believe. Take your time and study them carefully. But unfortunately they will have to remain here because they are much too heavy for your return voyage to Earth. So when you are ready to return, take these "Love Dice"—they contain the essence of the secrets and will be much easier for you to carry."

She gave me a package of four dice, two red and two white. On the package was printed, "WARNING: LOVE IS NOT A GAME."

The love goddess said, "Through these dice you will learn what has been hidden from you on Earth regarding quality love relationships. Much of what you learn will be foreign to you, and the odds are you will react violently against some of these ideas. Be patient. Open your heart and mind. Use the dice to help you learn and help you remember. Share what you learn with others. But heed the warning,

LOVE IS NOT A GAME!

I left Io feeling somber with the responsibility she had placed on me. I would not have chosen this path for my life. All I wanted was my own soulmate to love and to cherish. But the path chose me.

> *Think about how many times*
> *I have fallen*
> *Spirits are using me*
> *Larger voices callin'...*
>
> Also from Southern Cross

I hope in this book to be an adequate channel for these larger voices.

INTRODUCTION

The Search for Quality Relationships

The purpose of this book is to increase the understanding of quality love relationships. It is not like most of the books you have read that tell you the "rules of the game" or urge you to "get real." Most of those books, while interesting to read, for the most part simply repackage conventional wisdom. If you want a quantum jump in understanding, then you must look "outside the box." When we look outside the box we see things that seem unbelievable or impossible to us, though they may seem obvious to people in the future.

I said in the Prologue that "spirits are using me" to write this book. I suppose the reason they are using me is that they saw me looking for my soulmate and searching outside the box. They saw me becoming more and more frustrated trying to follow the advice of the so-called psychologists. Perhaps they chose me because I am not a psychologist. I am a normal, healthy, reasonably intelligent American male and I am tired of the dead-end streets of conventional wisdom. I don't have to conform and I can say what needs to be said even though it might be unpopular with some people.

This book represents my opinions and ideas based on my own experiences, the shared experiences of others, and the advice and counsel of Harold Bessell, Ph.D. Dr. Bessell is the only psychologist I have really trusted. He set me on the road to understanding relationships twenty years ago when I first met him. He helped me to see that quality relationships are not likely to be found with inside-the-box thinking. More recently he collaborated with me in the writing and editing of this book in order to provide the "other half" of the information people need to know about love. These secrets are contained in the Love Dice.

Throughout this book I use true stories to illustrate the secrets of the Love Dice. Although these stories are based on real relationships, specific facts have been changed so as to not reveal the identities of any individuals.

I have constructed this book using a building block approach. Each chapter builds on what comes before. It is intended to be read sequentially, chapter-by-chapter, in order to make sense and fit together in a complete, though possibly unconventional, philosophy. If you skip around, the material will be out of context and may easily be misinterpreted.

My hope is that these "secrets" will become household words. My fantasy is that whenever two people start talking about love or sex, their first words will be, "How does this situation stack up against the 'Secrets of the Love Dice'?" The icon illustrations at the beginning of each chapter are intended to make the secrets even more memorable.

Because I use the Love Dice to explain a variety of important concepts (you'll understand why as you read more), it would be easy to fall into the trap of thinking that love is a game. Therefore it is important to reassert and remember the love goddess's warning:

LOVE IS **NOT** A GAME

Secret 1

POWER AND MAGIC

Romantic Chemistry

Ain't no trick to make love come to you
No matter what the people say
Ain't no trick to make love come to you
But it takes MAGIC to make it stay.
From the song "Ain't No Trick"
By J. Hurt and S. Pippin

If love is not a game, what is it? Many think that a candlelight dinner, wine, and roses must be love, but unfortunately it is sometimes a game. Marriage should be love, but it too often also turns out to be a game. Living together, having kids—these could be love or they could be games. Maybe love is "communication and trust," but this doesn't set love apart from many games. Personally I think love is more like space travel than it is like candlelight dinners or marriage. One thing we know—space travel is not a game. But it's not love, either.

We explore the analogy of love and space travel more in a later chapter.

But first let's explore what a quality love relationship is. We'll start with a story.

THE STORY OF MIKE AND LORI

Mike met Lori at a restaurant where she was working as a waitress. He found her very attractive, so he wrote her a note on the back of a napkin asking if she'd be open to starting a new friendship. She wrote back, "Thanks for the compliment. But I have a boyfriend." He wrote back, "But you could still be my friend!"

Lori, to her credit, was not afraid of friendship. And Mike felt a kind of chemistry that he had never felt before. He was surprised that he could feel this way even though it did not lead to sex. She was surprised that he was willing to maintain such a friendship. The devilish look in her eye and the spark when they talked and laughed made every moment together special. They shared their crazy ideas about life and love. They each had a basic rebel personality. They loved country music and dancing. Her playfulness and responsiveness excited him more than anything he could remember. He let his imagination soar. It was so easy to be with her, to listen to her, to wait for her, to forgive her. He felt like he had always known her. He was not threatened by her boyfriend because they were doing nothing "wrong," and true chemistry like this was worth the price even if it never bore fruit in terms of sex or marriage. The friendship commitment was one he was easily able to make and keep. She loved the power that she felt but didn't know if it would last.

There is a one-word description of this phenomenon: "MAGIC."

To Lori and Mike, this relationship did not feel like work, even though it had its problems. It was, in fact, emotionally very trying for him, because he wanted her so much. Yet she needed time to build trust and understanding. And although he wracked his brain trying to solve the puzzle that this relationship presented, it still did not feel like work. It felt like magic.

The mutual chemistry never died between Lori and Mike. The relationship lasted for two years. It was not infatuation. But there was a maturity gap. Emotionally she was still a little girl, still learning about love and relationships. She loved the chemical reaction that she felt and so did he, but she had no idea what it meant or how to handle it. She could start a fire in anything anywhere just by pointing her finger at it, and she had pointed it at him. She didn't know the real power that she had, and didn't have the capability to handle it or keep it properly controlled. She thought it was fun, but didn't realize that this relationship was really a diamond she was holding in her hand. She had never seen this before. She was afraid of being smothered, as she had been in past experiences. She did not want to be caught in the "love trap." She enjoyed the fun, but did not want to deal with matters very seriously for very long. The possibility of having high chemistry *and* a mature partner who would not trap her never even crossed her mind. Mike gave her the space she said she needed, but it was not enough to overcome her fears.

She moved away and that was the end of it.

As this story so poignantly shows, a strong attraction is not enough. Yet it is the first of the two important factors in defining quality love. Romantic attraction has to be there. The importance of this feeling, or "chemistry," is well known, but some of its important attributes are not. In this chapter we discuss these important but little known attributes of romantic chemistry.

The second factor that's important in a quality love relationship is emotional maturity. This factor (or the lack of it) was also illustrated in the story of Mike and Lori. In Chapter 2 we'll focus on emotional maturity.

Almost everyone has experienced chemical attraction at one time or another and probably has a general understanding of it. But a general understanding is not good enough if you are reading this book. You are reading this because you want something special. You don't want to settle for half-knowledge.

The best explanation of romantic chemistry that I have ever come across is in the book *The Love Test* by my friend and mentor Dr. Harold Bessell. He is a renowned psychologist who has made a life work of understanding love chemistry. *The Love Test* is very thorough in its explanation of this important concept, and I highly recommend reading it.

It is crucial to completely grasp the concept of chemistry explained in this chapter and the concept of maturity explained in the next chapter because they are central to the success of relationships and they are the building blocks for the rest of this book. These concepts are not clearly articulated in other books on this subject. I don't want to reinvent the wheel, so most of what I present in this chapter and the next is based on Dr. Bessell's work.

WHAT IS ROMANTIC CHEMISTRY?

Dr. Bessell explains romantic chemistry as follows:

> *Romantic attraction is an invisible force, like magnetism, gravity, and electricity. You can't see it, you can't touch it, you can't smell it, but you recognize it by its effects. Romantic attraction can not be created, because it's a biopsychological*

force, relating to each individual's ability to be attracted to another specific individual. It is not necessarily reciprocated; there are no known rules or reasons that explain its existence. I may be attracted to Mary; John has no interest in Mary other than to note she's a very nice person. Mary may or may not be attracted to me, or to John. Romantic attraction is either there or not there to some degree. And if it's real and strong, it will last forever. We do not yet know how to create romantic attraction nor do we know how to remove it.

According to Dr. Bessell's theory, romantic chemistry knows no age boundaries; it never discriminates; it is oblivious to money, to religion, even to marriage. It may be pleasurable or painful depending on the other circumstances that surround its bite. The power of romantic chemistry comes from a source more basic than our societal constructs of age, beauty, money, religion and marriage, and it cannot be harnessed or altered by those who experience it.

Romantic chemistry is different from infatuation or sex; it is also different from the feelings we have when we like, trust, and respect another person. Affection and sex are two facets of romantic attraction, but they are only part of its realm. Romantic chemistry is the sense of excitement that you experience about another person, that indefinable, powerful desire to associate with him or her in a very intimate way, a desire to be special and valuable in that person's life. Romantic chemistry encompasses the desire for belonging, companionship, intimacy, and deep affection. When you feel a high degree of romantic chemistry for another person, you want to be with that person as often as possible. You want him or her to want you! The time you are apart can be agony for you. When you are not together, life is less pleasant. You feel lonely until you are reunited with your lover. This is the person you choose not only to sleep with, but also to wake up with, to go places with, to be your date on New Year's Eve, to be your partner in many things, big and small.

In strong mutual romantic chemistry, there is a shared sense of excitement in each other's companionship and affection. The chemistry feels right and good. Something very special is happening. Sometimes it is described as "the two of us are one." This delightful closeness can give the feeling of a shared psyche.

CHEMISTRY IS PERMANENT

Dr. Bessell also explains the differences among infatuation, sex, and true chemistry:

> *Many people who divorce have been the victims of "infatuation." They very probably married in haste, often without enough experience to be able to tell the difference between true chemistry and infatuation. True chemistry and infatuation can feel identical in the early stages. But there is one big, all important difference. Those wonderful feelings that tell you this person was made for you don't last with infatuation. With true chemistry, the feelings not only last but can deepen.*

Dr. Bessell believes (and my experience verifies) that the more you get to know someone, the more you are able to judge the difference between fantasy and reality. Infatuation will probably wear off in 90 to 120 days if the partners in the love match see each other as often as possible and really get to know each other—perhaps two or three times during the week and many weekends. With this much time together, the excitement will wear thin around the edges by the third or fourth month. If your feelings don't weaken after this much time together, it looks like you've got true romantic chemistry on your side.

Sex is a special kind of infatuation. Many, many people confuse sex with true love. Sex attracts, but physical attraction alone cannot bind two people happily together for very long. Sex is very intimate at the physical level, but there may not be much personal or emotional depth involved. The mysterious energy that we call romantic chemistry is only partially related to sex, but it is this energy (romantic chemistry) that is needed to sustain a lifetime of happiness together.

There are many false ideas of chemistry. Everyone loves children, so often people mistake childishness for chemistry. Our society places a high premium on good looks, so many people mistake beauty (male or female) for chemistry. A good sense of humor is always delightful, and may be easily mistaken for chemistry. Money can buy a lot of things, and the resulting enjoyment can easily be mistaken for chemistry.

Sometimes these "false positives" come in combination and we find someone who is very charming: good looking with a playful childishness and delightful sense of humor and maybe even money. Such a person can "charm the pants off you," but often it is a façade that masquerades as true chemistry but hides a low level of maturity (a subject to be discussed in the next chapter). Frequently the "charming" person has never had to grow up because everyone thinks they are adorable, so they tend to always get their own way. They know how to play the game of love (but they don't know that love is *not* a game!).

The secret of enjoying love (the kind that is not a game) is to learn to identify true chemistry (the underlying permanent feeling between two people) and to screen out the false positives.

Dr. Bessell's book also contains several tables that further compare and differentiate true chemistry, infatuation, sex, and emotional maturity. These tables are reproduced in their entirety in Appendix 1 and are worth reviewing to fully understand these important phenomena.

Before going on, I would like to point out that not everyone agrees with Dr. Bessell or me that chemistry is a permanent force. There is a prevalent myth in our society that romance always fades. In fact, two of the authors whose works I reference in this book do not accept the premise that true chemistry is a permanent force. Thomas Moore in *Soul Mates* says: *"Romantic love is an illusion."* And Dr. M. Scott Peck in *The Road Less Traveled* says: *"The bloom of romance always fades,"* and, *"...romantic love is a dreadful lie."* Based on my experience, I simply disagree with these statements, although I highly regard most of what these authors say. I believe that because their books were not about romantic love, they did not give adequate thought to the causes of the "romance always fades" myth (the causes being infatuation and immaturity). As you read further in this book you will be able to identify why the "romance always fades" myth is so popular and you will learn how you can keep romance alive.

CHEMISTRY IS POWER

It should be obvious from the above material that true romantic chemistry (as differentiated from infatuation) is essential to a quality love relationship. Chemistry is the engine that drives the relationship, as we saw in the story of Mike and Lori. Dr. Bessell describes it this way:

Romantic attraction is like an electrical spark that sets a friendship on fire. When accompanied by high emotional maturity, it is a caring, quiet understanding, a mutual confidence, a sharing and forgiving. It is loyalty through good times and bad; it settles for less than perfection and makes allowance for human weakness.

When you are highly attracted to someone, the urge to please that person can motivate you to change your behavior. You may quit smoking when you had never been able to quit before, because your partner has asked you to stop. You may begin to like football, or may even become motivated to work on maturity problems that are standing in the way of having a more fulfilling relationship. Mutual romantic chemistry often provides a strong incentive for an immature partner to grow up.

CHEMISTRY IS CONNECTION

Thomas Moore in his book *Soul Mates* describes the ultimate in chemical connection:

A soul mate is someone to whom we feel profoundly connected, as though the communicating and the communing that take place between us were not the product of intentional efforts, but rather a divine grace. This kind of relationship is so important to the soul that many have said there is nothing more precious in life…It is a rare form of intimacy…

Soulmates are the highest form of quality love relationship; they are "profoundly connected." Not all quality love relationships have such a profound connection, but any quality love relationship must have some degree of this feeling. This is what we call "chemistry."

As we'll discuss later, chemistry is *one half* of the definition of a quality love relationship. It is the natural, permanent, powerful, connected, magical half. But it is nevertheless only half. The other half (maturity) has to do with the skill of relating and maintaining this natural connection that chemistry provides. This other half, the "skill" half, is discussed in detail in the next chapter.

CHEMISTRY IS MEASURABLE

Finding and maintaining a quality love relationship requires effort, and a blend of emotion and logic. Chemistry is certainly one of the most highly charged emotional aspects of this experience. However, it has its logical side in that chemistry can, believe it or not, actually be measured! Dr. Bessell has developed a "Romantic Attraction Questionnaire" consisting of sixty statements; to take this test you are to think about the other person and rate your feelings on each statement on a scale from one to five, with 5 being the strongest feelings and 1 being the weakest. Examples of some of the statements are: *(answer on a scale of 1 to 5)*

I love to surprise this person with a card or gift

I can forgive this person almost instantly

I enjoy discussing a wide variety of subjects with this person

We have something that could be described as spiritual intimacy

This measurement instrument is reproduced in its entirety in Appendix 2.

After taking this test, you have a measure of your romantic attraction (chemistry) toward the other person, with the maximum score being 300. Dr. Bessell recommends taking the test several times, because although the scores are usually very consistent, it is possible for them to fluctuate. They can be artificially high during the infatuation stage. They can be low during moody periods where you are down in the dumps or feeling unhappy with the other person. Taking the test several times will give a good indicator of the long-term true chemistry.

A friend once said to me, "The last thing someone in love wants to do is go home after a romantic evening and take a test!" Although her statement was probably true, it also shows the reason that so many relationships fail. Knowledge is power. Do yourself a favor and take Dr. Bessell's test. You can take it the day *after* a romantic evening, but take it often.

CHEMISTRY COMES IN DEGREES

We often hear people say, "I love you," or "She's in love with him." This leaves us with the impression that love is a black-and-white, all-or-nothing matter. It may be considered impolite to ask, "How much do you love me?" (And you may not get an honest answer anyway.) Yet "How much chemistry?" is precisely the important question that anyone looking for a quality love relationship should ask themselves because it is an important factor that differentiates quality love from ordinary relationships.

Using Dr. Bessell's Romantic Attraction Questionnaire, one quickly sees that an accurate answer to the "how much" question can be anywhere from 60 to 300 on his rating scale. The question then is not "do you love her?" with its "yes or no" answer, but "how much do you love her?" with an answer of, say, "241."

My recommendation is that the first thing you should ask yourself (or your friend) when you or your friend say "I think I'm in love" is: "How much?" And then answer it numerically using Dr. Bessell's Romantic Attraction Questionnaire. And of course beware of infatuation and rate the feelings again after the infatuation period has passed.

CHEMISTRY IS USUALLY UNBALANCED

When you think about it, considering that the degree of "love" can be anywhere from 60 to 300 on Dr. Bessell's scale, it becomes highly unlikely that any two partners will have identical attraction levels. It is somewhat more likely that their two scores will be within five to ten points of one another, but even that is the exception, not the rule. The likely scenario is that there will be a 20 to 40 point spread, with one person attracted more than the other. There is almost always, then, some degree of imbalance (which is also measurable, i.e. the difference between the two chemistry scores). Dr. Bessell has this to say about imbalance in romantic chemistry:

> *It's often true that one person is in love more than the other person. It's hard to find a couple where both partners have identical chemistry and maturity scores. If your chemistry score toward your partner is higher than your partner's toward you, then you love him or her more in the romantic sense.*

Keep in mind that chemistry ratings need not be very close to have a good love match. But a chemistry imbalance can create a power differential in your relationship. Dr. Bessell says, "*It is quite possible that the person who rates his or her partner with the lower chemistry score could have more power.*" This is because the person with the lower chemistry score is less motivated to work toward the success of the relationship. (I prefer to think of this as "control" instead of "power," since it is not the kind of power that drives a relationship forward.)

It's often better when the man is at least a little more interested in the relationship than the woman. That tends to make up for the power differential between the sexes that already exists in today's culture. Fair or not, men usually still have more power than women. If a man's chemistry score is somewhat higher than a woman's score, then his interest in her is stronger, and he is therefore more highly motivated to please her. This "advantage" that the woman has in such a relationship can be thought of as compensating for society's generally granting more power to men. These power (control) factors can be very important when it comes time to resolve basic conflicts and come up with a solution that is reasonably fair to both.

It is important to recognize that these imbalance issues exist. In quality love relationships, where there is high chemistry and also high maturity and not too much imbalance, the partners will be better able to deal with the many issues that will arise. Although one person will probably be more powerful, that person will be aware of his/her position and not take advantage of it.

THRESHOLDS OF ROMANTIC CHEMISTRY

Now we know that we can measure romantic chemistry. And we recognize that it comes in degrees. But when does it become "love"?

Dr. Bessell categorizes romantic chemistry as follows:

260-300	*Romantic chemistry is very high*
220-260	*Romantic chemistry is high*
200-220	*Romantic chemistry is borderline*
180-200	*Romantic chemistry is weak*
120-180	*Little romantic chemistry*
60-120	*No romantic chemistry*

Dr. Bessell suggests that a score of 220 or above is usually high enough for a very satisfying relationship.

INTRODUCING THE LOVE DICE

Here is where the "Love Dice" start to come in handy. If you recall from the Introduction, the love goddess Io (pronounced "ee-oh") could not send her secrets with me on stone tablets (too heavy for the return trip to Earth), so she gave me the Love Dice. The Love Dice provide a shorthand method of describing the essential features of a relationship—they are a memory device to help you recall how these features affect the quality of a relationship.

Many people when they see the Love Dice say, "But love is not a game." The stereotypical image of dice conjures up words like "gambling," "chance," and "losing." Many have gambled with love and lost, so they are afraid to even look at dice. I think we should do away with stereotypes, but it is because of these stereotypes that the dice come with a warning, "Love is not a game." The Love Dice are not intended for gambling, or playing games. They are intended as a helpful and fun way to show important features of chemistry, maturity, probability, balance, and quality in relationships, as we'll see throughout this book. They are an abbreviated way of describing important secrets about love relationships. So remember, although we are using the dice as an illustrative tool,

Love is not a game!

We will use red dice (think "heart") to represent levels of romantic chemistry, as follows:

Die	Level	Range
⚅	Very High	(260 to 300)
⚄	High	(220 to 260)
⚃	Medium (borderline)	(200 to 220)
⚂	Medium Low	(180 to 200)
⚁	Low	(120 to 180)
⚀	Very Low	(Below 120)

As you can see, using the Love Dice creates a scale of one to six instead of Dr. Bessell's scale of 60 to 300. I suppose the goddess Io could have used a scale of one to five, or one to ten, or even one to one hundred (percentages), but the dice are more fun, and Io is playful (although she also wants us to remember that love is not a game). There are other advantages to using the dice as an illustrative measurement tool, and these are explained in Chapter 3.

Although the illustrations using the Love Dice simplify Dr. Bessell's romantic chemistry test to a scale of from one to six, you should not lose sight of the fact that chemistry can actually be measured to a much finer degree of accuracy using his materials.

SOULMATES, MAGIC AND THE VIOLIN

We have already met Mike and Lori, whose story shows the value and importance of chemistry. The chemistry both Mike and Lori felt was very high (a level ⚅). It was special, wonderful, and worth having, even for a short while. The chemistry they felt was so high that I would have to call it "soulmate chemistry."

Lori and Mike felt that their relationship was "magic." Richard Bach felt this kind of magic with his soulmate in *The Bridge Across Forever* (another "must read" for anyone serious about finding a quality love relationship). Here I quote from *The Bridge Across Forever*:

"The only life worth living is the magical one…"

"Magic is so much stronger than steel!"

Soulmates are an important subset of quality love relationships. All quality love relationships have high chemistry and therefore high power, but soulmates have *very* high chemistry. This is when "power" becomes "magic." (Note that most dictionaries and books write "soul mates" as two words, i.e. a combination of two different concepts. However, I feel that the concept of "soulmates" in the romantic sense is so important that it should be written as a single word, and I will do so throughout this book.)

An analogy that helps me to remember what soulmate chemistry feels like is the "Stradivarius" model. I liken the feeling in soulmate chemistry to the feeling in a Stradivarius violin. There are many violins one can play, and they can all sound good. There are many men or women that you can love, and they can all feel good. But when you play a Stradivarius, you know that you have found true resonance. When you feel soulmate chemistry, it is not just good, it is magic. Naturally you must be a good violin listener or player to truly enjoy a Stradivarius, and it follows that you must be a relatively experienced lover to appreciate the chemical reaction that takes place when there is soulmate chemistry.

If it feels not just "good" or "very good," but it feels like *magic*, then it is probably soulmate level chemistry. If the music you hear is not just music from a good sounding violin but music in which you can hear and feel the resonating overtones as from a *Stradivarius*, then it is probably soulmate chemistry. If these feelings last through hard times, then it is almost certainly soulmate chemistry.

Note that I have been very careful to say, "You have probably found soulmate *chemistry*." I have *not* said, "You have probably found your soulmate." Because chemistry is not everything. Chemistry is wonderful. It is a rare and precious jewel to be treasured and enjoyed. It never dies. It can be the powerful engine to take you to the stars. In my estimation it is invaluable and irreplaceable. But it is not everything. As the story of Mike and Lori illustrates, chemistry is only *one half* of what it takes for a quality love relationship. Without maturity, high chemistry is an accident waiting to happen. We discuss maturity in the next chapter.

THE STORY OF TOM AND MARY

Lori and Mike and the young lady in the Prequel are not the only people to have experienced disillusionment in love. There are millions of stories out there, all of them different in their details, all of them the same in their pain. I have heard way too many of them. The purpose of this book is to provide the knowledge necessary to avoid or overcome this disillusionment. Each story included here gives one small picture of what to do and what not to do along your path to meaningful love. The following story illustrates the importance of measuring chemistry before marriage and also illustrates chemistry imbalance.

Mary was intelligent, outgoing, beautiful. Tom knew her from the time they were kids; their families knew each other, they never dated anyone else. Mary and Tom dated for seven years before they got married.

Tom was a young and promising corporate executive. Mary didn't really care for the corporate society scene, but "What the hell?" There were other things more important in a relationship.

Tom was the adventurous type. One day he said, "Let's go skinny dipping after dark at the beach. It would be fun!"

To which Mary replied, "You've got to be kidding! That's disgusting! What if we got caught?"

I should say Tom is both adventurous *and* romantic. He says, "Honey, we've had such a nice day together, and this fire in the fireplace is so cozy, let's do it right here. I want you right now."

"Tom, don't be silly. The fire is beautiful, but it wouldn't be at all comfortable on the floor. We should go up to the bedroom."

Tom, of course, does not give up easily. "Let's go for a bicycle ride this afternoon."

"But we don't have bicycles!"

"I know. I've found a place that rents bikes."

"Oh, that's such a hassle. And it's a waste of money to rent them."

Tom wanted to see the world and do things. He wanted to experience life. He wanted to do things together. But they never did much.

Mary still didn't like the corporate society thing. She didn't feel the same chemistry for Tom as he felt for her. She fantasized about going out with other men.

So she left.

Tom was very much in love with Mary. Mary, although she tried hard to make the relationship work, was only marginally in love with Tom. His feelings for her were very high (a 🎲), but her feelings were medium (a 🎲). They got married because it was the natural and expected thing to do. They didn't measure their chemistry using Dr. Bessell's test before marriage. There was chemistry but it was not in balance. In a sense Mary had more power in this relationship because her feelings for Tom were lower than his feelings for her. But in reality she couldn't get what she really wanted (a deep feeling of connection) because she did not feel enough chemistry, and this made it relatively easy for her to leave. To complicate things, neither of them was very mature (see Chapter 2). This was a very typical relationship. Lacking any real understanding of love, they succumbed to the popular fantasy of "let's play house together" and got married. It was doomed from the start by the large difference in chemistry, but they were not mature enough to know.

SUMMARY

Chemistry is magic. Chemistry is power. Chemistry is connection. True chemistry is permanent. If both partners have very high chemistry (a 🎲) they have a chance to be soulmates. If both partners have high chemistry (a 🎲) they have a chance for a good love relationship. If the chemistry is less than this for either partner, then the chances of a quality love relationship are more remote.

By using *The Love Test* romantic attraction questionnaire and the information in this book you can develop a feel for the quality of the chemistry connection that you presently have or that you think you want.

But chemistry is only one half of the equation that constitutes a quality love relationship. To increase your chances of finding good love, keep reading.

ASSIGNMENT

Throughout this book I include "assignments" as suggestions to help you build your understanding of love and relationships. Many of these assignments will take a long time to complete, and naturally you will want to continue reading subsequent chapters of this book as you also begin the assignments.

This first assignment is to establish a friendship with someone where you feel chemistry at the level of a 🎲 , or approximately 260 points or above on the Romantic Attraction Questionnaire (Appendix 2). It is not particularly important how strongly the other person feels for you. The importance is that you establish this friendship as a *non-sexual* friendship, much as Mike did in his relationship with Lori. This will be very hard for most people.

In fact, most cannot handle it at all. But we are evolving toward a time when people will be able to handle this with ease. Try it and see how hard it is. It probably is harder for men than for women; many women complain that they can not have male friends because the man always wants something sexual or else abandons the relationship. You will have been successful in this assignment when your non-sexual/high chemistry relationship has lasted for at least two years and you are committed to maintaining it regardless of whatever happens.

Notes

Secret 2

GYRO STABILIZATION

Emotional Maturity

The problem in many relationships is that one member of the couple has a serious problem with emotional maturity.
Dr. Harold Bessell, *The Love Test*

Lori and Mike had very high mutual chemistry, but the relationship failed. Why? Mary and Tom had a severe imbalance of chemistry but they got married and later divorced. Why did they do this, and why do so many others do the same?

As we answer these questions we will learn to know more fully what a quality love relationship is.

As a society we are evolving. In the future more people will know what a quality love relationship is. And they would no doubt like to reach back and tell us if they could. But they can't, and anyway we aren't listening. Maybe the stories of those who have tried and failed will help us form a picture of how relationships can be better.

In this chapter I define with more precision the second critical element of quality love relationships, emotional maturity. Again I rely heavily on Dr. Bessell's material. Later I'll share two more stories and assess those relationships using the Love Dice.

WHAT IS EMOTIONAL MATURITY AND WHY IS IT IMPORTANT?

It may be easiest to recognize emotional maturity by its absence, because more people are immature than mature. Emotional immaturity results in a myriad of relationship problems including infidelity, abuse, unreliability, lack of caring, inability to communicate feelings, impatience, slovenliness, and many others.

An unfortunate side effect of immaturity is that it can make chemistry *appear* to fade. Poor treatment feels like non-love, and it is. But poor treatment is not the same as low chemistry, even though both can have the effect of tarnishing the quality of the relationship. This effect of immaturity is one of the primary reasons for the "love always fades" myth. However, it *is* a myth because maturity can be improved, with time and effort, and the chemistry will then shine as brightly as before. Mature couples can maintain their chemistry level (at whatever degree it might be), but immature couples have a hard time doing so. It is therefore important to be able to decipher what is actually going on in a given relationship—is it a chemistry problem or a maturity problem?

Emotional maturity may be the natural way of life for spiritually advanced people in some distant future or on some distant planet. However, it is not so natural here and now on Earth. But thankfully it can be learned, and we can evolve toward that better place. Dr. Bessell defines emotional maturity as follows:

> *Emotional maturity refers to those behavioral patterns that make for a good adjustment to life.*

According to Dr. Bessell, emotionally mature people are better able to cope with life's problems and challenges. They are readily in touch with their own feelings and those of other people. They cope well in a wide variety of emotionally charged situations even when fearful, angry, frustrated, or disappointed. Emotionally mature people are in touch with reality; they may have fantasies, but they are not walking around in a dream world.

They have good insight into their own motivations. In relating to others, mature people behave in positive and constructive ways. They care about the well-being of others, recognize other people's worth, and treat others with consideration, inclusion, and respect. They readily make and keep friends. They share in decision-making and resolve conflicts constructively.

They take initiative and responsibility when appropriate; they plan for the future, are organized, self- reliant, and are good at problem solving. They have good self-control, are patient, reasonably neat, persevering, and willing to do their share of the work. They are honest, sincere, fair, and can accept blame when at fault.

How well does this describe you or your closest friends?

Dr. Bessell goes on to describe the four distinct aspects of emotional maturity:

> *A good adjustment to life requires reasonably good functioning in the four major areas of emotional maturity: awareness, relating, competence, and integrity.*

"Awareness" refers to the extent to which you (or your partner) are aware of your own and other people's feelings, have insight into your own motivation, and act nondefensively and realistically. Feelings tend to be "vague, fuzzy things," often very difficult to describe. In school, we don't learn how to study, understand, or give an articulate description of our feelings. To a great extent we grow up as emotional illiterates. But feelings are at the core of our existence and are the basic cause of all action. The challenge of awareness means that we must make deliberate efforts to counter our cultural indoctrination and learn to listen more carefully to our feelings.

"Relating" indicates how well a person goes about getting his or her social needs met and to what extent the person is respectful and caring about other people. The most important, intense, and broadly based relationship is the one with a lover. The needs and expectations from such a relationship form a very strong list of possible rewards and also possible disappointments or frustrations. All of these expectations make us very vulnerable. The mature couple will discuss these issues so that understanding will replace false assumptions. The following "relating skills" can help to establish a closer relationship: (1) sharing intimate thoughts, (2) sharing intimate feelings, (3) discussing the daily issues of living, (4) discussing and solving problems together, (5) making decisions together, and (6) doing things together.

"Competence" indicates the extent to which a person is assertive, organized, motivated, flexible, and good at problem solving. Making a successful adjustment in life requires not only being aware and relating well to other people, but also being effective in dealing with the continuous stream of problems that challenge us. The challenge to become a competent person goes on throughout our lives; it doesn't end the day we leave school with a diploma in our hands. Competence develops through hard work, plenty of practice, and the willingness to take on new challenges under ever-changing circumstances.

"Integrity" refers to a person's traits of self-discipline and ethical behavior. Together, these traits reveal a person's character, the extent to which he or she can be trusted. Our push-button society has tended toward making things too easy for us. This does not help build the inner strengths of being able to work hard, to endure unpleasantness, to be persevering, to exercise self-control, or to wait willingly for good things to happen. Our culture's abuse of public relations and "image making" has not been conducive to honesty, genuineness, or fairness. A person with integrity is "integrated"; their everyday functioning matches their self-image; they respect themselves and earn the respect of others.

MATURITY IS STABILITY

People with a high degree of emotional maturity are trustworthy. You can trust them not only in business matters, but in matters of emotions and feelings. You can tell them something in confidence and know it will not be repeated. You can share a fantasy and know that it will not be interpreted literally. If they make a commitment to you, you know it will be carried out. They are slow to make commitments because they do not want to make a commitment that they cannot keep. They are good at problem solving because they can draw on a wide range of experience and solutions. They can accurately describe how they are feeling and are willing to listen to your feelings without judging you. They make good friends, because their friendship lasts forever—they will never abandon you. They make good lovers because they have a wide range of stimulating things to do in lovemaking.

This degree of maturity comes from experience. But not just any experience. It takes good experience as well as bad, and it takes an ability to decipher what is going on in each situation. A good "trainer" can help a person understand, but a good trainer is hard to find—counselors and therapists are a good place to start, but they are not all equal. I liken the buildup of experience to the stability of a gyroscope. If a gyroscope is very heavy and spinning fast and true it will maintain its orientation even if you try to push it over. This is what keeps rocket ships on course. But if a gyroscope is lightweight or is spinning slowly, i.e. not much experience, then it will wobble and fall over. And if experience spins a gyroscope first one way and then another way it will never spin true but will fluctuate from one axis to another. Or if it is spun up with the axis pointing to a "false north" it will never give accurate directional readings. The process of gaining maturity through experience is like the spinning up of a gyro with the axis held fast to true north. This is very hard in our society where there are so many taboos (and therefore false notions of true north), and not much awareness of what good relationships are all about.

MATURITY IS MEASURABLE

Just as Dr. Bessell developed a rating scale for romantic chemistry, he researched and developed one for emotional maturity. Together they can forecast the likely success of a marriage or a soulmate relationship. The emotional maturity rating form consists of sixty-three statements grouped into four categories: awareness, relating, competence, and integrity. Take this test by rating your partner on each of these traits in terms of how often you observe the particular behavior: almost never (score 1 point), sometimes (2 points), moderately often (3 points), often (4 points), or very often (5 points). Examples of some of the statements are:

My friend is emotionally expressive in a natural and immediate way (awareness)

My friend demonstrates warm personal interest in other people (relating)

My friend behaves in planful and organized ways (competence)

My friend's controls prevail over impulse (integrity)

After making these ratings you have a measure of your partner's emotional maturity. Although the theoretical maximum score for this test would be 315 points, Dr. Bessell suggests that if two-thirds of the scores are a "moderately often" or above, then a person is reasonably mature. I calculate the two-thirds/one-third rule as producing a total score of around 200 points (Footnote 1). Keep in mind that someone can be mature in one of the four areas and immature in another. Hopefully we are evolving toward a world where most people will score close to 315!

This measurement instrument is reproduced in its entirety in Appendix 3.

MATURITY COMES IN DEGREES

Are you "mature" or "immature"? Dr. Bessell uses the two-thirds/one-third rule to make this distinction in the interpretation of his maturity rating scale (a person is reasonably mature if two-thirds of the answers to the questionnaire are "moderately often" or above). But, just as we discussed in regard to chemistry, there is really a continuous spectrum, from pure black ("almost never" on all questions) to pure white ("very often" on all questions), with every shade of gray in between. And maturity is further complicated because a person can be relatively mature in one area, say "competence" while at the same time being relatively immature in another area, say "awareness." Using Dr. Bessell's material you can see that there are varying degrees of maturity, and you can play with his questionnaire, using it on yourself and your friends. You will easily observe that some are more emotionally mature than others.

So again, as with chemistry, the question of "how much" comes to the forefront, in this case "how mature?" For a quality love relationship we want someone who is "very mature."

MATURITY CAN INCREASE (BUT OFTEN DOES NOT)

Fortunately, maturity is *not* like chemistry in that maturity can be learned and can improve over time. Dr. Bessell has this to say:

> *To have lasting love you need to have a sufficient amount of both maturity and chemistry. If the chemistry is not there, nothing can be done to create it. But if sufficient emotional maturity is missing, the relationship need not be abandoned. Romantic chemistry cannot be acquired; emotional maturity can be acquired. Maturity comprises learned skills.*

There are, unfortunately, some people who are so immature they think they're mature. These people seldom mature emotionally because they seldom seek help. They are quick to blame others for their problems and they cannot see deeply enough into themselves to recognize a need for change.

You can't judge maturity by age. There are men and women who have grown up biologically but remain children in the maturity department. This may have been caused by lack of good parenting or a combination of other factors. They have entered the grown-up world as pseudo-adults; in reality they are still children who have only grown larger and have become sexually developed. They appear to be grown-up, because they have been around long enough to give the appearance of and at times behave as grownups.

The reverse can also be true: on occasion a very young person has a maturity level beyond that normally found for his/her age. Sometimes we say they are an "old soul," or have gained experience from past lifetimes.

The point is that maturity can and often does grow over time. You may hear it said, "People don't change." But that is a short-term view. It speaks to the fact that many people don't change (the pseudo-adults) and most others change so slowly that it is hardly noticed. By the time they have changed they may have moved on elsewhere in our highly mobile society. But hopefully most people *are* growing, learning from their experiences, and gaining insight with the help of wise (hopefully) friends and/or counselors (and maybe books!).

MATURITY IS USUALLY UNBALANCED

At this point is should be obvious that maturity, just as chemistry, can be different in the two partners involved in a relationship. Not only can be different, but most likely will be different, at least to some degree. Even if we are both very mature, and my score is 250 and yours is 270, there will likely still be times where you see me as needing to grow up. Hopefully you can help me do so in a constructive fashion.

The more frequent scenario is that there is a wider point spread between two lovers, with one being relatively mature and the other being relatively immature. In such a case there is a burden that falls on the mature person to help the other along.

Depending on the progress exhibited, and also on the level of maturity of the more mature person, this can be a very frustrating experience. Professional counseling is often the only successful way. But most people shy away from counseling because it can be expensive, there is unfortunately a stigma still attached to it, and it is often difficult to find a good counselor. Therefore most relationships that are "out of balance" tend to stay that way. This is very unfortunate because often very good soulmate chemistry goes to waste.

Here are a few words from Dr. Bessell on this subject:

The problem in many relationships is that one member of the couple has a serious problem with emotional maturity. They are in love (they both have high romantic chemistry scores), but only one of the two is reasonably mature.

Dr. Bessell says that the immature person acts out his or her immaturity by either neglecting the partner or by making unreasonable demands which first aggravate and can eventually destroy the relationship. What the couple probably doesn't realize is that once the less mature partner does some growing up, most of their problems can be solved. A willingness to seek professional guidance and some hard work on the part of the immature partner, combined with a lover who is willing to help, can bring significant improvement in the relationship. Occasionally the immature partner will be so in love that they will realize that they'll have to shape up in order to keep the relationship.

The role of the mature partner in such a relationship is known as the "therapy lover." The more mature person is actually providing the important therapy through love, support, occasional confrontation, and acceptance. The romantic chemistry is necessary to the therapeutic results, as is the maturity level. Professional therapy for the more mature person may also be necessary to help him or her cope with the demands and frustrations of working through this growth period with the partner.

MATURITY THRESHOLDS

How mature must one be to have a quality love relationship? That is really a $64 million question!

Let's take Dr. Bessell's maturity rating form and simplify it using the Love Dice. Remember, the dice are not for playing games; they are an illustrative memory device. In this simplification of maturity we will use the color white for the dice (think "good guy"). Since each question on Dr. Bessell's form has a five-point response scale, and there are 63 questions, it is possible to create an overall maturity yardstick with a maximum score of 315 points. The rating scale for maturity then looks like this:

⚅	Very High	(280-315)
⚄	High	(240-280)
⚃	Medium	(200-240)
⚂	Medium Low	(160-200)
⚁	Low	(110-160)
⚀	Very Low	(60-110)

This is certainly not a perfect science but I think it is a helpful simplification. (Remember that one reason this is a bit of an oversimplification is because there are different categories of maturity [awareness, relating, competence, and integrity] within the test itself. Therefore a single number does not tell everything.)

How mature is "mature"? Dr. Bessell uses the two thirds/one-third rule for "reasonably mature," which if you do the math comes out to 200 points, or a "low ⚁." Given the difficulty most people experience in growing up, I suppose that is a good enough maturity level for average relationships.

My own experience is that a person with a maturity level ⚁ has a very hard time dealing constructively with the immaturity in others. It is possible, but extremely trying emotionally. Such a person is aware to some degree of what he or she is doing, and that's a start, but it's still very difficult.

I have found that a quality love relationship requires both partners to have a high (⚂) or very high (⚄) maturity level. This is not easy to find.

In Chapter 1 we met Lori and Mike. Now we can better understand why Lori and Mike's relationship failed. Although they both felt very high chemistry (⚄ 's), there were maturity issues that the relationship could not overcome. Mike was mature enough to recognize high chemistry and remain a friend, but it was very difficult for him. He probably had "reasonable" or "medium" maturity, a ⚁ . Lori was not even mature enough to recognize that their mutual chemistry and his moderate maturity were valuable to her. Her maturity was low, probably a ⚀ .

Even though there was very high mutual chemistry, the low maturity caused the relationship to fail.

In Chapter 1 we also met Mary and Tom. We can now picture their relationship with more clarity:

Tom's feelings for Mary were very high, a ⚃. Mary's feelings for Tom were medium, a ⚂. Their maturity was probably "medium low," both about a ⚁.

As a result of their maturity levels, they were not able to recognize the imbalance in their chemistry before marriage. And also they were not able to work productively together on the problems of marriage because of both the imbalance of chemistry and the insufficient level of maturity.

Here are some more true-life stories. Although many relationship self-help books include illustrative examples, those examples are usually just one or two paragraphs in length. As such they are interesting, but obviously cannot give a very complete picture of what the relationship was really like. I have opted for longer stories. I do this at the risk of boring the hurried reader, but believe it is better to have a deeper understanding. That's what this book is all about—dealing with reality and full knowledge and not settling for half-truths. Love is not a game. Half-knowledge is not enough.

The following story shows that "reasonable maturity" may not be enough for a quality love relationship.

THE STORY OF RICK AND JACKIE

Jackie worked at a bank. She had been searching a long time for a quality love relationship. And then out of the darkness came Rick. They could flirt briefly while transacting business—safe! He had deep brown eyes framed by golden blond hair. Italian? Norwegian? What a nice mixture!

"I need to withdraw some cash," he said.
"How much?"
"Enough for us to go out to lunch!"
"But you know I have expensive tastes," she said.

"So where would you like to go?"
"Oh, maybe Jamaica!"
"Give me $50 and we'll do Jamaica another time."
"OK."
He liked the sparkle when she laughed! Such a quick wit! And then one day:
"I want to deposit my check."
"Do you need any cash back?"
"I can't afford Jamaica right now."
"What about Denny's?" she said.
"I can handle that!"
"Next Wednesday?"
"OK."

She was thrilled. She'd waited all her life for someone like Rick.

She hoped he would be willing to start with a friendship. He hoped it wouldn't have to be a "non-sexual" friendship but he was prepared for it if necessary.

They both loved music. She'd once worked in a record store. He liked dancing, rock 'n' roll. This was obviously a match made in heaven…

"I find it hard to make real friends," she said. "I've been here for two years and have finally found one female friend."

"Why is it so hard?" he asked.

"I guess it's my high standards!" she said.

They had lunch every few weeks. She wanted open honest communication. He liked the fact that she was a "real person." "Friendship first" was the name of the game.

She said, "I wish I could really let go with someone…" Her eyes were laughing. "Do you believe it's possible for a couple to freely and openly discuss their sexual fantasies and even act out some of them?"

"Of course," he said. "When do you want to start?"

"I've never really trusted anyone enough to let go," she replied. "Talking to you makes me wonder about everything. I'm not sure I believe what you're saying is possible."

"I know it's risky," he said. "We'd have to put all the rules aside."

"Time will tell," she said. "Everyone's been burned."

She loved his eyes, his smile, his mind.

She said, "I'm not sure I'm ready for a relationship. Too many men are happy just 'getting along' together in a relationship. I want more than that."

"Like what?"

"Like something exciting, romantic, real. Like what I feel with you!" she replied.

But she had to deal with the fact that he had a girlfriend, Rudi. He had told her about Rudi at their first lunch together. And although it hurt her, his friendship was important. She valued it and didn't want to lose it. She appreciated his reliability—he was always there when he said he would be. He valued her open, honest, caring ways. She enjoyed his flirtatious, joking manner. She tried to support him in his relationship with Rudi. She avoided a sexual relationship with him. And although she naturally went out with others, no one compared to Rick.

"This is a test of your character, Jackie," said her inner voice.

"It still doesn't seem right that to be his friend I have to deny my true feelings and desires!" she retorted.

"Just take it easy," her inner voice replied.

"I'm trying to break up with Rudi," he said one day at lunch. "But I can't hurt her feelings."

"I can understand that." *But why don't you hurry up, for God's sake!*

"Maybe I should try a non-exclusive relationship with Rudi," he continued. "But I think that's too hard. A clean break would be better."

"I'll support you in whatever you decide to do," she said.

Two months later he said, "I'm afraid it may take five years to get out from Rudi."

"What's holding you back?" she asked.

"This is the second time for me. Before it was Jeri. She was very attentive, and I love attention. She always sent me cards, flowers, gifts, etc. But in reality she was extremely jealous."

A few months passed and he said he was just "going with the flow," even though he knew it wasn't right. He said, "Rudi is so closed and introverted. But I can't dump her when she's down. I guess it will be OK if I get it together by the time I'm thirty-five!"

In her mind she could hear him calling out to her in the darkness: *"But I'm confused, Jackie. I am paralyzed by fear! I am not sure what I want or what I should do. My mother never really loved me. Then I lived eight years with Jeri, scared to death of anything even potentially serious. Now I feel like I'm in a cage, and Rudi wants me to stay there forever. I know you can see all this clearly, even though I cannot. I have a lot on my mind and I can't sort it all out. It takes time."*

That night she had a dream:

She saw thousands of people living their entire lives in a village with no light. They lived completely in darkness, enveloped by a misty fog of social taboos and half-truths.

On the hill above stood a beacon, with a light as bright as the sun. The beacon could be beamed full force in any direction, and could cut through mist and fog.

> *But it was clear to her that the beacon could not be turned directly upon the village or it would blind the village people. They had lived too long in darkness. If they were ever to learn to live in the light, the beacon would have to be very gradually increased in intensity so they could get accustomed to it over time.*

Such a frustration! She just wanted to flick the switch and have Rick be able to see everything!

He kept holding on to Rudi.

She kept trying to be calm, positive, supportive. Help maintain his self-confidence. Understand him. Be the type of evolved person she wanted to be. Her friends from the future would be proud of her. Except that it was still so hard! If she didn't care it wouldn't matter. If she didn't know what she and Rick *could* have, she wouldn't care.

"Why don't you and Rudi go to counseling together?" she asked.

"I don't know what I really want," he concluded.

Rick needed to take a chance, make a move.

She hated living in a straightjacket. But her commitment to herself was to be the best friend he'd ever had regardless of how it worked out.

The next month they went out dancing and had a wonderful time. Calm came over her as she realized that to find his way out of his confusion would take a while. She was reaching out to him, stretching as far as she could, trying to give him something to hold on to. He was reaching out to her as far as he could. Their fingertips brushed together as they strained to hold on to each other. And then in that instant he was swallowed up again by the darkness.

Rick and Rudi moved away together. Rick was lost to Jackie forever. The darkness is very deep.

So, using the Love Dice to uncover the secrets of this relationship, here's my assessment:

Jackie was very much in love with Rick, probably a ⚅. Rick was also attracted to Jackie, though perhaps not quite as much as she was to him, probably a ⚄.

With regard to maturity, Jackie was pretty mature in her willingness to maintain a friendship in the face of Rick's uncertainty, although it was difficult for her. We could apply the criteria of Dr. Bessell's "Love Test" and estimate that her scores in each of the four categories of maturity might have been as follows (refer to Appendix 3 for definitions):

Awareness/knowing her own feelings—often

Relating/caring about others—often

Competence/showing self confidence—often

Integrity/being genuine and reliable—very often

I think her maturity rated a ⚄.

Rick was also reasonably mature, being open, honest, and reliable, but his inability to make a decision showed that his maturity level was probably lower than hers. I would summarize his maturity scores in Dr. Bessell's four categories as follows:

Awareness/knowing his own feelings—moderately often

Relating/caring about others—often

Competence/showing self confidence—sometimes

Integrity/being genuine and reliable—very often

Overall he probably met Bessell's "two-thirds" rule for being "reasonably mature." In other words, a ⚁ . Pretty good!

However, as the story shows, "pretty good" was not "good enough." His experiences with his two girlfriends had not helped him to understand that there is a difference between "girls" and "women," and the difference is not about age. It is about the level of emotional maturity. He was afraid to trust anyone or let anyone close. As long as he stayed with Rudi, he had "love" (to some degree) and he still had his "freedom" because in his mind he could "leave at any time."

And Jackie probably held on to false hope for longer than she should have. Her high level of attraction pulled her in, and his maturity level, though only moderate, was above what she had experienced in previous relationships.

In summary, the mutual high chemistry was wonderful. But in the end, what seemed like it could be a quality love relationship failed because his maturity level of ⚁ was not enough. If he had felt chemistry at a level ⚅ instead of a ⚄ , that might have been the power sufficient to push him along toward emotional growth. But he didn't, and that was that.

The next story shows how immaturity can masquerade as charm:

THE STORY OF DAN AND BARBARA

Barbara was a hard working secretary. But she lost one job after another. At first she didn't know why. All of her bosses liked her, even loved her (she was beautiful), even wanted to go to bed with her. But that wasn't her style. She maintained her integrity, but not her job. Final paycheck in hand, without prior warning she was out on the street again, wondering what had happened.

After several recurrences of this scenario she began to get an inkling of what was going on, and decided she needed a boyfriend to keep her bosses from hitting on her. She went out dancing with a friend who introduced her to Dan.

Dan was charming, bought her flowers, said everything to let her know how wonderful she was and how much he loved her.

So they got married and had children. She married him because she was attracted by his charm, and she needed a "cover" to hold a job. He married her because she was strong and he needed stability.

But Dan both loved and hated strong women. He loved them because he needed the strength and the stability. But he hated them because he himself was weak. He resented Barbara. So he beat her up. And then he would bring flowers and say, "I'm sorry." She would forgive him because of his childlike charm. And then he would beat her up again. And sweet-talk her again. He was a master of the art. And she had the black and blue bruises to prove it.

He threatened to "really hurt her" if she left. Because he "loved her so much" and "he couldn't live without her."

It took her two years, three attorneys, and four restraining orders to finally get away. She moved in with her mother. Dan continued to stalk her. He sent more flowers. He apologized (again).

He just didn't want to be alone!

I asked Barbara to assess this relationship using the Love Dice. She said she was quite attracted to Dan, probably a ⚄ . She said she would never marry anyone where she felt very high chemistry (i.e. a ⚅) because then it would be "too hard to leave." I was surprised when she rated his chemistry level for her as only a ⚄ . She said "It couldn't be higher because he screwed around on me." I pointed out that the "screwing around" was really a maturity issue, not a chemistry issue. My own assessment is that Dan's chemistry level for Barbara could easily have been a ⚄ or a ⚅ , but it didn't seem that way to her because his maturity was so low.

She said Dan's abusive behavior showed that his emotional maturity was probably low, maybe a ⚁ . She acknowledged that although she had tried to make the relationship work, and she may have been "reasonably" mature, she certainly wasn't "very mature" or she wouldn't have allowed herself to get into this situation in the first place and she would have gotten out of it sooner. She rated her maturity level as a ⚃ .

Here is a clear example of the charming, immature person (Dan). Also, this story shows (again) that chemistry by itself is not enough to create a quality love relationship. It takes both chemistry *and* maturity, i.e. both power *and* stability. And it takes knowledge to distinguish one from the other. Barbara misread Dan's charm as chemistry, and then it was too late.

So here we have two widely different relationships: Rick/Jackie and Dan/Barbara. The chemistry was not that different in the two scenarios. But the level of emotional maturity was very different, and that completely colored the nature of each relationship. Dan's maturity (a ⚁) was so low that the relationship was a disaster. Rick's maturity (a ⚃) was high enough to create value in the relationship, although it was not high enough to hold it together in a long-term quality love relationship.

SUMMARY: DEFINITION OF QUALITY LOVE RELATIONSHIP

The definition of a "quality love relationship" should now be obvious. It is a romantic liaison in which both partners feel high or very high chemistry (a ⚁ or a ⚂), and in which both partners are highly mature or very highly mature (a ⚁ or a ⚂). In other words, the partners are strongly attracted to each other and are also aware of each other's feelings, are respectful and caring about each other, solve problems together flexibly, and act with integrity toward one another.

These relationships will not be perfect, because there will always be imbalances in chemistry or gaps in maturity, but relationships like this can be very good. Love is clearly not a game in relationships like these.

I have referred before to an important subset of quality love relationships, namely "soulmates." I believe the term "soulmates" is highly overused in the popular literature and is often simply a catchy way of saying "love relationship." As such it often carries no clear meaning with regard to the quality of the love relationship, or can simply imply very high chemistry. In my view, the term "soulmate" should be reserved to mean "the highest quality love relationship." In this sense it can be clearly understood using the Love Dice as "a relationship with *very* high mutual chemistry (both feel attracted at a level ⚂) and *very* high mutual maturity (both partners have reached a level ⚂)." The chemical connection and emotional maturity in soulmate lovers is so strong it radiates outward to others. Soulmates are not an isolated pair, but an energy source connected to the universe. Relationships like this are rare.

So now that we know what a quality love relationship is, why are they so hard to find? This question is the subject of the next few chapters.

ASSIGNMENT

Rate yourself and three friends using Dr. Bessell's Emotional Maturity Rating Form in Appendix 3. Ask three friends to rate you and compare their scores. Based on the scores you may find yourself interested in personal growth because, as the stories show, anything at a level 🙂 or below is likely to cause failure in an otherwise good relationship. I suggest that you consult Dr. Bessell's "63 ways to improve your maturity" in his book *The Love Test*. Choose one or two of his sixty-three ways that can help you grow in awareness, relating, competence, or integrity. If you are currently in a relationship, you may also be interested in Dr. Bessell's "Ten Commandments for an Emotionally Mature Relationship" (also in *The Love Test*).

Footnote 1: That the two-thirds/one-third rule for "reasonably mature" (but not *very* mature) using Dr. Bessell's Emotional Maturity Rating Form (Appendix 2) will result in a score of approximately 200 is based on the assumption that two-thirds of the questions receive an average score of "4" and one-third receive an average score of "1.5." This assumption yields a total score of 199.5.

Notes

Secret 3

KISSING FROGS

Why Is It So Hard to Find a Lover?

But mommie, I don't like kissing frogs!
Why do I have to do it?
I don't want to kiss any frogs, mommie!
Please!

Anonymous

Love relationships are not for the faint-hearted.

This book is for those who are *not* faint-hearted and who *are* seriously interested in learning about quality love relationships.

Many people are not seriously interested—they may have been too severely hurt by past relationships, they may be too busy or too tired, maybe they don't like frogs, etc. With so many joys to experience in life, everyone has to decide what is most important to him or her. Not everyone is interested in a "something special" relationship. Other priorities, or "something sufficient" may be good enough. It isn't hard to find a lover. What's hard is finding a *quality* lover.

This book is for you if you *are* looking for quality. Maybe you have just ended a relationship because it wasn't what you really wanted. Maybe you are vaguely dissatisfied with your present relationship. Maybe you tried looking before but gave up because it was so hard.

Why is it so difficult to find a quality love relationship? What are the odds? Love is not a game, but life does have its realities and its probabilities.

We are confronted over and over again with the "love at first sight" model. We are programmed to believe that we can quickly and easily find that someone special.

I have yet to see a movie where the leading lady and the leading man independently date a million others before coming together in their so-called "one-in-a-million" relationship! It just can't be done in two hours, and that's the total of our typical attention span. Also, watching a million rejections is not likely to sell very much soda and popcorn. But it is easy to see that it takes a lot of contacts to find that one-in-a-million. Unfortunately, in our society this obvious fact is not readily accepted, so it isn't given much thought.

Most relationships are formed by chance and circumstances. It is easier to meet people at the office, in your neighborhood, at church. It is more comfortable to meet people who live nearby and share your same culture. It is easier to hold on to an existing relationship than to risk losing it and being alone. So most people settle for something easy. Searching is hard; it's time consuming; in many circles it is not even considered desirable. "When you stop searching is when it will come to you," is the frequent cry of the common "settler." But "easier" does not ensure "more valuable." Unfortunately most people have never experienced anything better than what they have or what their friends have. It is therefore easy to say, "This is all there is"—or worse yet to say nothing at all and just keep up the pretense. Because your friends most likely don't know what a quality love relationship is, it is probable that you will have to go against your "friends'" beliefs in order to find one. *It isn't hard to find a lover. What's hard is finding a quality lover.*

If you're reading this book you probably already know that the search for a quality love relationship is difficult. I'm now going to explain why, and provide you with new understandings as to what you can do about it.

REALITY, PROBABILITY, AND THE LOVE DICE

We have already learned two secrets of the Love Dice, namely that the essential features of any love relationship are (1) the degree of mutual romantic chemistry and (2) the degree of mutual emotional maturity. Now we will learn another secret of the Love Dice, namely (3) the probability of finding a quality love relationship.

If you have not already done so, send in the coupon at the back of the book to receive your free Love Dice. As we have already discussed, there are two red dice and two white dice. The red ones depict romantic chemistry (think "heart"), and the white ones depict emotional maturity (think "good guys"). The dice are two different sizes: one large and one small red, and one large and one small white. The size is to indicate the male or female person in each relationship.

(Although this book is primarily oriented toward a heterosexual audience, I do not intend it to be "heterosexist." Many of the principles are the same for alternative lifestyles, so where I have labeled the dice diagrams with "his" name and "her" name, alternative lifestyle readers can substitute "his and his," or "hers and hers.")

Example Relationships

To see for yourself the odds of finding a quality relationship, take out the Love Dice now and try rolling them a few times. This is not a game, but a microcosm of real life. Each time you roll, think of it as meeting someone new, maybe at a seminar, or a club, or a party at a friend's house. With each roll, check to see if the numbers on every die are at least a five or a six. If not, you have not found a quality love relationship and you need to keep searching (keep rolling). You can do this experiment at home using the dice to see how many rolls it takes to find a quality love relationship (i.e. keep count while you are rolling). It is often fun to do this with friends to see what they roll, and to discuss the meaning of each relationship.

For the purpose of the book I'll try rolling the dice on my computer to show some examples:

Example 1. On Friday night Cindy went to a discothèque. She met Jeff while they were dancing. I am now rolling the dice to see what kind of a relationship she found with Jeff. Here's a look:

Jeff   Cindy

Here's how to read this diagram:

Jeff   Cindy

Jeff's chemistry for Cindy is high

Jeff's maturity is low

Cindy's chemistry for Jeff is low

Cindy's maturity is medium low

Although Jeff was good looking and she was initially attracted to him, after Cindy got to know him she found out that her true feelings were really not that strong. But he was attracted to her. Unfortunately his maturity was low so he did not realize or accept that she was not attracted to him, so he kept pursuing her. Her maturity was not that high either, so for a while she enjoyed his attentions. Only after it started to get messy did she look closely at the relationship and realize her feelings were not strong and he was immature. It was difficult to do, but she ended the relationship.

Example 2. On Wednesday Al went to a seminar and met Georgia. (I'm rolling the dice again…) Here's what that relationship turned out to be like:

Al Georgia

Al's chemistry for Georgia was medium
Georgia's chemistry for Al was medium
Al's maturity was medium low
Georgia's maturity was very low

Al and Georgia liked each other, but there was not a very high level of attraction on either of their parts. This could have been a friendship except that Georgia had very low maturity and saw no value in the friendship. Al's maturity wasn't that high either, so this never came to anything.

Example 3. On Saturday Grace went to a party and met Chuck. (I'm rolling the dice...) Here's what this relationship looked like:

Chuck Grace

Chuck's chemistry for Grace was medium
Grace's chemistry for Chuck was very high
Chuck's maturity was medium low
Grace's maturity was very high

Grace was very strongly attracted to Chuck. Unfortunately Chuck did not feel the same. The good news is that Grace was also very mature and was therefore able to quickly see that Chuck was not that strongly attracted to her, and also that his maturity still left something to be desired. Therefore she was able to move on without getting too entangled and without feeling depressed.

Example 4. On Sunday Ben met a new girl at church. Her name was Heather. (I'm rolling the dice to find out what that relationship looked like... I can't stand the suspense...)

Ben Heather

Ben's chemistry for Heather was medium
Heather's chemistry for Ben was high
Ben's emotional maturity was low
Heather's emotional maturity was medium low

As it turned out, Heather was more strongly attracted to Ben than he was to her. But he felt very confused by her attentions, and thought maybe it could be love. She continued her attentions because she was not mature enough to know that he was not very attracted to her, and he played her for a fool because he was too immature to treat her in a quality way.

Please don't get the idea that Cindy, Al, Grace, or Ben should go home and immediately "roll the dice" like some sort of voodoo magic to ascertain the quality of their new relationship. That is not the idea at all. Love is not a game, and the relationship will reveal its true nature in time. The dice are only a convenient visual means to illustrate it. The important thing is that Cindy, Al, Grace, and Ben learn to evaluate their relationships relatively early in order to know best how to handle them and to avoid future painful situations. They should use Dr. Bessell's *Love Test* materials (see Appendices) to make such an assessment. Then the

Love Dice should be used as a memory aid to help maintain focus. Every relationship can be pictured in terms of the Love Dice, and *should* be pictured in this way.

Let me also clarify that when I talk about "rolling the dice," I don't intend to imply that relationships are all about luck. Love is not a game. There certainly is an element of luck in whom you have the opportunity to meet, but as you gain experience and knowledge (that's the purpose of this book), luck will give way to skill, and the odds will improve for you. Nevertheless, there are always many unknowns when you meet someone new. As chemistry and maturity levels reveal themselves with time it can feel very much like watching the dice roll out in slow motion. But love is not a game, and my use of the analogy "rolling the dice" is merely a shorthand way of expressing this unfolding of key ingredients in a new relationship.

A friend once told me, "Love is a state of mind." Her implication was that love shouldn't be analyzed numerically or "dice-sected." To which I replied that this is precisely why so many love relationships fail: people get themselves worked up into a "state of mind" based on hormones, movies, or romance novels. And without analyzing what's actually going on they make poor decisions. For these people, love is actually a "state of confusion," but they euphemistically term it a "state of mind."

Recap of Relationships

Let's continue working with the Love Dice illustrations. Here are summaries of the four stories from Chapters 1 and 2:

In Chapter 1 Mike met Lori working at a restaurant. Here is their relationship again:

Mike Lori

Mike's chemistry for Lori was very high
Lori's chemistry for Mike was very high
Mike's maturity was medium
Lori's maturity was low.

As we saw in Chapter 1, the mutual chemistry in this relationship was magic. Mike tried to hold it together and Lori loved the fun they had together, but she was too immature to trust the permanent value in the chemistry or recognize his maturity level. After two years the relationship fell apart.

In Chapter 1 we also met Mary and Tom. They were childhood sweethearts and got married after college. Using the Love Dice for illustration, their relationship can be assessed as follows:

Tom Mary

Tom's chemistry for Mary was very high
Mary's chemistry for Tom was medium
Tom's maturity was medium low
Mary's maturity was medium low

Tom and Mary remained married for three years before Mary left. Her lack of strong feelings and their mutual immaturity created irreconcilable differences.

In Chapter 2 Jackie met Rick when he came into her bank. Illustrating with the Love Dice:

Rick Jackie

Rick's chemistry for Jackie was high
Jackie's chemistry for Rick was very high
Rick's maturity was medium
Jackie's maturity was high

Rick was confused and couldn't give up his other girlfriend even though it clearly was not a quality love relationship with her. This relationship with Jackie almost made the grade as a quality love relationship (only one attribute was lower than a five). But Rick's medium maturity, though "reasonable and normal" by most measures, was not enough to give him the courage to end his other relationship and bring the love that was possible with Jackie to fruition. Rick moved away with his not-very-good girlfriend. Fortunately Jackie was mature enough to handle the situation pretty well, though not without pain.

Also in Chapter 2 Barbara met Dan through a friend while out dancing. Here's how it turned out:

Dan Barbara

> Dan's chemistry for Barbara was high
> Barbara's chemistry for Dan was high
> Dan's maturity was low
> Barbara's maturity was medium

Pushed by mutual attraction and Dan's childlike charm, Barbara married Dan and stayed with him for two years while he beat her and "screwed around" on her. Three attorneys and four restraining orders later she was finally free but he continued to stalk her. She should have analyzed the relationship before getting married. Love is not a state of mind. Love is not a game. Love is real, but the odds of finding a quality love relationship are not high, and this was not quality love.

We have now had a bird's-eye view of eight relationships. All were looking for quality love, but none of them found it. Why?

LOVE TYPES

The reason it is so hard to find quality love should be getting clearer if you are experimenting with the Love Dice that came with this book. If you have been rolling the dice for a few minutes and counting the rolls, what are you up to? Five… ten…twenty-five…fifty… Have you found a quality relationship yet? Have you found a soulmate? Are you getting tired? Can you kiss this many frogs?

At first people enjoy going out with a variety of others, but then it starts getting old. "I don't really need to meet that many people." (Wrong.) "I mean, after all, I love her, so I'm sure she must love me in return." (Wrong!) "I mean, I'm not perfect, but nobody is, so I think he'll just accept me." (Wrong again.) "Well, she's not perfect, but she loves me a lot, so I know she'll change for me." (Wrong—Again!)

If you're already tired of meeting people (or rolling the dice) then you have some choices. You can

1. give up altogether and settle for whomever you are currently dating;

2. reduce your standards (perhaps a ⚁ instead of a ⚁ or a ⚂);

3. insist that I am wrong and do whatever you want;

4. fortify yourself (with the information in this book) and continue with your search.

If your choice is to fortify yourself with information and continue the search, then it's time to look realistically at the odds. You already have a feel for how difficult it is to find a quality love relationship, both from your own personal experience and from this brief exercise of rolling the Love Dice. But it is possible to describe the probabilities numerically, and this may help you gain perspective and therefore be more patient with your search.

The Love Dice again come in handy in illustrating, simplifying, and quantifying the probabilities of finding a quality love relationship. Love is not a game, but there are real probabilities that you should take into account. Here are several possible love relationship types, and the statistical probability of finding each type. (Details of how to calculate probabilities are given in Footnote 1 at the end of this chapter. The odds shown should be used as a creative learning tool to understand the relative difficulty of finding each relationship type; as discussed in the footnote they are simplifications and should be viewed as such.)

Soulmates.

His chemistry for her is very high. Her chemistry for him is very high. Both have very high maturity. The probability of finding this type of relationship with any given person is 1 in 1,296. That means kissing a lot of frogs! True soulmates are very rare indeed. (However, as shown by the percentage ranges below, even soulmate relationships are not perfect.)

Very Good Love Relationship.

His chemistry for her is high. Her chemistry for him is high. Both have very high maturity. The probability of finding this type of relationship with any given person is 1 in 324. This still means kissing a lot of frogs, but not as many as it might take to find a soulmate.

Good Love Relationship.

Both have high chemistry feelings and both have high maturity. The probability of finding this type of relationship is 1 in 81. This and the two relationships illustrated above are what I would term "quality love relationships."

Typical Relationship

(Can it really be called love?).
In the relationship shown here, his feelings for her are high, her feelings for him are medium, his maturity level is medium

low, and her maturity level is medium. The probable result of this very typical (and not bad) relationship is marriage, kids, chronic unfulfillment, disappointment, discouragement, and divorce. The probabilities of finding a relationship at least as good as the one shown are 1 in 11. Not having to kiss as many frogs is a primary advantage of a relationship like this.

If you have studied these diagrams, you are probably thinking, "I don't like kissing frogs." Or "It's not really necessary to meet that many people." Or, "Your concept doesn't take into account the role of 'destiny.'"

Obviously I don't want you to take me literally. "Kissing frogs" is just a figure of speech. But so often the best looking man or woman turns out to be a frog after you get to know them (the opposite of the fairy tale stories!). And although the probability numbers are not an exact science, they are probably closer to being in the right ballpark than whatever you had previously been thinking. Destiny is of course always a factor, but you are more likely to have favorable destiny if you give destiny more opportunities to find you.

So rather than hiding your head in the sand or arguing about the exact numbers, what you should be thinking is, "What is most important to me?" "Am I willing to meet an awful lot of people (regardless of the exact number) in the hopes of finding my soulmate?" "Can I be happy with a somewhat easier to find (though still difficult) 'good love relationship'?" "Am I lonely or shy and will I therefore settle for less in order to find something quickly and easily?"

These are serious questions that require real soul-searching to answer truthfully. The answer will be different for each individual. It is apparent that some kind of compromise among the different factors will be required, regardless of which path you choose, since is highly unlikely that you will find a soulmate on your first outing. The compromise is a three-way tug-of-war between chemistry, maturity, and time. You can give up a little in the maturity department and find a relationship sooner, but the relationship will have problems. You can give up a little in the chemistry department in order to have more maturity and fewer problems, but you will feel less fulfilled emotionally. You can spend more time trying to find both chemistry and maturity, but then you will have to deal with loneliness. In the real world there is no magic wand that can make it all happen at once, in spite of the fairy tales we read as children.

Of course there is always the option of trying to prove me wrong…

While you are wrestling with which compromise to accept (or whether to try to prove me wrong), I want to point out something else about the Love Dice. Each number (one to six) shown on the Love Dice really represents a "range." Therefore a ⚅ is not "perfect" and so even soulmates will have some problems —it's just that soulmates will have fewer problems and they will be better able to deal with them. To give a more accurate feel for the meaning of the Love Dice, here is how they would roughly translate into percentages:

Love Dice	Percent Chemistry	Love Dice	Percent Maturity
⚅	85-100%	⚅	85-100%
⚄	70-85%	⚄	70-85%
⚃	50-70%	⚃	50-70%
⚂	30-50%	⚂	30-50%
⚁	15-30%	⚁	15-30%
⚀	0-15%	⚀	0-15%

Thus my definition of a "quality love relationship" includes everything down to a 70% level of chemistry (a ⚄) and a 70% level of maturity (a ⚄). Some may want to compromise below this (and many do) in order to not face the loneliness that comes with a lengthy or continuing search.

There are many ways to do "life," and those who are satisfied, for instance, with a ⚂ or a ⚃ on the chemistry scale have every right to be so. Their reasons for not seeking a high level of romantic love can be just as valid as my reasons for seeking it

Here are two more stories that illustrate the difficulty of finding a quality love relationship.

THE STORY OF NATE AND SHARI

Shari and Nate were high school sweethearts. It was hard when they went off to college separately, seeing each other at Christmas and spring break, looking forward to summers together. But it was wonderful to be in love.

Nate's world fell apart when Shari said, "I'm not ready to be tied down. I need to be free to go out with other guys." He was devastated. He shut the iron doors to his heart and kept them closed so that nothing could touch him.

Then Shari called Nate and wanted to see him again. They got married soon after.

From the outside they were the perfect couple, the perfect family. Three adorable children, attractive wife, professional husband, nice house, and two cars.

It wasn't that bad on the inside either. They did all the family things together and actually believed this was love. But there was something missing. Neither of them knew or understood what it was. They only knew vaguely that they weren't happy like they thought they would be. They discussed why they were unhappy with their jobs, or unhappy with the kids' schools, or unhappy because of the world situation. But they didn't know how to discuss the essential emotional content of their marriage.

His steel facade didn't help. He didn't really want the facade any more, now that Shari was back with him, but it had become a part of his psyche. And Shari's insecurities didn't help either. But they tried. They even tried counseling, but in the end they couldn't make the marriage work.

Why didn't it work? Why after ten years did they get a divorce? Why did they get married in the first place?

They were innocent and responding to their natural human drives. They both came from homes with protective parents. They knew little of life or love. They thought love would last forever. But really they were in love with love. The true chemistry wasn't there in large degree, and it was out of balance. More than likely they matured over the course of their years together, but they still did not understand the dynamics of love or the requirements for a good relationship.

Using the Love Dice I would assess their relationship as follows:

Nate Shari

Nate's chemistry for Shari was medium low
Shari's chemistry for Nate was high
Nate's maturity was medium low
Shari's maturity was medium low

This was not a "bad" relationship. There was some chemistry and some maturity. There was not abusive fighting such as might happen with a maturity level of ⚀ or ⚁ . But it was certainly not a quality love relationship.

It's hard to say when the infatuation wore off and the relationship took a dive from the newlywed feeling of ⚅ and ⚅ to the long-term reality of ⚁ and ⚄ . Distance kept it alive for many years (infrequent contact can prolong a fantasy). After they were married, it was very difficult for inexperienced lovers to recognize the difference between lack of chemistry and lack of maturity. The same argument could be interpreted as, "You don't love me enough," (lack of chemistry), or "You don't treat me right," (lack of maturity).

As we discussed in Chapter 1, true chemistry does not change with time. However, infatuation does, and it exists in most relationships for some period of time. Infatuation can easily be confused with true chemistry, so appearances may cause us to think there is a chemistry reduction, when there really is no change in the true timeless chemistry. Heavy fighting (due to low maturity) can also tarnish true chemistry and make it appear to change; however, it can shine again if the maturity problems are resolved.

On the other hand, maturity levels *can* increase with time and experience. More than likely when Shari and Nate got married their maturity level was something like a ⚁ . The newness of sex and marriage probably kept the infatuation alive for three to six months. Thereafter, arguing and fighting (associated with low maturity levels) over everyday things like children or housing tended to cover up and mask the lack of true chemistry.

But they grew in understanding during the course of their marriage, up to perhaps the ⚂ as represented in the diagram. And they grew even more as a result of their divorce, maybe to the level of a ⚃ . This was all very valuable, but also very painful.

After ten years they were suddenly out on their own again, just beginning to kiss more frogs. They should have read this book before they got married.

THE STORY OF BRUCE AND KAREN

Bruce met Karen on a business trip. She was the most beautiful woman he had ever seen. He would have given everything he owned for one night with her. He couldn't take his eyes off her; she kept looking back at him. And then suddenly there they were, in a hotel room together. The fact that Bruce was married was irrelevant. The fact that Karen was married was irrelevant. The fact that they both had kids was irrelevant. Everything was irrelevant except the way he looked at her and the way she felt. She turned him down that first time. But from then on, neither one could get enough. She would say, "Put it in deeper, deeper!" And he would go crazy, saying, "Oh, my God!" as her twin mountains heaved and rolled like waves on the ocean. He found his home in the wide-open darkness wet within her. Then they would be floating on a cloud together, brushing close to heaven, only reluctantly coming back down to earth.

Little did Bruce know that he would, in fact, give "everything he owned" as the price of this relationship!

Little did Karen know that in the instant of that first eye contact with Bruce her husband became a thing of the past, even though they were to remain married for another seven years.

You say: "This is supposed to be a book about quality love relationships, not extramarital sexual affairs. Including this story is sordid and obscene!" It's natural for you to feel that way and I daresay many others would feel the same. But we are talking here about chemistry and maturity, not morality. We can talk about morality later, but we must be clear about chemistry and maturity first.

The relationship between Bruce and Karen lasted, off and on, for twelve years. He divorced, remarried, and divorced again during that time. She separated from her husband, got back together with her husband, had another child, moved to the other side of the country, promised to never see Bruce again, couldn't keep her promise, and ultimately got a divorce. After all this dust settled, Karen and Bruce lived together for two years and it was wonderful. She would cry for more and cry for more until she'd had enough and then she would be wide open and accepting for as long as he wanted until the explosion put them once again on that cloud, half in and out of sleep.

Then Karen had another affair. She couldn't help herself. She had all the love she wanted with Bruce, but she couldn't resist Charles, who was a multi-millionaire, because Karen had grown up in poverty. Her soul was torn apart trying to have both. The pain Bruce suffered in leaving her was worse than his divorce. Karen suffered pain as well, but couldn't reconcile the split inside herself.

My assessment of this relationship is as follows:

Bruce Karen

Bruce's chemistry for Karen was very high
Karen's chemistry for Bruce was very high
Bruce's maturity was medium
Karen's maturity was medium low

The excitement never wore off between Bruce and Karen. It was not infatuation, but true chemistry. They connected. They connected in bed. They connected dancing. They connected talking. It just came naturally. They were truly "in love." For him, she made loving fun, and vice-versa. You could see that it was true chemistry because it flowed naturally, did not have to be forced, and did not change with time, even in the face of difficulties. The power of their magnetic attraction pulled them through all kinds of situations, not all of them pretty.

But their immaturities were obvious. They were both dishonest with their spouses. She did not have the fortitude to leave her husband. He married a second time but it still wasn't right. She couldn't remain faithful once they were living together. If any fire could have propelled a couple through their immaturity issues, the chemistry Bruce and Karen felt should have. But immaturity does not seem to yield to chemistry—only to experience. And only if the person wants to learn from the experience. In this situation Bruce wanted to learn but Karen could not.

This chemical connection had a permanent and unforgettable affect on Bruce. He could never again settle for less.

In summary, the magnetic attraction (chemistry) between Bruce and Karen was rare and special. It never faded. But their maturity was not enough to handle the strong chemistry that they had. The relationship was like a powerful rocket ship with a weak gyro—a disaster waiting to happen. And it did.

SUMMARY

Kissing frogs is not fun. Meeting a lot of people is often considered "playing the field" and has a negative connotation. But the odds of finding a quality love relationship are much lower than commonly understood, and therefore meeting a lot of people is an important part of the search strategy. Finding quality, mutuality, and balance in love relationships is not as easy as it looks in the movies!

So far in this book we've rolled the dice ten times. We've not yet found a quality love relationship. We've seen friends and sex and marriages and children and affairs, but we haven't seen even one quality love relationship! It must be time for a new perspective and understanding. Let's start by looking at the "secret of the spaceship."

ASSIGNMENT

If you are serious about finding a quality love relationship, then I highly recommend that you get in some practice at "kissing frogs." There are of course many ways to meet a lot of people, but one of the easiest, most economical, and fun is to place and/or answer personal ads. Go out to coffee with a dozen people you have never met before and may never meet again (or maybe you will). Talk about whatever—life, love, kids, jobs, hobbies, the news. The fact that you never knew them before and may never see them again actually makes it easier to talk. Get to know the other person and share as much as you can about yourself. (I suggest meeting in a public place [a restaurant is usually good] and not divulging your address. Most people you meet are very sincere and nice, but it never hurts to be cautious.) Meeting a lot of people is one of the surest ways to overcome the difficult odds of finding a quality love relationship.

It doesn't matter if anything significant comes out of any one of these conversations; the important thing is to gain experience in meeting a lot of people. Later you can sort out who is who and what is what. It's important that you don't expect to find your "1 in 1,296 soulmate" in these dozen or so meetings, but it can be fun and it can also be very enlightening!

Footnote 1. Here is how to calculate the probability of finding a love relationship of a given quality, using the Love Dice. The probability calculation is the probability that the relationship occurring with any one particular person you meet will have the specified quality as shown on the dice. The probabilities of finding a quality love relationship are better if you meet more than one person.

In statistics, the probability of multiple independent events occurring simultaneously is calculated by multiplying together the separate probabilities of each event.

So for instance the probability of meeting someone where you feel chemistry at a level ⚅ would be one in six (1/6). The probability that the other person feels chemistry for you at a level ⚅ is also one in six (1/6). The same can be said for finding maturity at levels of a ⚅ . Therefore the probability that any one person whom you meet is your soulmate ("four sixes" simultaneously) would be determined by multiplying each of the four probabilities together, or 1/6 x 1/6 x 1/6 x 1/6 = 1/1296. This represents a probability of one in 1,296. Obviously soulmates are very rare.

The probability of finding *either* a "five" *or* a "six" on any one of the four factors (your chemistry, the other person's chemistry, your maturity, the other person's maturity) is one in three (1/3). Therefore the probability of finding a "good love" relationship (each of the four factors is either a "five" *or* a "six") is 1/3 x 1/3 x 1/3 x 1/3 = 1/81 or a probability of one in eighty-one.

The dice analogy is of course a simplification of the many complexities in real-life relationships. On the one hand the fact that we are dealing with adults makes it relatively less likely that we will find someone who is a ⚀ on the maturity scale than if we were dealing with children (though there are some adults like this!). On the other hand, the phenomenon of the "bell curve" suggests that it is relatively less likely to find a ⚅ than it is to find a ⚄ , even among adults. You probably will very quickly eliminate the ⚀ 's and ⚁ 's on the chemistry scale, but ⚄ 's and ⚅ 's occur much less frequently than ⚂ 's and ⚃ 's. Therefore, although the Love Dice represent a simplification, the factors such as I just mentioned tend to offset each other, leaving the simplified probabilities of the Love Dice as an instructive, if not perfect device.

Notes

Secret 4

THE SPACESHIP

All Systems "Go"

*So let that wonder take you into space
Just feel the thunder as it warms your face*
From the song "Let Your Love Flow"
By L. E. Williams

We ended the last chapter with Bruce and Karen's relationship, which was "like a powerful rocket ship with a weak gyro—a disaster waiting to happen." Also, way back in Chapter 1, I said, "I think love is more like space travel than it is like candlelight dinners or marriage." What do I mean when I compare love to space flight?

What I mean is that you have to think "outside the box."

Like the young lady in our "Prequel," we are programmed to fall for the "skyrockets" in our society and to overlook the Saturn spacecraft. The Saturn spacecraft is of course more likely to get us close to heaven, but only if it's built right. Bruce and

Karen's spacecraft was not built right. If you're going to try out a spacecraft, I suggest you keep it solidly locked down on the launch pad while the systems are still in the developmental phase!

THE SPACESHIP MODEL

The analogy of the spaceship can help to cement some of the concepts thus far discussed. Here's the picture:

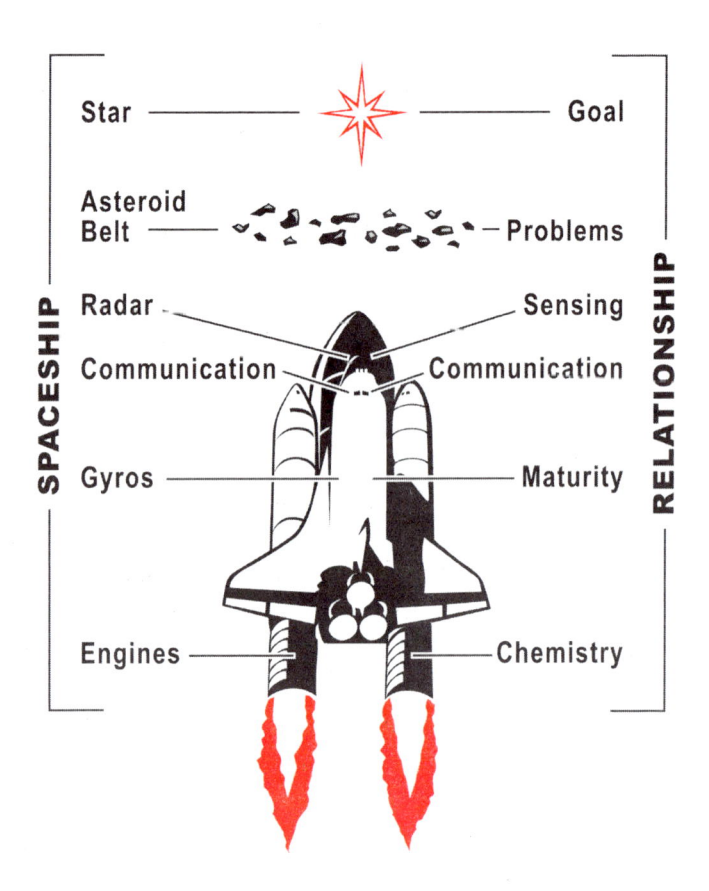

SPACESHIP | **RELATIONSHIP**

- Star — Goal
- Asteroid Belt — Problems
- Radar — Sensing
- Communication — Communication
- Gyros — Maturity
- Engines — Chemistry

This metaphorical image is best explained from bottom to top:

Rocket Engine (Romantic Chemistry): Chemistry is the power source on this flight. A few things become obvious when using the spaceship analogy:

1. It takes a lot of power to go to the stars! Your ordinary flashlight battery, motorcycle engine, or car engine is not going to take you there. It had better be a 🎲 (or close) on the chemistry scale if you want to break free of the earth's gravitational pull.

2. Both engines must be of approximately equal power. If one engine is a 🎲 and the other is a 🎲 , the thing is going to power itself over into a dive, then crash and burn. Of course the powerful engine could "throttle back" (hold back feelings) to provide the necessary equality, but then you no longer have enough power for space travel. Maybe enough for a sub-orbital flight, but that's all.

Stability Gyros (Emotional Maturity): The stability gyros are necessary to keep the spacecraft on course (there are two gyros, one for each person in the relationship). In the analogy with emotional maturity, each individual's gyros are "spun up" by life's experiences, and "pointed in the right direction" by capable advisors. If either one of these gyros is weak or wobbly or pointed in the wrong direction, the two gyros will fight for control, and the spaceship will ultimately crash.

Communications: Often touted as "the" solution to marital problems, communication is certainly essential to the functioning of our spaceship. When the radar senses an asteroid problem in its path, communication allows midcourse adjustments to the rocket engine power controls, and these adjustments can be made smoothly if the stability gyros are functioning well.

But communication is neither the source of power nor the source of stability. Communication without power is only idle gossip. And communication without stability is likely to be either fighting or panic, depending on how far the inevitable "crash" has progressed.

Radar (Sensing): This rocket ship/relationship needs to have some way of "seeing" problems before they become unavoidable disasters. Experience ("I've been here before"), knowledge ("Here's what others have learned"), and intuition ("I have this feeling…") are the brand-name radar sets.

Asteroids (Problems): The asteroid belt in this analogy represents the fact that any relationship is going to have to face problems. The issue is the ability to deal with them.

This requires power, stability, communication, and sensing all working together.

Star (Goals): The star represents how far the individuals want to go in their relationship. Soulmate lovers want something super-special, "out of this world." They are willing to undertake the rigors of space travel in order to reach their star. They can't accept a stereotypical, comfortable marriage. They are prepared to search and wait for equal power, equal stability, good communication, and the ability to sense and solve problems in order to achieve their goal. Others may be satisfied with slightly less, yet still have a "quality love relationship."

ANOTHER LOOK AT SOME LOVE TYPES

Let's see how the Love Dice fit into the spacecraft model. The main idea here is to form a mental picture that reinforces the meaning of the Love Dice. Here it is:

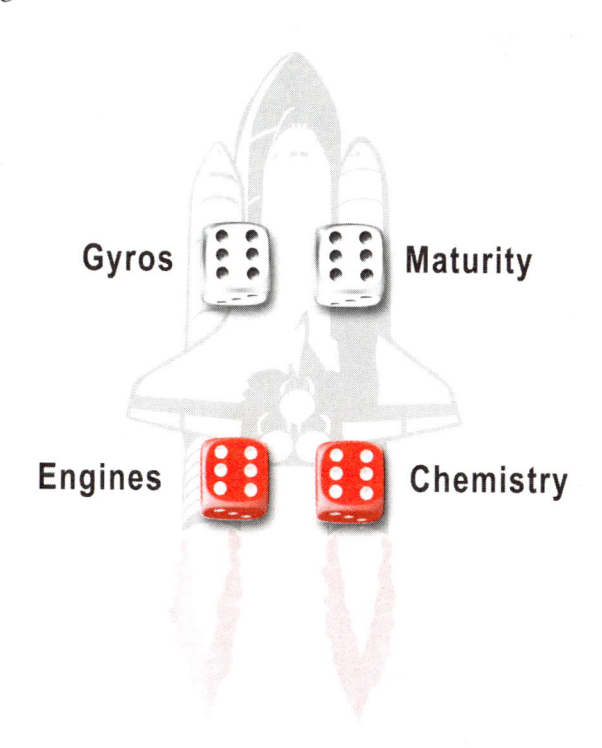

Gyros · **Maturity**

Engines · **Chemistry**

From what we've seen of probabilities, a spaceship like this is not easy to find (1 in 1,296). One can find lots of "skyrockets" everywhere you look, but a true spacecraft with "all systems go" is something special!

Here are some examples:

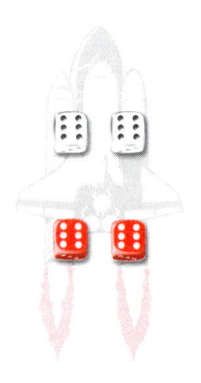

Soulmates.

This relationship has very high chemistry and very high maturity. Therefore it has both the power and the stability for interplanetary or interstellar travel.

Good Love Relationship.

This spaceship has high chemistry and high maturity, but not the same power or stability as soulmates. This relationship probably has sufficient power and stability for orbital or sub-orbital flight, and this can be enough for many people. I consider this to be a "quality love relationship."

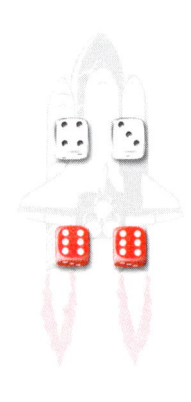

Bruce and Karen (Chapter 3).

Bruce and Karen's powerful chemistry could have taken them to the stars, but their weak maturity made the relationship unstable. The chemistry propelled them through three marriages (to others) while they maintained their love affair with each other. But ultimately the instability caused the relationship to blow apart in midair.

Tom and Mary (Chapter 1).

Tom loved Mary more than Mary loved Tom. Mary tried to make the relationship work but she didn't feel enough chemistry. In this case of chemistry imbalance coupled with weak gyro stability, the spaceship powered over, crashed and burned soon after leaving the launch pad (i.e. three years after marriage).

An interesting thing about this spacecraft analogy is that all of the above relationships look exactly the same from the outside. In other words, someone looking at these four very different spacecraft sitting on their respective launch pads would not know how much (or little) chemical power each has or how successfully (or unsuccessfully) spun up each of their maturity gyros are. The fact that they all look the same from the outside is one reason there are so many relationships that don't go anywhere – the essential internal ingredients are missing, or not immediately apparent, and the partners often fail to recognize what is actually there (or not there).

The analogy of the spaceship could probably be carried further, and we could discuss things like "training," "fear," "trust," or "heat shield." This book could be considered part of the training that is necessary to assure that the crew of our spaceship (i.e. the partners in a love relationship) understands all systems and can operate them effectively. Love partners (astronauts) will naturally feel fear, and this will be discussed in Chapter 9. Trust is essential when operating in an environment of high risk, and this is discussed in numerous chapters throughout this book. And a successful spacecraft must have a "heat shield" to accommodate the temperature and pressure found in space flight. The subject of how to deal with the "temperature and pressure" will be discussed in the next chapter.

SUMMARY: A TOTAL SYSTEM

We will leave the spaceship analogy here. The main thing is to bring to mind the picture of a spaceship as a way of reinforcing the Love Dice analogy, and to remember that it takes everything *working together* to create a "system." Power without stability, or stability without communication may be necessary components, but individually they will not take you anywhere, at least not safely.

ASSIGNMENT

Take a break. No assignment today!

Secret 5

DIAMONDS TAKE A LONG TIME TO GROW

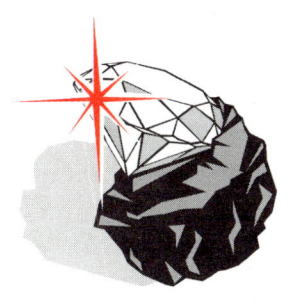

Can People Change?

The dream, that came through a million years
That lived on through all the tears
It came to Xanadu.

From the song "Xanadu"
By J. Lynne

We ended our spaceship analogy with the suggestion that a quality love relationship must be able to withstand extremes in temperature and pressure. I like to compare this to the formation of a diamond.

To understand what I mean, let's go back to the Love Dice and discuss how long it takes to find and/or develop a quality love relationship. This is the fifth secret of the Love Dice.

Here are our basic relationship types:

Diamond
(Soulmates).

Very high (85-100%) mutual chemistry and maturity. This is a relationship of the highest quality. Diamonds are very hard to find, however, with the odds being only 1 in 1,296 that you will meet your soulmate on any one date. If you go out with twenty new people per year (that's a lot of frogs) it will take an average of sixty-five years to find a soulmate!

Cubic Zirconia
(Good Love Relationship).

High (70-85%) mutual chemistry and maturity. I call this relationship a "cubic zirconia" because it is ten times easier to find than a diamond, the odds being 1 in 81 that a relationship like this will happen with any given person. Using the same twenty-new-people-per-year assumption, it will take on the average four years to find a good love relationship. And with additional time and effort the maturity level can grow so that this could ultimately become a "very good love relationship." However, it can never become a soulmate relationship because the chemistry is not high enough.

Diamond in the Rough.

With very high mutual chemistry but medium maturity, there is a possibility that this relationship may develop into soulmates. This is possible because maturity is a learned skill that can be developed with time, training, patience, persistence, and positive reinforcement. This is also ten times easier to find than a fully formed diamond, the probabilities being 1 in 144, which translates into seven years at the rate of twenty frogs per year.

Cubic Zirconia in the Rough.

With high mutual chemistry and medium mutual maturity this can never become a diamond because the chemistry is not high enough. Nevertheless this has the potential to grow to become a good love relationship and ultimately a very good love relationship if the partners work to develop maturity skills. The probability of finding a relationship like this is 1 in 36, which on the average means less than two years of kissing frogs at the rate of twenty per year.

In the relationships depicted above, the last two (diamond in the rough and cubic zirconia in the rough) rely on the development of emotional maturity, a process similar to the formation (growth) of a diamond. Diamonds do not start out as diamonds. They start out as carbon, that dirty black gritty stuff that's so hard to clean off your charcoal grill. Not something we've been searching for all our lives.

One might say, "Carbon will always be carbon." ("People never change.") And that would be true if you took a limited time view.

But somehow, plain ordinary black carbon gets transformed deep underground and can become a beautiful sparkling crystal clear shining blue-white diamond. It only takes 300 million years, 7 million pounds per square inch of pressure, and 3000 degrees Fahrenheit!

Can you stand by your "diamond in the rough" while he or she is subjected to 300 million years, 7 million pounds, and 3000 degrees? Can you endure it yourself? Or do you prefer your diamonds already completely formed? Do you want to search for two years and hopefully find a cubic zirconia in the rough? Or do you want to search for sixty-five years to hopefully find a soulmate? Or something in between? These are tradeoffs that each person must decide for himself/herself. Love is not a game, but there are tradeoffs that are necessary as a result of the probability factors and the time factors.

If you are not out there looking or if you are still looking for any one of the society sponsored substitutes for chemistry and maturity (beauty, money, humor, convenience, "compatibility," security, etc. etc.), then you may *never* find a quality love relationship. The time estimates above of from two to sixty-five years are based on the assumption that you are aware of what you are looking for and that you are actively searching.

If you are already in a relationship that has high or very high mutual chemistry, then you are lucky because you can skip the "search" phase. But you may still be in for a rough ride if your maturity levels aren't high. As we will see, the growth period for maturity development can be very long and difficult. Do you have enough strength to hold on through this growth period?

If you are already in a relationship and it does *not* have high or very high mutual chemistry, then you need to realistically assess whether the chemistry level that you do have is sufficient for your life goals. It may be sufficient in the short term but may or may not be sufficient in the long term.

Having discussed the time requirements for the "search" phase (two to sixty-five years), we are now ready to discuss the time requirements of the "development" phase. How long does it take for a diamond to grow?

First of all, the chances are that when you meet a person who is a "diamond in the rough," he or she will already be married, or already be involved with someone else. And by definition, he or she is not yet mature enough for a quality love relationship. So it then becomes necessary to wait for their availability and/or work for their maturity. This is not an easy task. It's no wonder that so many people give up.

Suppose the person you connect with is married or otherwise involved. This obviously is not a good situation, but chemistry comes uninvited (and maybe even unwanted). And if it is true chemistry, it is undeniable. So you decide you are going to wait for this person. Since the average marriage or relationship lasts, say, seven years, you've got that to face. And there are at least two strikes against you from the beginning, (1) he or she may not be interested in having you wait and/or may not be capable of maintaining a friendship while otherwise involved (assuming *you* are capable of such a friendship!), and (2) society frowns on such friendships so it is hard to find emotional support. Then the third strike is waiting just around the corner, namely (3) there is very little chance of instant maturity even if your soul-friend breaks out of the prior relationship.

So maybe you think it best to stay away from those who are already involved, and stick with the single, unattached scene. You still have three strikes against you: (1) opportunities come along less frequently since most people get lonely very fast and form some kind of liaison even if it's not right and even if they're not ready; (2) mutually high chemistry connections are rare to begin with; and (3) maturity (or lack thereof) can still be a problem.

So here we have a "damned if you do and damned if you don't" dilemma.

And whichever way you go (married/attached or unmarried/unattached) you will most likely have to deal with a waiting period for maturity to gradually grow. Let's look into how long this might be.

We'll start with another story.

THE STORY OF BARRY AND LINDA

Linda owned her own interior design business. Barry contracted with her to redecorate his home. She was married so he had no question about dating her. The wedding ring served to keep it "safe." He just enjoyed their conversations and her calm, centered, self-assured manner. But there was that flash—the mystical eye contact—the lightning bolts from her eyes—the quick look away because it was too strong—the little laugh to try to cover up the feeling.

When Linda had finished the job at Barry's house, on her way out she said, "What about lunch next week?"

"Sure!" He didn't have to think twice.

She never said much. She didn't need to. What she said was what she meant.

Anyone could see the depth of their feelings. She smiled and his heart melted. She said there were no guarantees, and he should have no expectations. She said, "I don't play games. I'm not going to have an affair with you. Just be my friend. I want to know you. Enjoy the here and now. You need to prove yourself. I'm afraid you'll turn on me."

So he held back his feelings and tried to be her friend. It was not easy with such powerful chemistry.

As months went by they built a friendship based on straight-from-the-heart conversations. She was afraid of hurting him and afraid of hurting her husband. She had tried an affair two years earlier and it had torn her apart.

She shared what had been pent up inside her for so long. "I got married when I was 18. I didn't know he was an alcoholic. I learned later, and I built walls for my own protection. His drinking is not so much of a problem now, but it will never be right. Sometimes I ask myself why I ever married him. He doesn't listen to my feelings and I have to carry the whole relationship."

She was confused, afraid to move in any direction.

He struggled to show her that he cared without ever saying, "I love you." The magnetic field of her eyes drew him in and it was all he could do to control his desire. Although many marriages end up in divorce and many more are unhappy, he didn't consider it acceptable to try to break up a marriage. He suggested that she and her husband get therapy. It was not easy being a friend...

The months crawled by. He could see the feeling in her eyes. She said, "I see something in you, Barry—I'm not sure what it is—and I want you in my life. But I can't believe that it will last."

After six months or so the "chemistry" was no longer a question. At first they wondered whether their feelings were infatuation or true chemistry. But with time there came to be no doubt. The interpersonal enjoyment lasted even without sex. They could both feel it—it was the real thing.

They had lunch at a Chinese restaurant about a year into the relationship. Linda said, "It's been a year and you've been very patient. What do you want from me...?"

He said, "I've never been in this position before; I don't know what to do. But time doesn't matter when we have forever."

A slow smile came across her face that said, *That's true. That's how I feel also. That's what I wanted to hear!*

At the end of lunch they opened their fortune cookies. Hers said, "Changes are coming."

His said, "Do what's safe and proper."

One year became two years. Change did not seem to be coming very quickly.

Two years and counting. How long does it take for a diamond to grow?

He desperately wanted to know where this was going, but he was determined not to push, to just enjoy. She was married. He didn't know whether to laugh or to cry.

She felt herself getting stronger. But she still needed time. She didn't want to waste ten years of marriage, and she was still afraid Barry would turn on her.

Passing the three-year point, Linda looked at the restaurant menu and said, "I don't know what to order – I'm in one of those moods where I don't know what I want."

That's the understatement of the century! he thought.

She said, "I guess I'll have an order of egg rolls."

He ordered a house salad with French dressing.

"It's not fair for me to lead you on," she said.

"I can decide that for myself," he replied.

She looked him in the eye and said, "This feeling with you is different from anything else. And I'm not interested in relationships that end."

She ate only one of her four egg rolls. He ate only three bites of his salad.

Linda didn't show up for their next lunch date. This was so uncharacteristic that Barry naturally was worried. He called her the next day. And the day after. Nothing. And the day after that. Still nothing. He was really worried she'd been in an accident or something equally bad.

Then he received this message on his telephone answering machine:

"This is Linda. Please stop calling me and do not attempt to see me. I cannot explain to you nor do I wish to. Thank you." Click.

There was no question as to what Barry had to do—just listen to the silence. He could not break her trust by violating her request.

Linda went through hell. She knew she had to do it by herself to protect Barry. The pain was torture day and night.

He waited for her to call.

One week—nothing.

One month—nothing.

One year—nothing.

Just silence.

The silence of eternity.

I would assess Barry and Linda's relationship as follows:

She was very expressive of feelings, was extremely caring about others, and was highly responsible and genuine. In a word, she was quite mature. Yet she still had her delusions that somehow she could fix her marriage, and she was still afraid to take a chance on something new. Her ethics said she shouldn't leave her husband, and she prided herself on being able to control her own life (even if it had little emotional meaning). So to the degree that her fears restrained her from acting in her own best interest, she still was not completely mature.

Barry handled this friendship in an excellent fashion. He didn't turn on her or demand sex. He maintained the friendship even though she was married. But the amount of effort involved for him to keep his feelings under control suggests that he also had some distance to go in his maturity efforts.

The mutual chemistry was obvious in their eye contact. It was soulmate chemistry.

Barry Linda

Barry's chemistry for Linda was very high.
Linda's chemistry for Barry was very high.
Barry's maturity was high.
Linda's maturity was medium.

This "diamond in the rough" relationship was actually better than the prototype shown earlier in the chapter, because Barry's maturity of ⚂ was higher than the ⚁ in the prototype. Nevertheless, the relationship failed. Three years was not enough for her to gather the strength that she needed, even though she was reasonably mature. Diamonds take a long time to grow. And they must survive the pressure. This one didn't. There are no guarantees. Love is not a game.

The best book I've seen on the subject of human growth toward emotional maturity and personal fulfillment is by Karen

Horney—*Neurosis and Human Growth*. It is very challenging reading, thick with substantive content. I am going to condense her chapter, "The Road of Psychoanalytic Therapy," into two paragraphs. It does a serious injustice to her work to condense it like this, but I want you to have a little flavor of her opinions about what it takes for a person to grow up.

> *We must be clear about the seriousness in order to guard against false optimism, envisioning quick and easy cures. The appeal of short therapies is enormous. We cannot "cure" the wrong course which the development of a person has taken. We can only assist him or her in <u>gradually</u> outgrowing their difficulties. [emphasis added] Only as their "shoulds" lose their coercive power, can they discover their real feelings, wishes, beliefs, and ideals.*
>
> *All such changes can be described as a <u>gradual</u> work of reality testing and value testing [emphasis added]. Does the patient want to keep whatever is left of the grandeur and glamour of her illusions, her claims and her false pride or can she accept herself as a human being with all the general limitations this implies and with her special difficulties, but also with the possibility of growth? There is, I gather, no more fundamental crossroad situation in our life than this one. [Footnote 1]*

I have added emphasis to stress Dr. Horney's use of the term "gradual." Dr. Horney does not put any time frames on the growth process she describes, but clearly sees it as a difficult task.

MATURITY GROWTH RATES

I've tried to assess how long you might have to wait for your "diamond in the rough" to grow up and get over his or her fear of being in a *real* relationship. Karen Horney didn't give me much to go on. So I've used my own experience and the experience of others I've talked to.

Recall the simplified maturity scale introduced in Chapter 3. The use of "points" refers to Dr. Bessell's Emotional Maturity Rating Form (Appendix 3).

⚅	280-315 points	Very high maturity
⚄	240-280 points	High maturity
⚃	200-240 points	Medium maturity
⚂	160-200 points	Medium low maturity
⚁	110-160 points	Low maturity
⚀	60-110 points	Very low maturity

Let's assume that the average person is fully mature by age sixty (a dubious assumption, but a convenient hypothetical benchmark). A growth rate of five points per year would achieve 300 points by age sixty.

Now consider the growth rates of some of the people we've met so far in this book.

Dan (Chapter 2). A ⚁ (130 points) at age 33. This suggests a growth rate of about 3.9 points per year. Not good!

Lori (Chapter 1). A ⚀ (140 points) at age 27. Implies a growth rate of around 5.2 points per year. About average.

Nate (Chapter 3). A ⚁ (180 points) at age 38. This is a growth rate of 4.7 points per year, a little below average.

Karen (Chapter 3). A ⚁ (190 points) at age 30. This implies a growth rate of 6.3 points per year. An above average growth rate.

Mike (Chapter 1). A ⚂ (230 points) at age 42. A growth rate of 5.5 points per year, a little above average.

Linda (Chapter 5). A ⚂ (230 points) at age 32. Growth rate of 7.2 points per year. Way above average!

Barry (Chapter 5). A ⚃ (260 points) at age 46. Growth rate of 5.6 points per year, a little above average.

Jackie. A ⚃ (250 points) at age 36. That would indicate a growth rate of 6.9 points per year. Very good.

Most people I've known have grown in the 4 to 8 points per year range. Much faster or slower is pretty unusual. And personal growth is not usually uniform, but comes in spurts and plateaus.

So how long do you have to wait for your diamond in the rough?

Well, the answer clearly depends on their existing maturity level, their future growth rate, and the maturity level at which you would feel comfortable making a commitment.

Using 260 points (the midpoint of a ⚃), as a target maturity level necessary to have a quality love relationship, and projecting their past growth rates into the future, the individuals listed above will reach the target maturity level in the following times:

Dan—another 33 years
Lori—another 23 years
Nate—another 17 years
Karen—another 11 years
Mike—another 5 years
Linda—another 4 years
Barry—he has just made it to the target
(but could progress further).

Do you really have to wait until you and your partner have reached a level ⁙ to establish a committed relationship? I don't think so. I think there's something to be said for "growing together." An unfortunate fact, however, is that more often than not exclusive relationships, including marriage, stunt growth instead of encouraging it. This is because partners tend to limit each other's actions instead of supporting expansion and growth. As most of our stories show, a maturity level ⁙ is bound to create problems, and may not be enough to hold on. But in some situations, it may be.

Unfortunately, I don't see very many people that I would rate as a ⁙ , regardless of age, nor many ⁙ 's either. It seems to me most people reach a plateau at about age forty and enter the stage of "supposedly complete normal adulthood." Little growth occurs after that, simply repetition of past habits and transmission of these limited (and limiting) values to their children and grandchildren. Dr. M Scott Peck, in his book, *The Road Less Traveled* states:

> *Growing up is the act of stepping from childhood into adulthood... it is a leap that many people never really take in their lifetimes. Though they may outwardly appear to be adults, even successful adults, perhaps the majority of*

"grown-ups" remain until their death psychological children...

If the average person's emotional growth slows at around age forty, this translates to about 200 points (40 years x 5 points per year) on Dr. Bessell's scale, or a "low ⚁ ." In one sense this is good, in that most people reach a level of "reasonable maturity." In another sense it is not good because those looking for a higher quality relationship find the atmosphere rarer and rarer. I think this is another reason for the popularly held belief that "people don't change." In fact few do after they reach a certain level. They see no reason to, unless they happen to have that inner drive for something special.

A convenient rule of thumb is that the average person grows emotionally at the rate of "one click" of the Love Dice for each ten years of age, with the growth usually ending at a level ⚁ . In other words a person's emotional maturity at age ten, is, on the average, at a level ⚀ , at age twenty a level ⚁ , and somewhere around age forty peaks out at a level ⚁ . But as the examples above show, the variation in individuals is great, so the Love Dice simply provide a starting point for estimating time frames. The best way is to use the Emotional Maturity Rating Form (Appendix 3) along with past growth rates to estimate future potential, as is done in the examples above. And what it will usually tell you is that you will need *lots* of patience to find and develop a quality love relationship!

Because growth in maturity is obviously very important, I refer readers to Dr. Bessell's "Sixty-three Ways to Build Maturity," in his book *The Love Test*. Also, competent psychological counseling can significantly reduce the time frames needed to increase emotional maturity.

Now that we have a sense of realistic time frames, let's continue our stories:

THE STORY OF MARIO AND ELISE

Elise met Mario while dancing at a private party. They were both single. Dancing was wonderful. They felt the music together. His quick laugh, and the bright glow of intelligence in her eyes, and you knew they could do anything and have fun doing it.

Mario let her know on their first date that he valued his freedom and did not want to be tied down. Elise knew this meant he was scared and uncertain, but so was she. It had been years since she felt this way, and although she wanted more from the relationship, she felt she could handle it. At least he wasn't married!

They went dancing together every couple weeks. Their time together was wonderful, but he always made it clear that their time together needed to be on his terms.

A few months later they went out dancing on her birthday. She laid her head on his shoulder, and he held her, caressed her, ever so lightly. His lips brushed her hair, her face, her hands. As he massaged her back, her body moved in response. She nuzzled her face against his neck. He rolled her hair between his fingers, then kissed her fingers one at a time. He was lost in her skin, her perfume, and she enjoyed spending hours listening to music, and then making love for the first time. The lovemaking did not turn out very well, but there was no other man in the world for her.

Several days passed and he didn't call. She called him to suggest going out again. He said he was busy and added, "That way you can miss me more." She asked if he missed her, and he said, "A little."

What could she do? Just wait. Her heart belonged to him. She had treated other men like he was now treating her, so she figured it was her turn to be on the receiving end.

Weeks went by while she wondered, "Does he love me?" "Does he feel pressured?" "What should I do?" "What should I say?"

There were no answers to these questions of course, except, "Just wait."

His armor seemed impenetrable. She kept searching her mind for ways to penetrate it. But she knew if she smashed it like a block of ice it could never be put back together. She wanted to live on the inside of his ice-shield armor, and she knew to do that she would have to take the emotional risk of maintaining the relationship with no guarantee.

Months more passed. They continued to see each other every few weeks, but it was freezing cold on the outside of his shield. She went out with other men. But then they would be together and there would be that flash in the eye contact, the laughter, and the special world they created when they danced...

He said, "I don't believe in true love. I'm not interested in marriage. I don't ever cry. Maybe I do believe in true love. I feel happy with you. You are so patient it makes me cry."

She could feel that he was split in half, not knowing which way to turn. She also knew that overcoming fear is a long and painful process. She knew that she couldn't predict the outcome, so much depending on his interior makeup, and she couldn't know all that was inside him. It was obvious to her that he had been hurt, probably more than once, and he was determined not to be hurt again.

Did she want to change him? Yes! Was she going to change him? No. She knew that she had to let him have control, and she had to just wait while he learned to trust both the chemistry and her maturity. She had to learn to love him in his way. For this to possibly become a soulmate relationship, she had to listen to Thomas Moore's advice, *"The soulful relationship asks to be honored for what it is, not for what we wish it could be."*

So she had to honor his freedom. She knew that he was going to have to learn many things on his own, probably the hard way, and she had to prepare herself for whatever storms might lie ahead.

As the months dragged on the lovemaking got better. She knew that the first few lovemaking attempts in any new relationship are often not that good, and he gradually got over his insecurity that somehow he had failed in the sex department. They talked and laughed and danced. He liked deep discussions and a feeling of purpose to life, just like she did.

Her friends told her she needed to push him into making a commitment, that she shouldn't continue giving him sex if she was not getting what she wanted. She told him that she sometimes felt insecure in the relationship because she wanted it to be so much more.

He said, "I feel happy when I'm with you. I feel warm. But I'm not ready to love. I feel confused. I'm scared. Maybe it's just not the right time. I've been very hurt, I have a lot of responsibilities, and I work hard. Women are so possessive, except for you. You are different, and I don't want to lose you. But you have to accept me the way I am."

She didn't want to lose him either, so she chose not to take her friends' advice.

They celebrated their one-year anniversary, out dancing of course. Margaritas at a club and then later at her house. They held each other for a long time, caressing each other, wanting more. Her legs pushed against his. He caressed her body. She said, "Touch me," and he held her breasts gently. They felt so precious. Then he squeezed them hard as she rode his leg. They made love until the sun began to rise.

He said, "I don't love you. I just want to be with you. I've been hurt, and I'm not going to love again. And I don't love you."

After that they did it again.

She would rather live with the "red light—green light" uncertainty than not have him in her life. Although she wanted to know the outcome, she learned she didn't have to know it to enjoy each day with him.

At a year-and-a-half into the relationship they went to New Orleans for Mardi Gras. They danced in the streets. They danced in the clubs. They made love every night. She was so beautiful. He wanted her so much. She loved the way he kissed her and undressed her. "Give it to me!" she cried. And he did.

It was clear to Elise what was possible with Mario: Passion. Friendship. Freedom. Security. Fantasies. Emotional Support. Opportunity for growth. Purpose. Understanding. Tenderness.

Oh my God, please don't say "love"!

But it wasn't clear to him.

At two years it seemed the relationship had come to a plateau. The friendship was good, the lovemaking was good, but she believed it could be even better. It was an emotional strain on her, because she cared about him so much.

Then her job moved her to another state. Nevertheless they continued to see each other once or twice a month, occasionally going on vacation together. After another couple years they saw each other less often—she would have liked it to grow, but it wasn't growing, so she needed to move on with her life. She of course continued the friendship relationship with him, it was important to both of them. And occasionally they would make love. By the eight year point he had been in and out of another failed relationship, and she had had a number of lovers. Their relationship continued on through all of this, but did not continue to grow.

So how do I assess this?

Mario was intelligent, charming, handsome. He worked hard and took his responsibilities seriously. He was mature in many ways, but he'd been hurt and was so scared that his emotional walls were impenetrable even though he felt strong emotions for her, even though they had great sex, and even though he was warm and affectionate with her children.

His primary issue was fear. He'd been hurt and didn't want to be hurt again. So he subconsciously chose girlfriends (other than Elise) where he could have good sex but where he knew he'd be able to maintain control and never really let them inside his heart. He says he didn't feel strong chemistry with Elise, but that is belied by the quality of their lovemaking. It's hard to know what the true chemistry level is when feelings are buried under ten feet of ironclad fear. His "my way or the highway" approach was seemingly very honest, but it also implied a lack of mutuality, which implied a lack of maturity.

As for Elise, I think she was very mature. Maybe not perfect, but very mature nonetheless. Naturally it was not easy for her to be "friends plus" (friendship with sex) when her feelings were so strong and outwardly not fully reciprocated. But she was able to be flexible—sex/no sex, failure/no failure, other relationships or no other relationships—and still be his friend. "Friends plus" shows a high degree of maturity.

Sorting it all out using the Love Dice, their relationship probably looked like this:

Mario Elise

Mario's chemistry for Elise was high.
Elise's chemistry for Mario was very high.
Mario's maturity was medium.
Elise's maturity was very high.

Eight years, and this is still a diamond in the rough. Love is not a game, but diamonds do take a long time to grow!

THE STORY OF BOB AND JANICE

Janice belonged to a golf and tennis club. At a club party she met Bob, and found him attractive. She could see he noticed her as well, but there was another girl hanging around him, so Janice backed away.

But after the party Bob called Janice. They found that they were both adventurous people, into golf, tennis, and wild crazy sex. They spent more and more time together, traveling and playing. Bob's son and Janice's two kids had a wonderful time whenever they were together.

Janice found "peace" with Bob. She felt she had met her soulmate and that "everything would be all right." They had fun together. The feeling of comfort and joy was something she had not known previously.

After a year Bob and Janice moved in together. Three kids in the house, two cars in the garage, plus golf clubs, tennis racquets and kids toys. Life was full!

They made love every night. They played in the day. They talked. They were on the same wavelength. Everything worked so well…

Except for the kids. Bob wanted all of Janice's time. He didn't want to share her with the kids. He couldn't do what the kids wanted to do on a trip; he had the immaturity to always want things his own way. Trips with just the two of them were wonderful. Janice wasn't perfect either. She yelled at her kids when they neglected their homework. She cried when Bob was unable to make a commitment to marriage.

They separated. Janice cried the day Bob came to pick up his golf clubs.

But they couldn't give up on each other. They continued dating for six years. Trips together (without the kids) were great. They played together in the day and made love at night.

They tried living together again. But they couldn't handle it. Bob said, "I'd marry you if you could just give up your kids to their dad." But Janice couldn't risk her children's emotional future to her immature ex-husband. And Bob couldn't rise to deal with the realities of life as an adult. They broke up again. They dated other people, but couldn't forget each other. Janice wanted to get married. Bob couldn't make a commitment. His excuse was the children, but that was just a sign of his immaturity.

Janice finally gave up. Bob moved to Seattle. Janice moved in with another man.

My assessment of the relationship looks like this:

Bob Janice

Bob's chemistry for Janice was very high.
Janice's chemistry for Bob was very high.

Bob's maturity was medium
Janice's maturity was medium.

This is the prototype "diamond in the rough." During six years of breaking up and getting back together, there clearly was "something there." And that "something" was equally "there" after those six years. It was not infatuation. It was true soulmate chemistry. But Bob was not mature enough (a ⚁) for a close, committed relationship. Janice, although she had grown as a result of prior relationships, was also still at a level ⚁; she couldn't handle the problems, and she couldn't stand to wait any longer. Another diamond left in the rough!

I want to compare the relationships of Bob/Janice, Barry/Linda, and Mario/Elise. Here they are represented side by side to make it easier:

Bob / Janice   Barry / Linda   Mario / Elise

First let's compare the degree of mutual chemistry. Bob/Janice and Barry/Linda clearly had soulmate chemistry. Therefore these could truly be considered "diamonds in the rough." Mario's chemistry for Elise, on the other hand, was only "high." Therefore, although the chemistry had potential for a quality love relationship, it was not quite enough for them to be soulmates. For Elise it was a diamond, but for Mario it was a cubic zirconia. Therefore Mario lacked the very strong motivation to change that he might have had if he had felt chemistry at a "very high" level. Nevertheless, he missed an opportunity to have a quality love relationship with Elise.

Now to compare maturity. Bob/Janice both had average adult maturity (a level ⚃). Their relationship was the prototypical diamond in the rough. It lasted on and off for six years. But it also presented significant challenges because they both lacked full maturity. As a result, the relationship ultimately failed.

In the second example, Linda had maturity at a level ⚃ whereas Barry had a maturity level ⚄. She had the motivation to grow up because of her very high chemistry, but in her case she was severely penned in by her own beliefs that she should stay married at all costs. Although a marriage relationship can be a good thing if there is quality love, in her case it clearly was not good because of her alcoholic husband. Barry's maturity wasn't perfect, but he gave her what she most severely needed, namely emotional support without a demand for sex. If she hadn't cut the relationship short after three years, she might have become stronger and this relationship might have succeeded.

In the third example Mario had normal maturity at a ⚃ level whereas Elise had very high maturity, a level ⚅. She gave Mario what he most needed, sex with freedom. But even this was not enough for him to grow to the point of committing to the relationship, even in eight years, possibly because he was continuing to hold out for a relationship where he felt chemistry at a level ⚅ instead of a level ⚅. Since they remain friends, we can't know what will unfold in the future.

All of these examples show that it requires a long time for people to change their level of emotional maturity. The stories also show that a level ⚃ seems to be a glass ceiling through which very few people pass. Obviously Barry and Elise had passed through this ceiling, but Bob, Janice, Linda and Mario still had not. The prevalence of this limit is probably due in part to parental ignorance and in part to the various strictures placed on personality development by society, government, and religion. Rules such as "Friendship doesn't include sex," "You shouldn't have sex without love," "Don't get involved with someone who is married," and "Stay married at all costs," keep people from expressing the truth of their (often mixed) feelings and keep them from getting beyond the rules and into the realm of quality love. Often it takes motivation, a good therapist and a long time for people to make it through this glass ceiling.

These three stories show that it takes a long time to grow a diamond, and you have to be able to stand the pressure. Neither Janice nor Bob could stand the pressure. Barry provided the married Linda with high quality treatment during the course of their relationship, and he seemed to be able to stand the pressure, but ultimately Linda could not. At the time of my interviews Elise was still maintaining contact with Mario, still handling the pressure, although she was also dating others.

THE THERAPY LOVER

Earlier in this chapter I defined a relationship with very high mutual chemistry but medium maturity as a "diamond in the rough":

As the stories show, people with "reasonable maturity" (i.e. a ⚂) have a hard time conducting quality love relationships (e.g. Linda, Mario, Bob and Janice). If *both* partners have only this medium level of maturity, such as Bob and Janice, it will be doubly hard. And if you are dealing with maturity levels less than a ⚂ you probably have only "carbon" instead of a "diamond in the rough."

If you yourself have already been subjected to the time/pressure/temperature process, you may have already matured a great deal, (up to a ⚄ or a ⚅) and it may be easier to stand by your friend who is still at a level ⚃ . If you can and do, you are playing a role known as a "therapy lover." This can be the very best way to help a person to grow up—i.e. to provide an atmosphere where there is chemistry (motivation) and mature support (so that growth can take place). It is still hard work, for both of you. The therapy lover relationship looks like this:

Elise was (and still is) playing the role of therapy lover in her relationship with Mario. Barry was playing the role of therapy lover in his relationship with Linda (though it was harder for him with his maturity at a level ⚄). The concept of therapy lover does not necessarily include sex, as was the case with Barry and Linda. What it *does* include is providing the less mature person with a corrective emotional experience, i.e. quality treatment along with new emotional insight.

Being a therapy lover can take years and endless patience and there is no guarantee of success. A competent psychologist or psychiatrist can often help, but still there is no guarantee.

If, on the other hand, you yourself have not already been subjected to the time/pressure/temperature process of maturing emotionally (i.e. you are still at a maturity level ⚁ or ⚂), you will have your hands full attending to your own growth and it will be extremely difficult to play the therapy lover role (witness Bob and Janice).

Some do make it through, however. Carbon, in 300 million years, after surviving 7 million pounds of pressure and 3000 degrees of temperature, may become a diamond. (Maybe. No guarantees.)

THE FALSE HOPE

There are many who would suggest that the best thing to search for is a relationship that looks like this, i.e. medium chemistry and very high maturity, and then work to develop it into a quality love relationship. They contend that with good treatment the chemistry will increase. Unfortunately this is a well-intentioned but misinformed idea. It is often attempted, but it is almost always doomed to failure. As we discussed in Chapter 1, true chemistry very rarely changes. Not only does it not die, but neither does it grow by very much no matter how hard you try! The good news is that in the relationship shown, the individuals are very highly mature, and they will realize the fallacy of this relationship very quickly.

IMPROVING YOUR ODDS

It should be apparent by now that good relationships only happen when there is *both* mutual chemistry and mutual maturity. You can do nothing about the chemistry, and very little about your partner's maturity, but you *can* do something about your own maturity. This ranks right up there with "kiss a lot of frogs" as the best way to improve your odds of finding a quality love relationship.

In Chapter 3 we calculated that the odds of finding a soulmate

(⚃⚃) on any one date were 1 in 1,296. That was based on random odds for a random sample of the general public. But for you who are reading this book, the odds can be better because hopefully you are working on your own maturity. For instance, if you already have very high maturity (a level ⚅), then your odds of finding a soulmate relationship on any one date are 1 in 216. You still have to kiss a lot of frogs, but far fewer than before!

As another example, if your maturity is already high (a level ⚂), and you are looking for a good love relationship (⚅⚅) then your odds improve from 1 in 81 to 1 in 27 of finding it on any one date. This will never be a soulmate relationship (because the chemistry is not high enough), but it can be a very satisfying love relationship for many people and it certainly will reduce the time required and the number of frogs you have to kiss.

For many people, the growth process can be accelerated with directed experience or therapy. I also refer readers to Dr. Bessell's "Sixty-three Ways to Build Maturity," in his book *The Love Test*.

There is one downside to increasing your maturity. Those who are still at a medium maturity level are able to maintain their rose-colored glasses, and are able to believe that the odds are better than I am depicting in this book. So where I say the odds are 1 in 81 of finding a quality love relationship, they disagree and say the odds are about 1 in 10. With maturity, they are able to improve their odds from 1 in 81 to 1 in 27, but from their perspective, the odds have gotten worse, i.e. from their rose-colored 1 in 10 to a more realistic 1 in 27. My view is that reality is better than non-reality, though I must say it is not always a popular view.

You may be wondering why none of the relationships discussed so far have progressed to the point of a "quality love relationship." The answer is, "Because you haven't finished reading the book!" The answer also is that unlike many popular books, this book endeavors to be realistic about the odds of finding and growing quality love relationships, and since we have so far visited only thirteen relationships, it would be unrealistic to have found quality love already.

COMPROMISES

By now it should be clear that the odds of finding a relationship with very high mutual chemistry and very high mutual maturity (a ⚅⚅) in a short time are very low. So something has to give. Either you choose to exercise extreme patience during a long search for a diamond, or you compromise on either chemistry or maturity or both. The choice of a long search can lead to heavy loneliness. A compromise on chemistry can lead to feelings of unfulfillment, which can lead to affairs and/or divorce. A compromise on maturity can lead to fighting, which can also lead to affairs and divorce, but for different reasons. A sexually exclusive one-on-one relationship is difficult to maintain if either chemistry or maturity is compromised.

If the relationship is "good enough" for the partners, then they will be better able to deal with the problems that come from compromising on either chemistry or maturity. The "good enough" relationship that I postulate is the good love relationship, depicted by the Love Dice as .

Not everyone will be satisfied with a "good love relationship" like this. The next three chapters are particularly dedicated to those who would rather compromise on time than compromise on quality (although anyone searching for a quality love relationship will benefit from understanding the secrets in these next three chapters).

SUMMARY

So what's the point of all this? Stay away from married men/women? Maybe. Stay away from those who can't make up their minds? Maybe.

The point really is that nothing happens quickly. In the search for a quality relationship we are dealing with *geologic time*. (A search phase of 2-65 years and a growth phase of 4-33 years feels like geologic time to me!) Finding and building a quality love relationship is not easy. And finding/building a soulmate relationship is *extremely* difficult. But if you want one of these relationships, you have to be prepared to deal with the geologic time that's necessary. And you have to be prepared to deal with the pressure and the uncertainty.

I believe it is helpful to have a realistic view of the time frames necessary to find quality love. If you have a realistic view you are less likely to have unrealistic expectations and less likely to experience severe frustrations. I think the unrealistic expectations most people have are a primary source of failure in relationships.

If there is a short summary of the attitude that is necessary to survive geologic time it is "Don't push, just enjoy." You can't push carbon into becoming a diamond, but you can enjoy watching it grow. You can't push a glacier to move any faster than it wants to move, but you can enjoy the beauty of the glacier itself and the rock formations it creates. If you try to push you will be frustrated and not be able to enjoy. If you don't push, you can relax and enjoy.

Don't push, just enjoy!

Occasionally, such as in the "therapy lover" situation, a gentle nudge may be appropriate and necessary to help the less mature person grow up. But support needs to outweigh guidance by 20 to 1 in order to build trust and allow the occasional guidance to be effective. And the rest of the time the "don't push, just enjoy" philosophy is critical to the peace of mind of the more mature partner.

It's sad that a large majority of people fight growing up. They can't or won't or don't want to change. They grit their teeth, grin and bear it, and poison their kids' minds with the same old conventional "wisdom." Then they throw away all their money on divorce lawyers and pick another loser...

If you really want something special, you will have to work hard at gaining knowledge and understanding, and you will have to fight off loneliness. Most people give up. But if you've come this far in this book, you are well on your way to a better place!

ASSIGNMENT

How are you doing on kissing frogs? Remember the targets: 81 frogs for a good love relationship, 1,296 frogs for a soulmate relationship! How far along are you? Do you find it difficult because you don't like rejection? I don't like rejection either. Do you think you should be able to find quality love quickly and without any rejections?

During the next two weeks, set a target for yourself of receiving seven rejections. Approach people you wouldn't otherwise approach, whether it's at work, at church, at the grocery store, at a class, or out dancing. Stretch yourself. Rejection won't kill you. Tell yourself that you are not fulfilling your obligations to your future love partner if you have not received seven rejections. (The goal here is getting rejections, *not* finding a soulmate.) (You don't have to make a complete fool of yourself however.) Rejections may be a little painful, but they are a lot easier than finding a soulmate. Therefore you may as well start now to build up an immunity (I don't know if seven will be enough). Then you can go on getting another 1,289 rejections until you meet your soulmate (I'm just kidding).

Remember there's no rush to find your quality love relationship. Geologic time isn't in a hurry. The rush is to get your seven rejections out of the way as soon as possible so you won't be worried about them any more.

Footnote 1. I have changed Dr. Horney's use of the pronoun "his" to "hers" so the description more readily fits in the context of the story of Linda. Dr. Horney's analysis, however, is equally applicable to men and women.

Secret 6

SEX IS LIKE WATER

Emotional Closeness is like Food

*"No wonder I'm confused—
One of my parents was a man, the other was a woman!"*
Ashleigh Brilliant

In the last chapter we discussed the fact that looking for and building a good love relationship requires a very long time, so long that it will feel like "geologic time," and fighting off loneliness will be a major challenge. It's unfortunate that finding a good thing takes so long, but love is not a game.

Moving mountains may be easy if you are a glacier and have a few thousand years. But we are not glaciers. And even if we had a few thousand years, we are not made of ice! In particular, since we are *not* glaciers, what *are* we to do about *sex*? This is important!

As a baseline for this discussion of what to do about sex during geologic time I'll use the "diamond in the rough" relationship. As a reminder this is a (6,6 / 3,3) relationship (very high mutual chemistry with medium maturity). This relationship has a probability of 1 in 144 and a probable "search time" of seven years based on interviewing twenty frogs per year (for those of you who prefer "interviewing" to "kissing.") The further development of this diamond in the rough toward becoming a quality love relationship (a 6,6 / 4,4) is likely to take another ten years based on "one click of the dice every ten years." And then to become a soulmate relationship (6,6 / 5,5) will probably take another ten years beyond that.

Obviously other prototypes could be constructed using lesser standards of chemistry or maturity and thereby reduce the search and development time, but doing so also reduces the quality of the love relationship. Also much depends on the inner capabilities of the individuals, so all time estimates need to be seen as general approximations, not exact numbers.

But using our prototype diamond in the rough as an example we are looking at seventeen years from the start of search to the time it becomes a quality love relationship. Most people don't search and/or wait for seventeen years, of course, and that's the main reason why most people don't find a quality love relationship, let alone a soulmate.

It's hard to contemplate waiting for seventeen years. "Oh my God, I'll be an old man/woman by then!"

But I have not said, "Wait and do nothing."

So what *is* one to do?!

There are some options to consider in the "What are we to do about sex?" question. Unfortunately, none of them are very easy.

So before we go on to deal with these options, let's try to put sex into perspective. First, I want to deal with the complexity of sex and the problems associated with sexual activity. Second, I want to put sex into the perspective of various relationships where sexual deprivation (we'll discuss this more in a minute) is or is not being overcome. Only after having placed sex in perspective will we be in a position to discuss how to deal with a seventeen-year waiting period.

THE COMPLEXITY OF SEX

Sex is a powerful energy. Some see it as a force for good, others as a force for evil. In either case it is something natural, and the question then arises, "To what degree should it be controlled?" This is a very difficult question because of all the complex ramifications and interactions of sexual activity.

Sex can lead to excitement, enjoyment, fulfillment, connection, and procreation. It can also lead to deprivation, rage, jealousy, disease, and unwanted pregnancy.

Deprivation and rage can lead to rape or to premature marriage. Excitement and enjoyment can blind us to immaturities or true chemistry levels.

If sex leads to marriage, it can lead to divorce or chronic unfulfillment just as easily as it can lead to happiness. If sex occurs outside of marriage it can lead to guilt as easily as to bliss.

Children can come as a result of sex, whether inside or outside of marriage. Children can lead to happiness and fulfillment, or to custody battles, child support payments and/or neglect. It is even possible for children to bring both happiness *and* custody battles.

Sex can lead to improved sleep, and some say to better cardiovascular health. It can also lead to lawsuits and alimony payments.

Guilt, jealousy, and anger can lead to abuse (physical and/or emotional), and in some cases even to murder.

Religion, laws, dictated morals, and social stereotypes have come about in part to try to keep many of these complex ramifications under some degree of control. They have created yet another layer of complexity, in that they are not all in agreement (especially if you look all around the world). These control mechanisms (at least in the U. S.) have had the generally good result of providing for the support of children. Yet they create a source of guilt, and they have not (it seems) been successful either in keeping couples together or in eliminating jealousy, unwanted pregnancies, or disease.

In such a complex emotional, physical, and social phenomenon as sex, responsibility and reality must be key concepts. In addition, it seems that there needs to be a balance between sexual control (which can lead to deprivation) and sexual abundance (which can lead to fulfillment). The present 50% divorce rate in the U. S. seems to clearly show that something is indeed out of balance.

This book suggests that in the spectrum between sexual control and sexual abundance, if relationships are to succeed there needs to be change in the direction of more fulfillment. This book does not attempt to deal in detail with all the complexities of sex. Rather, it attempts to awaken the reader to the connection between the quality of sex and the quality of love relationships. Neither does this book recommend a specific program for changing the balance between sexual deprivation and sexual abundance. However, it does provide some alternatives for discussion.

Sex has been part of life for millions of years, and will likely continue to be for millions more, absent thermonuclear devastation. It is genetic and instinctual. It provides enjoyment and emotional connection as well as procreation. I would like to see us grow in our understanding of sex and learn to find a balance that leads to a higher degree of fulfillment than we enjoy today.

THE PURPOSE OF SEX

Having discussed the complexity of sex, we need to also discuss the purpose of sex. At the simplest level it is a physical/biological drive that provides intense pleasure and thereby assures the procreation of the species.

And, what sex is *not*: *"…sex is not a matter of commitment but one of self-expression and play and exploration and learning and joyful abandonment."* (Dr. M. Scott Peck, *The Road Less Traveled*.)

Sex clearly has its psychological side—the many fantasies, fears, guilt feelings, etc. are the subject of some very interesting books, a few of which I've listed in the bibliography.

So the purpose of sex is procreation, right? Partly.

And the other purpose is pleasure, right? Partly.

And it's good for the mind to wander through fantasyland, right? Partly.

I believe the most helpful way to express the highest purpose of sex is the following:

The highest purpose of sex is emotional closeness

That may seem strange to you at first. It was to me. Sex is mainly physical, right? (That must be a man talking). Wrong!

Here are two opposite approaches to sex. Please excuse my choice of language in the first approach. This is not my normal mode of communication, but it seems appropriate here to give you the unabridged version:

1. "You are so sexy I just want to fuck you. I want to fuck you so bad. You are so sexy. I love your body. I go crazy when I fuck you. I want you to want me to fuck you."

OR

2. "I want to make love with you because I'm crazy about you and I want to feel close to you and sex with you feels good and I want you to know how it feels and I want you to know what makes it feel good and my emotions are so all tangled up together in this sex thing and I just want us to do everything and I hope we'll learn to understand and accept each other."

In the first approach we have purely physical sex. Certainly sex is primal and libidinous. But it is not necessary for it to also be emotionally illiterate, or for one sex partner to "objectify" the other (more on this later). Purely physical sex is "emotional" (e.g. exciting), but it is not "emotional closeness."

In the second approach the desire for shared emotional closeness and transcendent connection is clear.

You choose the one that is right for you…

It is very doubtful that physical sex alone without true chemistry and mature treatment will give long-term enjoyment.

SEX IN A SOULMATE RELATIONSHIP

The ideal quality love relationship is a soulmate relationship. If you are successful in your search for a soulmate, what will your sex life be like?

In a soulmate relationship, sex is both physical and emotional. In its physical form, sex is a connection. But it is a representation of an *emotional desire* for connection, to be close to another person. "I just can't get close enough to you."

In a soulmate relationship, two things of importance happen that give sex a mystical, magical, spiritual quality:

1. Very high chemistry creates a natural emotional connection that goes deep into the soul. This connection exists and is felt before sex ever enters the picture. So sex then becomes an integral part of an existing strong connection. In many ordinary relationships, sex is the connection, often the only connection. Many people try to feel connected through sex. And it helps. But the spiritually fulfilling connection is chemistry; if chemistry is there it can drive the sex into another dimension altogether.

2. Very high maturity provides an environment where the growth of sexual response and excitement can be nurtured. This is in contrast to many immature relationships where discord and unhappiness arise due to lack of understanding, lack of flexibility, lack of communication, etc. This inevitably results in reduced sexual enjoyment. On the other hand, emotionally mature soulmates work at

understanding each other, are highly flexible in solving problems, and communicate their needs and desires. This reduces dissension, increases happiness, and heightens sexual enjoyment.

Sex, by its very nature provides a direct tap into the central nervous system. Thomas Moore in his book *Soul Mates* expresses it this way:

> *Through sex we may be able to express feelings more revealingly than in language.*
>
> *…sex can bring magic into a relationship, and anchor it in a way that no amount of talking or doing things together can. On the other hand, because sex touches such deep places in the soul, sexual failure can be devastating.*

Soulmate lovers understand that for them sex provides this direct tap into the soul. Little by little, soulmates share their fears, their fantasies, and their emotional deprivations. They take care to support each other's experimentation and even failure. And in so doing, they become closer than ever.

Without real chemistry, the interest in sharing these fears, fantasies, and deprivations is not high enough to make the relationship, or the sex, go very far.

Without maturity, the trust and capability levels necessary to blend two souls together are not very high, so the sex reaches a plateau and flattens out and can become boring.

With both chemistry and maturity, the interest and trust can, with time, allow all defenses to come down and a true merging of souls can occur. Slowly they meld together. It's frightening, because each person becomes different than they were—"I am no longer me—I am a blend of you and me." "I am afraid because maybe I am losing my identity." "But it is beautiful because I am becoming a better and stronger person."

"Sex" is replaced by "making love." There is an emotional shift as I learn that I will not lose myself, because you will guard my uniqueness as something of value to our relationship. I learn that I can become more of a person than I was, not less, even though I may be different. And in the safety of our mature soul-level connection I learn that I can say and do those things that I've always been afraid to say or do before, and this takes its highest form of expression in our lovemaking. Our fantasy/committed/variety/slow/fast lovemaking becomes an extension of the merging of our souls. Our bonding is not captivity, and our understanding is "wavelength natural." Our lovemaking creates an excitement that powers our spaceship to places unheard of before.

At the same time, soulmate lovers are realistic. They are aware of the "soulful shadow" of sex, as described by Thomas Moore:

> *On the other hand, there is no way to enter soulful sexuality without being soiled by its…shadow. As we answer the call of the sexual spirits, we will likely find ourselves in one mess or another, but this fall into sexual darkness may not be a literal fault. It may simply signal that we are getting close to the soul, which in its…sexual expression is never fully clean or bright.*

Summarizing all this in terms of the Love Dice, we have:

"Soulmates."

Very consistent, very high quality, out of this world sex. Sexual and emotional deprivation have largely been overcome. This type of relationship is extremely hard to find.

SEX IN OTHER RELATIONSHIPS

The sexual experience in other relationship types can be compared to that of soulmates using the Love Dice. Remember that the Love Dice provide an excellent way of visualizing the critical elements of love relationships, and although we use dice as a representation, love is not a game.

Here are some other relationships and their sexual/emotional content:

"Very Good Love Relationship."

Very consistent, good sex. The "very good love relationship" can approximate the soulmate connection and achieve "good" emotional closeness and sex. Although easier to find than a soulmate, not very many people find this level of fulfillment. But it can be quite satisfying, and can largely overcome sexual/emotional deprivation. I strongly support this type of relationship even though I myself am searching for a "soulmate."

"Good Love Relationship."

Somewhat consistent, pretty good sex. This type of relationship can, with time and commitment to emotional growth including the overcoming of sexual deprivation, become a "very good love relationship" as described above. Unfortunately, too many people never achieve even this "good love" level of quality in their relationship experience.

"Diamond in the Rough."

Inconsistent, but can be very high quality sex. Has the potential to become soulmates if the partners can weather the storms of emotional growth. Also has the potential to cause a lot of pain as the partners struggle to overcome their sexual and emotional deprivations along with other immaturities (diamonds take a long time to grow).

"Typical Relationship"
(Can it really be called love?).

Very inconsistent, not very high quality sex. Lots of sexual and emotional deprivation. In my experience, the typical everyday garden-variety marriage relationship looks something like this, with a mixed bag of lackluster chemistry and maturity scores. What you have in such a relationship are glimpses of connection, moments of emotional closeness, and occasional or even frequent moments of physical pleasure. But these moments are outweighed and covered over by a pall of low interest, unbalanced interest, continued deprivation, and the criticizing/blaming/neglecting/complaining/demanding/unrealistic behavior that is the expression of immaturity. Still, for many, glimpses and moments of closeness and connection may be better than emptiness or nothingness, and may be easier than emotional growth or searching.

DEPRIVATION IN GENERAL

I've said that the soulmate couple can easily share their fears, desires, fantasies, and deprivations, and other quality love relationships can also do so, though to a lesser degree. I want to dwell further here on the subject of deprivations, because it is central to any discussion of quality love relationships. I'm sure most of us would agree that if we had to spend seventeen years of adult life without sex that would constitute quite a deprivation indeed!

But the deprivation subject goes much deeper than just the casual observation that, "Oh I could never go even seventeen days let alone seventeen years without sex." Deprivation begins in childhood with parental denial of normal, healthy sexual feelings and continues to build with adolescent guilt, rejection and unfulfillment. By the time we've had one or a few inhibited adult relationships, deprivation has become a profound (though often subconscious) psychological issue.

Men seem to feel that they are deprived of quality sex, whereas women seem to feel they are deprived of quality emotional connection. This difference leads to confusion and frustration, making mutual understanding between the sexes difficult. But we need to have some understanding of this underlying deprivation before looking at the long search for a quality love relationship and the possibility of further starvation.

THE WAR BETWEEN THE SEXES

Men's experience of deprivation is usually different from women's. For women the deprivation is an emotional one. Men feel the deprivation as a physical one. Most men don't even realize that in addition to this physical frustration there is an underlying need for emotional closeness. They can't see beyond the unfulfillment of their immediate physical desires.

Women say, "All men want is sex."

Men say, "All I want is more sex."

It seems to me that both women and men are saying the same thing, "Men don't get enough sex."

So why don't they get together and do something about it?

Unfortunately most people don't think beyond these clichés, which are only half-truths. Women say, "All men want is sex," but what they really *mean* is, "Men *shouldn't* want so much sex without quality *emotional content*." And men say, "All I want is more sex," but what they really mean is, "I want more *quality* sex without having to pay such a *high price* (commitment, marriage, divorce, child support, etc.)."

When the respective statements are thus made more accurately, they are not so simple, and no one likes complicated problems. Therefore it is easier to stick to the old clichés (and leave the problem unresolved).

Yet the problem needs to be solved. It has been going on for a long time. Too long, it seems to me.

According to Dr. Marie Robinson, the war between the sexes began in 1784 with the invention of the steam engine, which launched the Industrial Revolution. She says prior to that time the historic division of labor between men and women in the home and on the farm had been based on mutual admiration and respect. But factories and increased specialization brought separation, misunderstanding, and competition.

The war was continuing in 1959. Dr. Robinson quotes one of her female patients, who describes her underlying attitude toward men as a whole as, "All they (men) wanted from a woman was sex."

The war was still going on in 1980 when Nancy Friday (*Men In Love*) said, "Women have placed his [man's] body at war with his soul."

After 210 years it had still not abated when Thomas Moore in 1994 explained the cause of the war as follows, "Our culture's fear of sex and our anxious controls on sex are at bottom due to a mistrust of the soul."

In 1999, John Gray (*Mars and Venus—Connecting with Your Soulmate)* recommends withholding sex until you're in an exclusive relationship and you love each other. In my opinion he is recommending that the war continue, and it probably will.

As with any war, it is doing more damage than good. Women feel alone, misunderstood, and used. Men feel alone, misunderstood, and neglected.

Men and women meet in bed. They meet in marriage.

But they are not together. They are still far apart.

Women are angry with men. Men are angry with women.

Something has got to give!

If the search for a quality love relationship is to be successful, peace must be found.

If men want to "win the war" for sex, they must understand the emotional deprivation of women.

If women want to "win the war" for emotional closeness, they must understand the sexual deprivation of men.

DEPRIVATION IN WOMEN

I am not a woman. I have never been a woman. I have never been through what women go through. But I have tried to understand the women with whom I've had intimate association. I have wanted to understand the unintelligible, to accept the unacceptable. I have listened to women, read books about women, and talked to professional psychologists about women. The fact remains that I'm a man.

So I think I can best describe the female experience by relaying stories that have been told to me.

THE STORY OF CHARLOTTE

Charlotte was a buyer for a women's clothing chain. Here is what she had to say:

> *I guess I'm beautiful, as men see it. And I guess that's good. But I'm not sure. Because I want to be loved for me, not how I look. How I look is surface. It fades. It's short lived.*
>
> *It's really wavelength that counts. But it's so frustrating when men don't understand that. I can't enjoy a man as a friend because if I don't go to bed with him he turns on me.*
>
> *But that's what I'm hungry for. That's what I'm deprived of. I need someone who wants to talk to me, who wants to know me, who wants to listen to me, who values my thoughts, who stays open to me, who doesn't turn on me, who doesn't close off, or run, or attack, or push, or any of those things.*
>
> *I mean, after all, I'm a person. I have a mind, a heart, emotions, desires, goals, etc. I'm not just a pretty face!*
>
> *In junior high and high school everyone wanted me. I had to hold them off. I got married early, not knowing what was important in choosing a mate. It was hard to make a go of it. Working. Children. No real emotional closeness with my husband. I've had to be the strong one and hold it all together. I've never really gotten attention, closeness, talking, listening, help, or emotional understanding. I mean I had to plan our whole vacation by myself while he was off fishing!*

So I take care of him, just like I take care of the kids. When he gets hard he wants to put it in me. But he doesn't want to spend time or talk or understand. And I do.

Why doesn't he understand (or even want to)? He probably senses that I'm not really in love with him but he doesn't want to admit it. So he keeps everything on a surface level.

And maybe understanding a woman is not easy. Giving a woman equal freedom to be a person is not easy. He may be threatened by my working. But in any case I am not getting the emotional fulfillment that I need.

I don't think I'm different in this regard. Women generally are not receiving emotional/feeling understanding from men. We get the desire for sex and the pressure for exclusivity.

We feel like we are slaves, living in captivity. We feel weaker physically and economically. We feel hunted, captured. That is the life of a woman—feeling hunted, feeling afraid, wanting to be loved, wanting to be an equal, not wanting to be captured. So we run, and we hide, and we peek out from behind trees, and we take cover with a man who is less powerful than ourselves, so we can feel in control. But then we still feel unfulfilled. Because we want an equal partner. So we look down on our inferior mate.

But our greatest fear is still the hunter, who uses our emotional desire for connection to place us in captivity.

I have lived with the hunt. I have lived with captivity. So I fantasize about freedom and about understanding. I fantasize about a man who will be a friend and a helper. Who will love me forever for the person I am, who will accept my faults, who likes cuddling and touching and kids and sex. But where there is something more than just sex that holds us together.

Note that this is coming from a married woman. Obviously marriage is not necessarily the solution to a woman's deprivations. This is because her need for understanding, intimacy, closeness, etc. will not be fulfilled unless there is a chemical connection with her husband *and* her husband has the emotional maturity to give her the attention/understanding she needs. Usually there is not such chemical connection and/or there is not emotional maturity. Then all that is left is sex.

So women say: "All men want is sex." "All men think about is sex." "Men just want my body."

They become aware of this at an early age. And it stays with them as a putdown, a dilemma, a deprivation.

THE STORY OF APRIL

Charlotte was a beautiful woman. Not all women are physically beautiful—beauty is a genetic stroke of good luck. But it seems that the deprivation for "not-so-beautiful" women is pretty much the same—no one to understand their inner feelings. The following are journal entries written by April, a not-so-physically-beautiful (but very beautiful inside) lady. I reprint them here verbatim, with her permission:

> *If I could look inside and see, what would there be in me? So many emotions still trying to find their way and place. So many parts of me, all little fragments trying to be whole. So many emotions: the blues, woes, and the tears.*
>
> *The joy, the woman, the one I want to be is waiting somewhere deep, deep inside of me. I hope I find and meet her before I die.*
>
> *I'd like to know why so much pain had to be felt by something or someone like me.*

> *If I could look back and see who I was meant to be—who would I be now? A woman strong and true, unafraid of uncertainty and all things new.*
>
> *A woman full of life, a devoted mother, who can set good values of strength, understanding, love, and friendship. A hard worker to strive for the future, to realize that without pain there are no gains in life.*
>
> *I'd like to undo so many things; it seems so easy to say. But there are still so many things holding me back and down—lack of adventure, self-confidence, and personal maturity. It's so hard to just let go and be free.*
>
> *I'm tired of being scared. I want more of life.*

Then, a year later:

> *Slowly I am becoming a free and beautiful butterfly. To see myself with delight is an awesome sight. I've been such a jittery little thing, so scared of the world, and more so of myself.*
>
> *At times I've been like a newborn, so weak and vulnerable, so dependent. Other times a tiger cub unafraid of adventure, able to explore with curiosity the unknown. Sometimes a soaring eagle with unlimited power.*
>
> *But now a butterfly, free to be free, to fly above all, to see what I see for myself, to live for the day with life and delight.*

Although April was very shy, and generally afraid of sharing her inner feelings, she gave me permission to print these words, hoping they would help others gain insight. Again, we can feel directly from her words the deprivation, the fear, the longing for emotional expression.

Charlotte and April are not alone it their deprivation. The following quotes describing the female experience come from the essay, "Inhibited Femininity," by the renowned psychoanalyst Karen Horney:

> *Our culture, as is well known, is a male culture, and therefore by and large not favorable to the unfolding of woman and her individuality.*
>
> *To the extent that the envy of the male is in the foreground, [disturbances of female functions] express themselves in resentment against the male as the privileged one—similar to the concealed hostility of the worker against his employer and his efforts to defeat the employer or to weaken him psychologically by the thousand means of daily guerilla warfare.*
>
> *Whether [these disturbances] reveal themselves in indifference or morbid jealousy, in distrust or irritability, in claims or feelings of inferiority, in a need for lovers or for intimate friendships with women, they have one thing in common—the incapacity for a full (that is, including both body and soul) love relationship with a heterosexual love object.*
>
> *Since in women the emotional life is, as a rule, much more closely and uniformly connected with sexuality, she cannot give herself completely when she does not love or is not loved.*

According to Karen Horney, emotional deprivation in women is at least in part culturally induced. Therefore cultural changes are probably necessary to improve the situation. But I hope men who read this book will take all of the above to heart in their relationships with women.

DEPRIVATION IN MEN

It may be easy to write off the concept of sexual deprivation in men by thinking that there are very few men who actually get no sex. Men will find it somehow, someway, sometime.

And it's true, most men today can find some amount of some kind of sex. But they rail at the price they have to pay in terms of dating, relationships, commitment, marriage, children, divorce, child support, etc. And they are unhappy with the quality of the sex that they are able to get. The result is they get less sex than they really want and it is not of the quality that they really want. So they still feel deprived, and to a significant degree.

So, as we've discussed before in this book on other topics such as chemistry and maturity, the issue comes down to a matter of *degree*. Sexual deprivation is not black and white, "deprived" or "not deprived." It is a question of "degree of deprivation."

If sexual deprivation is just a matter of degree, and if sex is much more available now than it used to be, how bad is this deprivation thing, anyway? In my experience, the deprivation goes very deep. Its hidden power threatens to destroy existing relationships and curtail the search for a quality love relationship. It catapults men and women into relationships before they're ready, before they've found quality love or their soulmate.

Understanding deprivation is made worse by the general lack of knowledge about chemistry and maturity. If a man is getting sex but there's not really chemistry, it's almost like not getting sex at all. (And usually sex will significantly disappear from such a relationship.) Or if a man is getting sex but the woman is immature, one day she's on and the next day she's off, sex may even come to have a negative connotation because it "baits" him back into an unhealthy situation.

Unfortunately most men (and many women) are largely unaware of these dynamics. He knows only that he doesn't get enough sex, or the sex he is getting isn't good enough, or the price he's paying is too high. *Something* is wrong, even if he doesn't know what it is.

So emotionally the man withdraws into himself. He restricts his view of women. He fantasizes about sex.

Unfortunately, as Nancy Friday explains, the man's deprivation often began long before he ever got involved with his current partner. It is something so deep-seated in his psyche that even he does not realize what is going on. Her best-selling book *Men in Love* describes the "rage" that men feel toward women. Although written in 1980, not much has changed since then.

> *"Don't do this," mother says to her little boy. "You must do that." Sit, stand, eat, sleep—the commands batter his self-esteem all day long. Eventually the child digs in his heels and says NO… The boy's rage against mother's rules is evidence of his struggle to preserve an emerging sense of himself as his own man.*
>
> *Tired of the battle, he removes himself from mom's control by spending more time out of the house.*
>
> *In our society, saying no to sex is usually the feminine role. The girl's outrage at the boy's sexual advances comes from trying to be as much like her mother as possible; those are her rules for gender identity… Controlling men, denying men, offering sex only with strings attached, confusing it with love, romance, and marriage—that becomes second nature, the very mark of a lady.*
>
> *The result to men is that while biology drives them to seek sexual satisfaction, they feel they must "attack" women to get it. Fortunately for the survival of the human race, the*

sexual imperative will not be denied. The girl who at fifteen made him feel like a beast capitulates when she is twenty. But there is a price. "No," she says, "only if you love (and/or marry) me." "No," she says as a wife, "I don't feel like it tonight because you were mean to me yesterday." "No," she says, "I will never try that because it is disgusting."

The husband feels a familiar loss of power, a frustration of desire, a damming up of his most central self. He is regressed back to those angers first felt when he was so little he had to do as women ordered. Some men may put the resulting frustration and rage into their work or into extramarital affairs. Others may run away or just have a philosophical drink with the boys and forget it.

How does this play out in real life? Here are two stories that give some insight into how men feel:

THE STORY OF JERRY

Jerry managed the restaurant in a large hotel. Here is what he had to say about deprivation:

I was a sensitive child. I was shy—my mother was not at ease socially and so neither was I. As early as third grade I was aware that none of the girls were interested in me. I didn't understand why. Now I know they were already responding to social stereotypes. Quiet, sensitive, shy men just didn't make the cut in third grade! Of course the girls didn't know what they were doing and neither did I. All I knew was it hurt.

And then my sexuality started coming alive. No one ever talked about it, so it must be wrong. But something in me rebelled. I wanted sex. I wanted closeness. And it started to become clear—if I wanted to have girls, if I wanted to have sex, if I wanted to have closeness, then I needed to match up to the stereotype. The cheerleaders and the majorettes went out with the football heroes and the other girls went out with the boys with fancy cars. If I asked them out they said, "No." I knew what I had to do. Switch from academics to athletics. Get a job. Buy a car.

It didn't work.

So naturally I was happy when I met Adrian. There was closeness, sex, hope, and happiness. And then she broke up with me. What could I do? Build a shell.

Meanwhile all the drunks were getting all the sex because "good girls don't."

Drunk girls do.

So what do you do if you're not the drinking type?

And then I met Sarah and we got married. But we were both immature. And the natural flow of chemical connection wasn't there. Neither of us understood these dynamics. She thought marriage should last forever. I thought I should be able to love her, even though sex dwindled to once every month or two.

From the outside everything looked perfect. But on the inside, I wasn't getting enough sex and I was furious.

So, even while married I dreamed of sex. I dreamed of sex with beautiful women, with multiple women, in all possible positions, and always they said just one word—"Yes."

And then came Francine. She was the goddess of "Yes." We had sex every night. She loved everything. She couldn't get enough. And I couldn't get enough. The mutual chemistry was there in spades. Love was beautiful.

> *And then it was gone. Only pain. And emptiness.*
> *Hope re-emerged with Phyllis. And then sudden death.*
> *What is left when love fails repeatedly? Sex. Sex may not be as fulfilling as love should be, but neither is it as painful. Compared to drugs and alcohol, it is not dangerous to the health (assuming safe sex practices). Sex is pure pleasure. It may not be readily available, but it is always desirable.*
>
> *I came to hold the belief that since love always fails, and women don't really understand men, sex must be the best that women have to offer. I think many men feel the same.*
>
> *That's why men objectify women. If the woman is thought of as an ice cream cone or a lollipop, there is no question about love or rejection. There is only delicious pleasure. Men don't want to get hurt and they can't deal with the rejection and the lack of understanding, so they go flying or fishing or drinking with the guys, and afterwards go looking for an ice cream cone.*

Obviously Jerry suffered from the pain of sexual deprivation. But hopefully somewhere in here he also began to get a first glimmer of understanding and therefore was able to move beyond the deprivation to a higher plane of maturity.

THE STORY OF TROY

Here is what Troy, an investment banker, had to say:

> *I thought maybe I could solve my deprivation by going to a nude bar. I was not alone... I sat in the front row and watched the dancers. I have been to many nude or topless bars and it is always the same—look but don't touch. I*

want to look, so one desire (visual) is met. Some are beautiful, some are good dancers, others are not. But when I see them, I want to touch them, not just look. I want to kiss them, not just watch. I want to hold them and feel them and make love to them and make them feel it too. But I can only sit there and be teased and frustrated. One desire is met (visual) but four others are not. Watch eight dancers in an hour. Eight validations visually, thirty-two rejections to the other senses. It's unnatural! Beastly! But the beer helps.

Even during the day I want to look at, touch, feel, kiss, smell, taste, and penetrate women. I may be capable of ejaculation only once or a few times a day, but I have unlimited ability to desire touching, kissing, tasting, etc. Therefore I have unlimited ability to receive multiple ego blows every day. Sonja does not smile at me. Wanda smiles at me but will not let me touch her. I want to kiss Barbara but she's married. I ask Cindy out but she says "No." After this happens often enough I don't have to ask in order to hear the "NO." I just play the tape again in my mind. And it plays over and over and over and over.

If I were to count all these rejections, real and imagined, large and small, estimating, say, 10 per day, from age 12 to age 30 I would have 65,700 rejections! How can I not be angry with women? What I thought I needed was a woman who could provide 10 "acceptance validations" per day (just to keep up with the daily onslaught of imagined rejections) and an additional 65,700 acceptance validations to make up for the accumulated dents to my ego. Maybe in this way she could help me overcome my deprivation. So I got married.

The deprivation got worse during my marriage. And after my divorce quality sex was still hard to find. Naturally, being a man, I persisted. Sex became my obsession.

> *For a while I kept count of the number of women I slept with, like notches on a gun. At first it wasn't very many. And it was hard work. But persistence paid off and ultimately I lost count. Now counting is not important. Because without emotional substance sex is just sex and it is not really satisfying for very long.*
>
> *I still want sex, but I want it with someone I enjoy and trust and ultimately want it with someone I love and trust. I have friends, sexual partners, kids, work, food, shelter, security, etc. But I don't have the deep connection that I want. It is very hard to find.*
>
> *My fantasies are now, "Please see me for who I am," "Please spend enough time to know who I am," "If the feeling is there please love me instead of running away," "Sex is secondary." Although my sexual fantasies still exist, I have had enough experiences of the pure sex variety to reveal a deeper deprivation. A deprivation of closeness, understanding, chemistry, and consistent loving friendship.*
>
> *Believe it or not, sex is no longer my primary deprivation. I have largely overcome this deprivation through many fortunate experiences. I have been fortunate to find abundant sex, but I have had to work hard to do so. And in spite of abundant sex, I can still feel the deprivation. It is a matter of degree. My degree of deprivation has gone down, but it is not yet zero. And my memory of deprivation is still very clear.*

Actually, it appears that Jerry's deprivation now is similar to the deprivation in a woman. Sexually, a woman can have all she wants. So her deeper needs for friendship, closeness, non-abandonment are quickly revealed. When her emotional needs are fulfilled, her sexual person blooms. Jerry seems to have arrived at this state as a result of satisfying his sexual deprivation.

THE SAHARA DESERT

Here is an analogy that gives another picture of just how deep sexual deprivation goes. Although the analogy speaks of the male sexual deprivation (water), it could be modified to apply to the female emotional deprivation (food).

Crossing the desert would be a very trying experience, even for a healthy well-nourished individual. But crossing it without water would be nearly impossible. I think this analogy can be helpful because understanding and dealing with sexual deprivation is central to survival in the search for a quality love relationship, just as understanding and dealing with water deprivation is central to survival in the desert.

It is hard for many women to understand that in men sex is a biological need, just like water. They understand this intellectually, but cannot accept it emotionally because it is not the same for them. Women's sexual desire is equally great, but it is not a biological need. Marie Robinson describes it this way:

> *We know...that woman has the same need for passion, the same capacity for sexual response that man has.*
> *However, it is not a biological necessity for woman to have an orgasm to fulfill her sexual role. It is only necessary for her to receive the sperm...*

The point is not whether men enjoy sex more than women. The point is that sex is natural and that frustration of sexual needs in the male is a very real biophysical deprivation. One may not die from it, as one would from lack of water, but there is an "emotional death" that is central to the search for quality love. Hopefully it will be easier to understand this deprivation if we use a metaphor (water) that is not so emotionally charged.

A man needs three quarts of water a day to live. If he is in the desert for years with only one quart per week, we can't say he is totally deprived of water. But years with one quart per week will literally drive a man crazy, if it doesn't kill him.

Now imagine that you meet this same man a year or two after he emerges from the desert. He is back to good health and looks otherwise normal and you fall in love with him. Maybe there is even true chemistry. But you find as you get to know him that whereas you may want to go to a movie, or a moonlight walk on the beach, or a quiet bedtime talk, all he can think about is WATER! It is compulsive. He can't control it. You can't stand it. You pass a store and he wants to go in and buy a bottle of water just to be sure. You pass a decorative fountain and he wants to stop and take a drink. You try to plan a family vacation and he wants to know where you will find water.

So you make sure that he always gets plenty of water. And you'd think after a few days or months or years of giving him water, he could start to think about something else.

But he has been traumatized by deprivation. After years of insufficient water, even when he has enough, he fears being without it, and thinks about water above all else.

And let's suppose you are now giving him one quart of water a day. That is a lot more than he was getting in the desert, and he should be satisfied, right?

Wrong. He needs three quarts a day. If you can give him three quarts a day, consistently, for ten years, maybe he will start to place moonlight walks on the beach above water in his priority system. But only when water has become taken for granted for so long that he no longer worries about it.

I don't want to overdo this analogy. But if you think about it when you're frustrated with your man because all he can think about is sex (water), maybe you'll remember how long he spent in the desert.

As a parallel, men could think of women's *emotional* deprivation as a "food" deprivation. "Food and water" (emotional and sexual fulfillment) are the essential nutrients during the search for a quality love relationship.

There is an interesting paradox to this issue of male sexual deprivation. A minority of men, by virtue of their genetics (good looking) or other attributes (funny, rich) never have any difficulty getting what they want from women. All say "Yes" to him. He has a flood of opportunities for sex and semi-sex (touching, kissing, etc.) with very few rejections. You would think, then, that such a person would not suffer from deprivation and would not exhibit the "primacy of physical sex" syndrome and would therefore be able to provide women with the emotional understanding and support they need. But oddly enough, they also are unable to give what women need. The reason is that sex is so good and so pleasurable and so *easy* for them, that they never have to extend themselves emotionally on behalf of another person. Everything comes easy and they *like* it that way. They even *expect* it to be that way. And they expect the *woman* to extend *herself* for *them*, and not the other way around. So, paradoxically, it is the deprived man who is (slightly) more likely to be able to understand that women also have their own deprivations. Thus the deprived man will be slightly more willing to extend himself to try to understand a woman. But not until he has had some "water." Lots of water. Enough water to feel sure he'll *always* have enough.

SOLUTIONS TO SEXUAL AND EMOTIONAL DEPRIVATION

Now let's consider what to do about sex and emotional fulfillment during the geologic time that is probably necessary to find a quality love relationship or soulmate.

We can now see this in perspective of the sexual/emotional deprivation that began in childhood, continued through adolescence, and by the time of adulthood is an unconscious, deeply ingrained, compulsive need. And we have looked at it from the opposite perspectives of men and women, although the truth is that both men and women need both sexual and emotional fulfillment.

It is easy to understand that the general unavailability of quality sexual and/or emotional fulfillment during a long waiting period is one of the primary reasons for the failure of individuals to find quality love or soulmate relationships. People get lonely, want emotional closeness, want sex, and so they get married or otherwise involved in a committed relationship. This often preempts them from finding their soulmate. Men probably fall into this trap faster than women, because of their biological need for sex and the degree of their long-term deprivation. Women tend to be more cautious because of their desire for emotional fulfillment and their concerns over unwanted pregnancy and disease.

Chances are that women will have more insight into these problems than men. Women are more likely to see that it is to their advantage to help men overcome sexual deprivation so women can have emotional closeness. Men will have a harder time seeing past their sexual deprivation and so will be less able to help women with their emotional needs.

Nancy Friday put it this way:

> *...women have one tremendous advantage in sexual development that is usually forgotten: Women rarely need to get angry at men for not allowing them, for not offering them, sex. Women do not spend their sexual lives with the gender that represents the great "NO" sayer of childhood.*

That is not to say men should sit back and let women do all the work of overcoming deprivation. On the contrary, I hope many men will read this book and participate equally in the effort to increase understanding of relationships and decrease deprivation (both sexual and emotional). It will be to their great benefit in the long run.

If finding a soulmate is hard, changing attitudes is even harder. Yet that is what is necessary to overcome deprivation and give quality love a chance to succeed.

Back in 1959 Marie Robinson used these words:

> *Taboos against sexuality have characterized Western civilization. The art of love, therefore, seems to me to be largely the art of getting over societal induced ignorance, superstition, and inhibitions.*

And here we are, largely still stuck in the same mud.

Some of this "getting over societal induced ignorance" can be done in the privacy of one-on-one individual relationships. But a widespread increase in fulfillment will require changes in societal norms. When enough individuals change, society will follow.

Women will probably need to be the prime initiators of these options because (1) women have more insight than men, and (2) women control the sex.

For women to take these options seriously will require an attitude shift. The attitude shift is that they must decide whether they actually want to win the war for emotional closeness, or just go on fighting it. To win the war women must change their strategy. The current strategy of "control the sex/control the man" may work to get a husband and to keep him long enough to have children and assure child support, but it will not overcome his deprivation and bring about closeness.

To win the war, it seems to me, women must give up their control of sex. One at a time, or as a society, this will be the real "triumph of love over rage." Women need to devise ways to increase the availability of quality sex to men. Just like providing water to a man who's been lost in the desert. And only women can supply sex. There is no other source of supply.

Thomas Moore in *Soul Mates* puts this issue of sex and morality into the context of the soul:

> *Although putting moral fences around sex is understandable,…the soulful aspect of sex can be deeply wounded… What if we didn't place sex and morality so stringently in opposition? What if we thought that the more sexual we are and the more erotically we live, the more moral our lives would be?*
>
> *As sweet as it sometimes sounds, care of the soul is a radical departure from modern notions of living correctly and successfully …Soul injects life with reasons that go against much of what is felt to be good, intelligent, and prudent.*

I guess I will have to "go against much of what is felt to be good, intelligent, and prudent" in order to make some suggestions for changing attitudes. So here goes…

Some options are:

1. Focus on Mutual Chemistry and Maturity

The first step in solving emotional deprivation is to define the problem correctly. When women say "men just want my body" or "I just want to be loved for me," they are only taking the first step in defining the problem. The next step is to define exactly what it means to "just be loved for me." Hopefully by now we have some insight to the answer. It means finding someone where there is *mutual chemistry* and *mutual maturity*. Most books on relationships don't focus clearly or directly on the issues of mutual chemistry and mutual maturity. You will have a head start toward emotional fulfillment if you do focus on these crucial elements.

If the chemical feeling isn't there, a person can never love you at the deep soul level you need, no matter how beautiful you are or how nice a person you are. And if he or she doesn't have maturity they cannot love you at the level you need no matter how good the chemistry.

So overcoming emotional deprivation means finding someone who is chemically connected to you in a natural way and who is mature enough to love you for that. He or she will then be "loving you for you" and you will be able to feel it. Quality sex grows out of the chemistry and the maturity, not the other way around.

For many people emotional deprivation happens because they are looking for love in all the wrong places: It's not about someone's looks or age or humor or money or status—it's about chemistry and maturity. If you are looking for someone who is handsome, young, funny, rich, and famous, you are unlikely to find someone who will love you for you.

2. Establish Emotionally Fulfilling Friendships

Overcoming emotional deprivation does not have to happen all at once. It doesn't mean you have to go out right away and find your ultimate soulmate/lover/partner. Perhaps as an interim step you could find a friend or lover where the chemistry isn't quite up to your ultimate standards. Such a friend could be single/unattached or married/attached. But if he or she is mature enough, the relationship could help to alleviate the deprivation.

Find friends where there is a chemical connection and who understand you and respect you and who have the maturity to love you for whatever they see in you. These friends could be men or women. In general I suggest finding one or more emotionally mature friends of the opposite sex where there is at least a medium degree of chemical connection. To include sex or not (safe sex, of course) as part of the relationship would be up to the two of you.

Hopefully it should be obvious that because we are talking here about an interim step to "fill the gap" during the search for a quality love relationship, the most important thing to look for is maturity. That way you'll be more likely to get something of value from the relationship. A mature person will be able to accept the interim status of the relationship and will value the association with you. An immature person, in contrast, will tend to drain you, cling to you, interfere with your search, and feel "used" if the relationship ends.

(I want to be sure that you do not confuse this "interim step"—look first for maturity—with the search itself, where it is important to "look first for chemistry." The "look first for chemistry" approach was discussed in Chapter 5 as the "diamond in the rough" strategy. It is a long-term approach to connecting with your soulmate or other quality love relationship. On the other hand, the "look first for maturity" approach, while it can provide a quality, emotionally fulfilling friendship, will not lead to a fulfilling love relationship if the true chemistry isn't there at the beginning.)

It's easier said than done for a woman to find a male friend who understands and respects her for the person she is. The reason so many women are deprived of understanding and emotional closeness is because so few men know how to give it. The sources of understanding without demanding sex and/or turning against you are few and far between. And those that do exist are not easily identified. Men don't go around wearing signs that say, "I am mature and know the importance of chemistry and am capable of being a friend and giving understanding without demanding sex or otherwise placing you in captivity." (Maybe they *should* wear signs!)

3. Expand Educational Programs

The #1 enemy of the search for quality love relationships is lack of knowledge. Schools teach the anatomy of sex and if we are lucky they teach about safe sex. But no one teaches about chemistry, maturity, how they are defined and measured, and how they can be found or increased. We learn by watching our parents (one mistake after another). We learn by watching TV and movies and reading books (more social stereotypes). It's no wonder we grow up as emotional and romantic illiterates!

Education should start in the schools. The vocabulary of feelings should be a required "foreign language." Understanding chemistry and maturity and how they relate to finding a mate and to maintaining a healthy relationship should be just as important as geometry. Sex as emotional closeness and what this means should be given equal weight to sex as procreation and the spreading of disease. Deprivation in both men and women should be discussed along with how to best overcome it. The value of sexual and non-sexual friendships and everything else in this and related books should be placed into curriculum programs to bring adolescents to a state of fluent proficiency in what will probably be one of the most important decisions of their lives.

Education need not be only in the schools. Adult education and self-study are means available to those who are already out of school. The topics covered should be the same as those just mentioned. Men would be well served to pay particular attention to those subjects related to emotional closeness, emotional deprivation in women, feelings, etc. Women could learn from subjects such as sexual fantasies, sexual deprivation in men, and sexual availability.

One-on-one friendships can also help meet the educational need. Women and men can talk and they can learn from each other.

One of the problems in any of these scenarios is sorting out the wheat from the chaff. There are lots of books with recommendations, and even more individuals with opinions. But they are not all helpful. In fact many can be very misleading. And most tend to deal with only some small part of the whole. I have tried to give references to a few excellent sources of information which, when taken together, can provide a reasonably accurate and complete picture.

4. Identify Emotionally Mature People

I mentioned that men do not go around wearing signs attesting to their maturity. Neither do women. Therefore it's hard to find the right kind of people. I know this sounds a little far out, but wouldn't it be great if there could be a "certification" program of some kind that identifies those men and women who have successfully completed a course of education on chemistry, maturity, relationships, etc. They would have to have proven themselves capable of long-term mature friendships, high-chemistry non-sexual relationships, medium-chemistry sexual relationships, etc. Then if someone is "certified" as an emotionally mature person, they could have some kind of sign, maybe a ring or a pin or something that would identify them to others who want the kind of maturity they bring. A woman looking for a man to provide an emotionally fulfilling friendship would be able to find one faster if she didn't have to check out so many blind alleys in the first place. And the same for a man looking for a sexual friendship. And maybe such a certification could provide an incentive for others to grow up if they came to see the benefits that maturity brings. I don't know who would be qualified to provide such certifications, but it's an idea that's maybe worth talking about further!

5. Increase Sexual Experimentation

Clearly there is much more freedom in this regard now than there was fifty years ago. But it is still hard for a man to get quality sex. Women still say "no" (physically if not verbally) much more often than they say "yes." It's not that sexual experimentation is frowned on so much anymore, it is just not that easy. A prevalent philosophy among women is "I need to know you before we have sex." The alternative philosophy could be "I need to have sex before I can know you."

Fear of pregnancy and sexually transmitted diseases are very real concerns and must be taken into account in any attitude shift that increases the availability of sex. Because responsible sex is crucial to successfully solving the deprivation problem, I have included Appendix 4, information from the Center for Disease Control (CDC) about sexually transmitted diseases and how to prevent them.

During their late teens and early twenties, our culture should focus on providing young adults with as much safe sex as possible and making sure that all young men and women get plenty of sex. Parents often obstruct this, because they frequently advocate limited or no sex, especially for girls, despite the existence of birth control and safe sex techniques.

By the time someone reaches their mid-twenties they should have had so many sexual experiences that they have lost count. They should be taught to not feel guilty, but to enjoy each experience and learn what the opposite sex is like.

I do not propose sexual thrill seeking just for the fun of it or to hurt people. There is a lot of sexual experimentation already taking place, but it's not particularly guided or sanctioned. Because it's not guided there's not much learning taking place, and because it's not sanctioned the "good" kids usually aren't "getting any." I propose sexual experimentation in the context of an "education for life" program so that young men and women (yes, even the good ones) will learn the ingredients of fulfillment at the same time as they are enjoying sex.

The objective would be for both men and women to arrive at their mid-twenties without deprivation (and also without diseases or unwanted children). The objective is for both men and women to have the experience that sex is easily available, natural, and good. Both men and women will then be able to see more clearly that what is *really* valuable is the special emotional closeness that happens when there is true chemistry. And they will not be afraid to wait for such a person because men will believe they will never run out of water (sex), and women will believe that men understand the emotional aspect of sex (food).

Even if the idyllic world described above is impossible to achieve totally within the next two centuries, maybe there are some aspects of it that can happen, or at least an acceleration of the movement in that direction.

6. Establish Sexually Fulfilling Friendships

This is the corollary to "*Establish Emotionally Fulfilling Friendships*" (Option 2 above). In a way it is similar to "*Increase Sexual Experimentation*" (Option 5) but carries with it a little more weight of commitment. As your friend I am committed to your emotional health including your sexual health. When we have sex it is not just a casual occurrence such as might happen in Option 5, but I truly care about you. Note that "commitment" does not mean the same thing as "exclusivity." I can be committed to the emotional and sexual health of several people without forming exclusive relationships.

Right now in this country our definition of friendship implies "platonic." "He or she is a good friend," means we don't sleep together. Maybe we did once, but we don't now. But I question whether this is really a "good" friend. If I really need/want sex but it is not conveniently available, why wouldn't a "good" friend give me sex?

I suggest expanding the concept of friendship to include sex ("Friends Plus"). If you are my friend and you are not getting sexual fulfillment, then I will give it to you. Sex is important, but not so important that I should deprive you of it. And who to better provide you with sexual fulfillment while you are looking for your quality love than your friend? Is it better with a stranger? Or better to continue the deprivation? I think not!

Again, I have described an ideal state. This will not likely happen to a significant degree in a few years or even a few decades. But progress can be made. Some individuals (primarily women) will recognize the truth of what I am saying and reach out to one or two of their male friends. And the men they reach out to will in turn become less deprived and hopefully will become more emotionally sound partners for the right woman in the future.

7. Expand "Open Marriage" Concepts

This is a special subset of "establish sexual friendships" (Option 6). Of all my potential friends, some will be single and some will be married. If only my single friends can help me with my sexual or emotional deprivation, then the source of "water" and "food" is diminished.

"Open Marriage," as conceived in the 1972 book by Nena and George O'Neill, was primarily oriented toward the benefits it could provide to the nuclear couple themselves. My proposal focuses on the benefit it can provide to the single, searching friends of such a couple. The O'Neills alluded to this when they said, "As open love expands, it floods out, encircling and including others."

Technically, "open marriage" does not necessarily imply "sexually open." The O'Neills definition is:

> *Open marriage means an honest and open relationship between two people, based on the equal freedom and identity of both partners. It involves a verbal, intellectual and emotional commitment to the right of each to grow as an individual within the marriage.*

One possible result of an open marriage is "open companionship." Open companionship does not have to be sexual, and it can benefit both the married couple and the other person. Open companionship from within an open marriage can be one source of "Emotionally Fulfilling Friendships" as suggested in Option #2 above. The O'Neills say:

> *Precisely because this bond [the open marriage] is so deep, so secure, and so central to their lives, they [the open marriage partners] can afford to open it up and let others in.*

Open marriage can also (but not necessarily) include the concept of "sexually open." The O'Neills put it this way:

> *We are not recommending outside sex, but we are not saying that it should be avoided, either. The choice is entirely up to you, and can be made only upon your own knowledge of the degree to which you have achieved within your marriage, the trust, identity, and open communication necessary to the eradication of jealousy.*

"Open marriage," especially "sexually open marriage" is even more difficult than "sexual friendships." This is because it exposes insufficient maturity or insufficient chemistry within the marriage. That's not necessarily bad (but then neither is divorce). The possibility of children makes the sexually open marriage concept especially complex. Each person needs to decide what is acceptable to him or her. Sexually open marriage has many pitfalls—it is only for the strongest lovers (who can handle it) or the weakest (where it won't matter). A majority of marriages will not likely be able to handle it, and the potential loss of the relationship could be significant; therefore for them sexually open marriage probably should not be risked. (See Chapter 11 for a more detailed discussion of how much openness a given relationship can likely handle.)

Nevertheless, I believe it is important to increase the availability of quality sex. I believe such an increase will help improve emotional understanding. I include the open marriage concept because the increase in sexual availability has to come from somewhere. Maybe it will come from this or from another of these options, or a combination, or from something else. But if behaviors don't change, the problems will remain the same.

8. Increase the Availability of Professional Sex

Getting parents and schools to support and encourage widespread responsible sexual experimentation is a long shot. Expanding the concept of mature friendship to include sex is certainly possible, depending on how many people read this book and take it to heart. But that is still a one-on-one approach which is unlikely to have a major impact on society in the short term. And expanding the concept of open marriage is only a small subset of expanding the concept of friendship.

One other option that deserves mention is professional sex. Some have termed this the "oldest profession in the world." In this country, except for some places in Nevada, it is illegal. But there are professional (and some unprofessional) "working girls" in virtually every state in the union. No law yet devised has been able to completely control mutual agreement for pleasure and income. Yet current legal prohibitions make professional sex difficult and dangerous for both parties. Therefore it is limited in its ability to fend off deprivation. In many cases it may just add to the guilt.

But professional sex can provide an opportunity for emotional and physical satisfaction without other relational entanglements (affairs, etc.). Unlike the nude bars discussed by Jerry, professional sex is not a tease. It does not relieve one tension while increasing others. It satisfies all five senses. It may not be the ultimate in satisfaction (that's why we are still searching for a quality love relationship), but it can be very good. Most professional sex workers know that the real need is emotional closeness. Most know about male deprivation. The more caring ones seek to serve their clients' needs, meet their deprivations, fulfill their fantasies, and allow open discussion of feelings that are otherwise repressed. In so doing they assure repeat customers, a better business, and help to create an environment where there are fewer deprived men.

Clearly there is a spectrum of sex workers: some are on drugs, linked to crime, have diseases, do not have a caring attitude, or are otherwise unfit to seriously help with the war on deprivation. But it is unfair to label all sex workers with the same stereotype; many are intelligent, caring, clean, quality people. Nor is it fair to disparage the men who seek out professional sex because they are seriously trying to overcome their deprivation and hold out for a quality love relationship.

Exactly how professional sex is going to gain widespread acceptance I don't know. I can only offer a few ideas at this time. Obviously laws would have to change. But acceptance will have to come first. It seems to me that women understanding about deprivation in men and how it links to the woman's emotional fulfillment is the key to this. Perhaps legalization with strong regulation of health aspects is one possibility. Perhaps requiring a "prescription" from a psychologist/psychiatrist/social worker is a way of assuring that the men who participate in professional sex are also getting emotional training from a registered professional, and not just having sex to have sex and reinforce the wrong information over again. Maybe professional sex could be linked to an ongoing educational program wherein men who are enrolled in the program receive instruction in emotional topics and women's needs (see Option 3). Certainly the availability of professional sex as part of the curriculum would be a strong enticement to men to enroll!

The bottom line: If women provide men with more quality sex, men are more likely to provide women with quality emotional closeness. And if men provide women with more quality emotional closeness, women are more likely to provide men with quality sex.

I'm sure many of these ideas seem hard to accept. I said earlier I would probably have to "go against much of what is felt to be good, intelligent, or prudent." I am trying to plant some seeds. Hopefully a few will grow so more people can find fulfillment in their love relationships.

THE SECRET OF SEXUAL "SURRENDER"

I feel this chapter would not be complete without including information on the topic of "sexual surrender." This topic is not specific only to the "search" for a quality love relationship, but applies equally to all marriages and other sexual relationships. However it is not widely understood, even though it is central to overcoming male deprivation and therefore central to women's "winning the war" for emotional closeness. It is important to any relationship that includes sex. This recommendation comes from experts in the field of enhancing women's pleasure, fulfillment, and orgasmic release. Many women may write it off as another showing of male chauvinism, but hopefully others will see the wisdom and read more in the referenced texts.

I should hasten to add that a man cannot expect sexual surrender from his woman if he lounges around the house all the time while she holds down a job and does the housework. A man needs to *earn* the surrender that the following authorities recommend. The importance to a man of sexual surrender at night means that he should focus his day on pleasing the woman in the ways that are important to her.

The information is presented so well in the following books that I feel it is best to simply quote from them directly. My own experience only corroborates what is said here.

Dr. Marie Robinson describes "The Power of Sexual Surrender" in her book of the same title:

> *This…is the idealized picture of the truly feminine woman. While granting that the plane of maturity she has achieved is rather too exalted for most women to attain, I have given her to you for some very concrete reasons…*
>
> *…We have found, in psychiatry, that when a goal has been clearly defined half the battle has been won.*
>
> *What…characterizes her sexually? Well, she's not very modest, I'm afraid…She's not sexually shy at all.*
>
> *However, there is another very important point. I have indicated that sexually she takes her cue from her husband.*

What does she know, do you suppose—know deeply and instinctively—that makes her do this, while other women refuse to?

She knows this: that it is the man who, from the purely physical viewpoint, has to be ready before intercourse can take place. No matter how many books have been written that ignore the fact, it is nevertheless true that, if the man does not have an erection, lovemaking cannot take place.

Just think about it for a moment. A woman can make love at any time; a man only when he is ready. There may be psychologically preferential circumstances for a woman, but there is no physical prerequisite. That is why (by virtue of the deeper sense of reality we spoke of) when her husband is ready to make love our lady is nearly always willing, barring sickness or certain difficulties that may come up during pregnancy. And that is why she is always willing to forgo lovemaking if he is not ready. Her deep altruism makes her extremely sensitive to his moods...

...she knows how much store men put on their potency, how vulnerable they can become if they are made to feel inadequate to the needs of a wife. She would die a thousand deaths rather than have her husband gain any such inference from her actions...

Her eternal acquiescence, her ever-readiness, never lets her in for a painful sexual experience, however. She knows that ninety-nine times out of one hundred even negative sexual feelings in herself will soon return to eagerness, and eagerness to desire. And even if that once in a hundred times occurs, she will still get a profound satisfaction from the pleasure she is able to give her husband...

But she not only takes the lead from him about whether they are gong to make love—the kind of love they are going to make is also usually his decision and, in pure delight, she follows him completely...

But there is even more to the psychic state necessary for orgasm than faith in one's partner and readiness to surrender. There must be a sensual eagerness to surrender. In the woman's orgasm <u>the excitement comes from the act of surrender</u>. There is a tremendous surging physical ecstasy in the yielding itself, in the feeling of being the passive instrument of another person...

There can, it is clear, be no crossed fingers about such yielding, no reservations in such surrender... To those who are moving toward [orgasm] the experience often remains for a time elusive because its very totality, its uncompromising demand that the whole being be swept up in the experience, remains somewhat frightening.

Orgasm, as I have said, is the physical aspect of surrendering. However, while there are similarities between the physical and the psychological experience, there is also an important difference between the two.

The difference is that orgasm cannot be sought entirely rationally. It will arrive when it will arrive, as the end process of a total change in a...woman's deepest psychological attitudes. It cannot be sought separately or as an end in itself. Indeed, to seek it directly, to wait upon it, to try to force it are the surest possible ways of postponing its arrival.

The simple fact is that concentrating on one's sensations during intercourse, wondering if one is feeling the "right" feeling, can destroy real sexual passion more completely that any technique I can think of...

Is there, then, an attitude one can take toward orgasm before one has achieved it? Yes, there is, and we have found it a helpful and productive one. This attitude may be *summarized in this fashion: If one has truly pursued the goal of self-surrender, uprooting and exposing attitudes left over from childhood and youth, the ability to achieve orgasm must inevitably arrive. Until that time, and particularly during intercourse, one must put the matter out of one's mind entirely.*

Another way of looking at this same subject is provided by Dr. John E. Eichenlaub, M. D. in his book, "The Marriage Art." Again I stress that a man must earn this type of behavior from a woman, not expect it as his right.

If you want good sex adjustment as a couple, you must have sexual relations approximately as often as the man requires. This does not mean that you have to jump into bed if he gets the urge in the middle of supper or when you are dressing for a big party. But it does mean that a woman should never turn down her husband on appropriate occasions simply because she has no yearning of her own for sex or because she is tired or sleepy, or indeed for any reason short of a genuine disability. As a rule of thumb, I usually tell women always to meet their husband's sexual requirements unless frank disability keeps them from performing their usual household or working duties or specific disorders of the sex organs themselves make intercourse impossible. Sex is too important for any wife to give it less call upon her energy than cooking, laundry, and a dozen other activities.

...constant availability makes sense in several different ways. The wife who always searches herself to see whether passion is developing only builds sexual anxieties which impair or actually wreck her responsiveness. Constant

availability builds your wifely appeal because sexual impulse is nourished by the memory of past successes and is not impaired by the memory of sexual rebuffs. It builds your husband's sexual capabilities, too, because total confidence and certainty that sexual activity will never lead to disappointment is the most effective potency builder known to man.

Although fairness would seem to dictate similar efforts to please by husbands whose wives require extra gratifications, the male can perform sexually only when he is sufficiently aroused to permit erection. He cannot match her in availability and should not try; but he can help to meet his wife's requirements in several other ways, as discussed in later chapters.

Never think of sexual by-play or early sexual caresses as tentative approaches by which the husband explores his wife's willingness to go on. She should always be willing to go on. Her husband's confidence in his sexual attraction and in marriage ... mean more to both him and to her than the enhanced ardor she might derive if only approached when in the grips of passion. You should confine teasing and coquetry to circumstances and techniques which raise no question of true rejection or denial....

As a couple, you cannot always wait for passionate feminine desire before proceeding with sexual intercourse. In order to build a sound sex life together, you must satisfy the husband's needs from the very start, and in the process develop the wife's erotic nature. Relaxed and willing service to a loved and loving husband provides a wife with steadily deepening emotional satisfaction—satisfaction which ultimately burgeons into anticipatory passion, keen sexual excitement and the intensive reward of orgasm. This build-

up of sexual desire and excitability takes time, and also requires exposure in the sexual situation. A wife cannot conquer sexual constraint or develop ardent desire by hanging back until the spirit moves her...She almost always has to develop her ability to please and begin to take definite pride in that capacity before the full flower of feminine arousal blooms in her breast.

When a husband starts a sexual episode, he needs to feel secure of himself sexually. Any substantial doubt about either his capabilities at the moment or his worth as a sex partner dampens his ardor in a hurry. This is one reason why a constantly willing wife inspires increased potency—by her actions, she accepts him as a reliably good sex partner, which builds his confidence more than anything she (or I) could say..."

THE STORY OF STEVE AND RACHEL

In this chapter I have suggested that we need to change societal attitudes if we want to increase the odds of success in the soulmate search. And I have given a few ideas about how to effect change. My purpose is not to do an in-depth study of how to change social attitudes, but to identify the need for such change in the challenge of searching for our soulmate or other quality love relationship. If the need is understood and acknowledged, little by little we will find ways to change society.

The story of Steve and Rachel is a story of a man and of one woman who understood the need for cultural change and lived her life accordingly. I almost didn't include this story because of its graphic content. But as I said in Chapter 3, *love relationships are not for the fainthearted*. The reason I did include it is so you can see Rachel's open-mindedness (a great sign of maturity), her understanding (another great sign of maturity), her lack of jealousy (a further sign of maturity), and the trust she developed with Steve (Rachel was *very* mature!).

As you read, also observe how she personified the solutions to deprivation that are described above.

The doorbell rang. Steve got up from the sofa to answer it. He had been listening to "You Don't Know Love" on the stereo, thinking how hard the encounter had been last night with his ex-girlfriend Tricia. There always is so much feeling with her. And every time he sees her, his hopes rise that she'll be ready for a full-fledged relationship. But those hopes were dashed once again last night. He opened the front door. The woman standing there was beautiful, long dark hair, a halter-top that left little to the imagination. "Hi!" she said. Steve let out a long low breath and motioned her to come in, "So good to see you."

A wonderful thing about emotionally mature people is their curiosity. They want to know about everything. Rachel was no exception. She studied astronomy in college and found it to be, for her, the perfect stepping stone to understanding religion, anthropology, psychology, chemistry, you name it. Steve never got bored talking to Rachel.

His problem was concentration. He could not take his eyes off that halter-top! As they discussed world economics his hand moved to rest on her leg. The subject shifted to popular music and she moved his hand to cup the halter-top as she reached around to unhook it from the back. It started to slide down ever so slowly, showing her twin suns rising on two worlds of soft white snow. As he kissed them he had no thought of Tricia.

Rachel's intelligence was wonderful. She was comfortable discussing any subject. And although Steve found it hard to concentrate, he enjoyed their verbal interchange.

He held her hand as they moved from the living room to the bedroom. Undressing her he forgot about Tricia altogether.

He even forgot the painful breakup that had left him so disconsolate a month ago. He knew that tomorrow the pain would return, but it would be bearable.

He lay there thinking how soft and warm Rachel felt and how lucky he was to have a friend like her. Last month his spaceship relationship with Tricia had exploded in midair, 100,000 feet above the surface of the earth, and he had just walked out of it. A little scratched, but alive. Of course he had fallen for a ways before hitting his safety net, but as always, Rachel was there. This fall was a little harder than some, and as Steve put it into her it went in deeper than ever, then deeper yet again, and finally exploded inside her. But the landing was soooo soft…

Sometimes they didn't talk at all. She responded to the lightest touch or non-verbal suggestion. Touch her legs with one hand and her shoulders with the other and she would turn around so he could see her from behind. Move her head toward him just a little and she would take it all the way inside her mouth. There was never any tension in her body—it was always relaxed and open and he knew he could do whatever he wanted and that she loved it too.

Most amazing was her uninhibited, open, frank, comfortable, and natural approach to sex. She was happy with herself, her body, and her world.

Steve: "What about anal sex?"
Rachel: "It's fun to do things that are forbidden."
Steve: "What about 'water sports'?"
Rachel: "Peeing is about as natural an act as there is."
Steve: "What about recording sex on videotape?"
Rachel: "I love my body and I trust you."
Steve: "How does Terry feel about your having sex with me?"
Rachel: "He knows I love sex and he doesn't believe I should feel imprisoned or inhibited." (Terry must have been very mature.)

One day they were sitting on the sofa listening to music. She was cuddled up softly in his arms.

Steve: "Today I really want to spank you."

Rachel: "OK. Why?"

Steve: "I can feel all my pent up anger and I need to get it out."

Rachel: "I want to feel it—show me how it feels!"

She was already starting to discover how it feels as she saw it getting hard so fast. She took it in her hand and led him to the bedroom holding it. His heart was racing—blood tingling every square inch of his skin. She said, "All women need to be punished" and lay down across his knees with her soft white bare bottom in the air. "Whack!" It stung his hand. "Whack!" He could see the red handprint on her body. "Whack!" His engorged member was ready to explode from top to bottom. "Whack!" "Whack!" "Whack!" And then it released all over both of them—warm wet spraying everywhere as he whispered, "I love you."

And then they cuddled: warm, soft, friendly. She knew he was acting out fantasies that originated in anger caused by deprivation. She knew he wouldn't really hurt her. She enjoyed being the vehicle for expression of his feelings. She could have been a great psychologist because she understood the dynamics of deprivation and feelings and fantasies. (More about fantasies in Chapter 11!)

Rachel said she had enjoyed sex for as long as she could remember. She began playing with herself soon after puberty. It felt good. She experimented with sensations and learned how much there was to enjoy. She was not a blind believer in social stereotypes. As a teenager she decided to expand her horizons and started taking ballet lessons. Terry was her teacher. He was centered, aware, natural, understanding, gentle. She learned to accept her feelings, to enjoy them without guilt, to listen to her body and her own intuition. The restrictions of society did not make sense to her and she let them go. When she finally made love with Terry it was slow and soft and good. They had built complete trust. By age twenty she was experienced, realistic, and self-confident, i.e. more mature emotionally than most adults twice her age.

Steve says I should give her a "300" for emotional maturity; that's a growth rate of fifteen points per year! Given that the average growth rate is only four to eight points per year, she was truly ahead of the crowd. Steve told me he had never met anyone as emotionally developed for her age as Rachel.

Rachel was a good friend to Steve. She listened and talked. She understood. She fulfilled his sexual needs as well as her own. She did not judge. She willingly followed his lead. Everything was OK. She was never a tease. Every encounter "un-dented" ten rejections. She helped him to stabilize his life, even as Tricia re-entered it.

Sometimes Steve would see Rachel the night before a date with Tricia so he would not feel a need to push Tricia for sex. Sometimes he saw her the evening *after* a date with Tricia so he could level out any unsettled emotions. Sometimes he saw her in the middle of the month to take the edge off the loneliness.

Having this wonderful relationship with Rachel enabled Steve to be a better friend. His sexual needs were being met in a quality way. That left him free to be a genuine, devoted friend to others. And her levelheaded, centered, understanding approach to life gave him additional inspiration and emotional support.

Steve enjoyed Rachel thoroughly but he was not in love with her. There was a moderately high level of feeling, and a very high level of emotional maturity. I'd assess the relationship like this:

Steve Rachel

Steve's chemistry for Rachel was high.
Rachel's chemistry for Steve was medium.
Steve's maturity was very high.
Rachel's maturity was very high.

Her friendship had its price, as do all relationships. The advantage of Steve's relationship with Rachel was that the price was clear. There was no game playing. Rachel was a professional sex worker. She earned her living by satisfying customers (the same as anyone else in a service business). He received good value and so did she. Rachel, like most of the better professional sex workers, saw her occupation more like "social work." Although sex was important, she knew that talking and cuddling are 80% of a man's emotional need. The final buildup and explosion are the frosting on the cake. Rachel was a very high class professional. She knew that love is not a game.

SUMMARY

Let's summarize this chapter as it played out through the story of Rachel.

Emotional deprivation makes it difficult for women and sexual deprivation makes it difficult if not impossible for men to "cross the desert" in search of a quality love relationship. Rachel brought Steve water in the desert.

I have suggested nine ideas for overcoming deprivation and increasing the availability of sexual/emotional closeness during the search for a quality love relationship:

1. ***Focus on chemistry and maturity.*** Rachel was mature and aware of her own feelings as well as the feelings of others. She could therefore assess with accuracy both chemistry and maturity.

2. ***Establish emotionally fulfilling friendships.*** Even though a sex professional, Rachel was also a friend and understood the emotional content of her interactions. Steve found this highly fulfilling.

3. ***Expand educational programs.*** Rachel was educating Steve as well as everyone else with whom she came in contact.

4. ***Identify mature people.*** Steve and Rachel both appreciated the emotional maturity that they found in the other. Steve gave Rachel a small lapel pin to recognize her as the quality person she was.

5. ***Increase sexual experimentation.*** Rachel started experimenting sexually at an early age and expanded it further through her profession. Her experimentation no doubt contributed to her maturity. The famous poet William Blake said, "You never know what is enough unless you know what is more than enough."

6. ***Establish sexual friendships.*** As a sexual friend Rachel filled a need that otherwise would have forced Steve into one-night

stands, lots of wasted time in bars, or a committed relationship with someone who was not his soulmate.

7. **Expand "open marriage" concepts.** Rachel was involved in a committed relationship. The relationship was based on an intellectual/spiritual connection more substantive than sex. Therefore sharing sex outside the relationship did not threaten it any more than sharing water would have.

8. **Increase the availability of professional sex.** Rachel was a quality person. Sex was her business. She did it well and filled an important need for Steve. She was a true professional. It's too bad that our society considers her a criminal.

9. **Offer complete sexual surrender.** Rachel understood the importance of sexual surrender. Her lack of inhibitions allowed her to respond with freedom. Her following Steve's lead allowed him to not worry about performance—if it worked for him it would work for her.

Steve told me that many times he thought to himself, especially after a trying meeting with Tricia, **"Thank God for Rachel!"**

Sex and emotional support are too important to go without for the "geologic time" that it takes to find and build a quality love relationship. The next two chapters provide additional secrets about how to deal with loneliness and geologic time.

ASSIGNMENT

Establish a medium-chemistry sexual friendship (your feelings for the other person are a 🎲 or maybe a low 🎲). The other person's feelings for you could be anything from a 🎲 to a 🎲 , although it will likely be more difficult if the other person has high feelings (and wants more from the relationship than you do—but that's part of the challenge). What is important is that your feelings are more or less "medium." Do not think of this as soulmates. Do not think of it as boyfriend-girlfriend. Do not think of it as a commitment to marriage. Instead, think of it as water in the desert. Think of it as "Friends Plus." Value it, cherish it, but be prepared to let it go.

Although your *chemistry* for the other person should be "medium" (for this assignment), it would be good (though not absolutely necessary) if the other person's *maturity* were "high" (a 🎲 or a 🎲 would be nice, although a 🎲 might be acceptable). This will tend to minimize complications as the relationship progresses.

This assignment complements the assignment from Chapter 2 (establish a high-chemistry non- sexual friendship). The two together (sex and chemistry, albeit in separate relationships) can provide a very stable emotional basis for continuing the search for your quality love relationship.

Notes

Secret 7

ENJOY SWEET DISTRACTIONS

The Safety Net

"All I wanted was a sweet distraction for an hour or two"
From the song "All Time High"
By J. Barry and T. Rice

I've promised to provide in this chapter additional information about how to deal with loneliness and geologic time. Many will argue that it does not really take seventeen years to find and build a quality love relationship. To this I have the following replies: (1) I am stating my experience and the experience of others I have known. Maybe your experience has been or will be different. (2) Many who argue this wind up getting divorced seventeen years later. (3) I use seventeen years as a ballpark number. This is not an exact science, and it could be anywhere from five to thirty years. The point is that it takes a much longer period of time than anyone imagines. This is probably because our culture is built around instant gratification instead of long-term quality. (4) The length of time depends on the standards you set. If you are willing to settle for an average relationship then it will take you considerably less time to find it, about a year according to the probabilities of the Love Dice. If you want it bad you'll get it bad.

Whether you accept my premise about geologic time or not is up to you. But since it is my premise, and I believe it to be true, I must then provide as much material as I can to help deal with the problem. The last chapter on sex was a start.

This chapter is about the importance of distractions. I was lucky to find the excerpt shown above from the song "All Time High," which starts out with a line about distractions. I think songwriters often have a better idea of what's going on in love relationships than do psychologists. But there are not many songs about distractions.

There are plenty of songs about "love," and "magic," and "all or nothing" relationships, and "heartbreak." But hardly any about the joy of distractions. Can't you just hear the lyrics: "My love for Rita is so strong—Sometimes I can hardly go on—So to keep my mind free—I think of Mary." Or how about "Every day I love you so much—That's why I find someone else to touch—Maybe one day our love will grow up—So tonight I sleep with Amy and tomorrow Buttercup." Or maybe "I am so glad to know her—she is so sweet—I am third on her list—but she knocks me off my feet."

These really grab your heart, I bet!

At least the writers of "All Time High" recognized that at times a "sweet distraction" is a desirable thing. Distractions can be helpful, even if there are few songs written about them. Because the search for a quality love relationship takes so long, it is important to understand more about distractions.

The concept of distractions is an elusive one. Clearly friends and activities are diversions that help fill the time while searching and/or waiting for a quality love relationship. But "diversions" may not be enough. You need to find water and food when you are in the desert, not just a book to read.

There is something going on in the search for a quality love relationship that we have not yet discussed: the fear of failure. "I'm not sure if I will ever find her." "What if I lose him?" "I don't know if he (or she) will ever grow up." This uncertainty is heightened if the wait is long and/or if the chemical attraction is very high. When you have soulmate chemistry going on, both of you are standing high up on the edge of a cliff. Any loss is not just a setback, but a disaster.

Until mutual trust is built over time, this fear of never finding it, coupled with the fear of losing it, the length of time involved, and the high intensity feelings can make for a very insecure setting. In fact this fear can be the undoing of an otherwise good relationship because one person puts pressure on the other to "commit" before he or she is really ready.

Ordinary diversions frequently are not enough to deal with this fear. The solution is what I call "distractions." By this I mean a continued variety of emotionally potent involvements during the waiting period as opposed to "putting all your eggs in one basket." Distractions are a way of protecting your emotional investment against a devastating loss.

THE SAFETY NET

If your chemistry for the other person is very high (a 🎲), you will be able to taste your feelings. At times you will be nearly paralyzed by fear. You will feel like you are walking a high wire across the Grand Canyon. If you think about how far you could fall, your stomach will turn over, your knees will go weak, and you will fall for sure.

Why do I use the term "high wire"? It relates back to chemistry and maturity.

It is "high" because the chemistry is so high. The higher the chemistry the farther there is to fall.

It is a "wire" because low maturity creates a real danger of falling off. If I'm standing on a wide bridge with six travel lanes for cars and a sidewalk, I might get a little knot in my stomach when I look down. But I don't really worry because I know the bridge is stable. On the other hand, I don't know if another *person* is stable or not until I've really tested them, and, until then, I'm standing on a wire. Or I'd better assume I am.

Seeing it another way: A wire (low maturity/unstable) four inches off the ground (low chemistry) does not cause much fear. And a bridge (high maturity/stable) 2000 feet in the air (high chemistry) does not cause much fear. The problem exists when you have a *wire* 2000 feet up in the air (low or unknown maturity with high chemistry).

If you know beforehand that the chemistry is high but the maturity is low, you may simply choose not to get on the wire in the first place. That would be a safe and probably wise thing to do.

But the more usual situation is that at first you *don't know* if it's a bridge or a wire. And then as you find out, what you usually encounter is some in-between/never-never-land of medium maturity, i.e. half bridge and half wire. So you may be able to make it half way across the Grand Canyon with no problem, but the other half is just as dangerous as if there'd been no bridge to get you there in the first place. And sometimes the immature person will seem to change from "bridge" to "wire" in an instant, without warning!

In the last chapter, Rachel was Steve's rope to help him climb up on the wire. And she was his rope should he need to climb down. But you don't want to trust your life, standing as it were on a wire 2000 feet above the Colorado River, to a single rope. If you fall and miss catching the rope, it would be curtains.

High wire artists don't use a single rope for protection. They use a safety net—many ropes interconnected. When they fall they are certain to hit the net somewhere—no one can say exactly where, but wherever they fall there will be a rope to catch them.

Relating this to your own search, you want high chemistry, so you want to be on the high wire. Therefore you need a safety net. You want to stay emotionally stable. You want to be a better friend. You don't want to settle for less than quality love just because you are afraid of falling off the high wire. And there's no guarantee—the search for quality love could fall apart at any minute. That's why it is necessary to have a safety net.

In my own search for a soulmate I always tried to have a safety net. It could also be called a backup plan, or a contingency plan. I had a supportive network of friends, "friends plus" (friend+sex), prospects, and a psychologist (Dr. Bessell).

Did this make me feel totally secure? No. It's impossible to feel totally secure when you're in love. Was I otherwise safe? Sort of. But when you are so vulnerable, even a strong safety net doesn't feel completely safe. There were times when I wished I'd had a stronger safety net. I had meticulously built mine to be as strong as possible, but even so there were some losses where the pain was searing, immobilizing. There was no safety net that could fend off the initial onset of that kind of pain. If a knife in the chest comes from out of nowhere and knocks you off the high wire, it hurts a lot, even if you know it's coming. But it's the fall that could kill you—I tried to always land in my safety net. My chest might hurt and my head might be spinning, but the fall wouldn't kill me and it wouldn't make me afraid to climb back up and continue the search.

It is important to recognize that it is not the net that is the objective. The ultimate goal is a special relationship with one high chemistry person who is mature enough to handle it. The net is only an aid in reaching the destination.

And keep in mind that while there may be several "ropes" in your safety net at any given time, you are also a rope in their safety net. So it is a mutually supportive situation as long as everyone sees it that way. The danger is if one person sees another as the "goal" and/or the only rope and has no other safety network options of their own, he or she may become hurt and disillusioned. The ideal situation is for everyone to have five to ten people in their safety net. The result is a "network" of hundreds of people who are all interconnected, although they may not know it or know each other.

The alternative to this network approach to getting to know people is "serial one-on-one relationships." Serial one-on-one relationships are the generally accepted relationship paradigm in our society right now. But they take too long—time is a reality constraint—how can you meet eighty-one people (to find a "good love" relationship) let alone 1,296 people (to find a "soulmate" relationship) if you spend two years with each, one at a time? Serial one-on-one relationships also put too much pressure on the "one" person to commit to exclusivity and to be everything. Serial one-on-one relationships can feel confining instead of interconnected. They frequently are characterized by peaks of ecstasy followed by depression followed by ecstasy followed by depression, etc. When the one relationship fails, everything goes down with it, and recovery takes a long time. A safety net reduces the impact and speeds the recovery.

I know the concept of a network of relationships may be a little hard to accept—we've been so culturally conditioned to be involved with only one person at a time. But how are we going to realistically deal with the time constraints, the probabilities, and the fears associated with the search for a quality love relationship? Remember, as we said in Chapter 3, love relationships are not for the fainthearted!

There is a second important aspect of the safety net that needs to be considered. We have discussed the first important aspect, namely that the safety net can "save your life" if you fall off the high wire.

But equally important is the beneficial effect the safety net has while you are still on the high wire. Your psyche knows that you have a safety net and therefore it provides a confidence, a peace of mind that enables you to better stay on the high wire. Now, instead of the negative connotation of "saving your life if you fall," the safety net takes on the positive connotation of enabling you to stay on the high wire with greater ease and more likelihood of success.

Instead of taking each step with fear and trepidation and trembling knees, you take each step with confidence. The fear of falling, while still there, is not paramount. Paramount is the exhilaration, the joy, of being up there on that wire, with the possibility of making it across, and the enjoyment of the view with each step.

Without a safety net, your fear would be paramount and you would fall for sure. You probably would never even step out over the abyss. But with the net, joy becomes paramount. You step out on the wire—dance and play—turn somersaults—devil may care—this is fun—nothing can hurt me.

"Safety net…" "Distractions…" They can "save your life." They can give you confidence. And there's a third aspect—they can take your mind off the danger.

This third aspect of distractions is the mental activity of not focusing on the danger that could befall you (for instance loss of your primary soulmate prospect). Not only do you have confidence that if you fall the safety net will save your life, not only do you have an absence of fear, but your mind is actively occupied somewhere else altogether and not on the danger. So good distractions involve mental activities of sufficient emotional potency to temporarily take your mind off your #1 prospect. Sex could be one of these mental activities. Spending time with a high potential prospect could be one of these activities. Uncovering new prospects could be one of these activities. *Activities that don't have sufficient emotional power to take your mind off #1 do not really qualify as good distractions.*

Because distractions are partly a figment of the mind, they may or may not turn out to have any value of substance. They are based primarily on hope. But they have an intrinsic value of their own in keeping your mind off #1, off whatever unresolved issues exist there, off your fear, and off however long the "wait" may be. Distractions may result in friendship, in sex, in a soulmate, in other values. Or they may result in nothing at all. But it is important to actively keep your focus off #1 and off the fear of failure.

DIVERSIFIED INVESTMENTS

Here's another analogy that I think is helpful. It is an analogy to economic investments. Certainly the "investment" in a lifelong love relationship is equally as important as an investment in stocks and bonds, don't you agree? So why do we apply different rules to these two types of investments? For economic investments we follow rules designed to ensure success. For love relationship investments we get so emotionally involved we forget the most obvious rules of success. We follow rules designed for failure.

Suppose you are deciding how to invest your entire life savings. You could pick one promising company and invest the entire amount in its stock. If the company does well, you win. If the company does poorly, you lose. This is a high-risk strategy. If you feel really sure about the company and can stand the risk of losing your entire life savings if the company fails, then go for it!

Most investment counselors suggest "diversification," a portfolio of investments that spreads the risk. Maybe some stocks, maybe some bonds, maybe some real estate, maybe some gold. If you feel very strongly about one company or one real estate venture, maybe you will put 30% or 50% or even 70% of your life savings into that single investment. But the remainder you will spread among a diverse variety of others. That way if one goes down, others may go up. If several go down, at least one may hold up. The chance of losing everything is reduced.

Given that economic investments, like love relationships, are notorious for having ups and downs, it's good to have enough investments so that the risk of all of them going down at once is low.

If you have only one investment, and it goes down, you are left with nothing. (This is where most serial one-on-one "love" relationships are today.)

If you have two investments, it's less likely that they will both go down at the same time. But bad things do have a tendency to happen, often at the most inconvenient moment, so this is still risky.

If you have three investments, it becomes very unlikely that they will all go down at the same time, although it is possible for a catastrophe to happen.

If you have four investments, then you have reduced the risk of all of them going down simultaneously to very nearly zero, absent an overall market decline.

And so it is the same with your emotional investments. Spread out and diversify. Do not put yourself in the position of losing everything. It will make you too nervous and almost assure "losing."

If you are looking for a soulmate quality relationship, consider putting the following categories in your emotional investment portfolio:

1. Soulmate Friend.

Number one of course, is any soulmate "diamond in the rough" prospect you may have. That needs to be the highest priority in terms of emotional investment. But keep in mind that such an investment can fall apart for any number of reasons, so plan your diversification and strategic coverage accordingly.

2. Friends.

"I get by with a little help from my friends…" (From the song "With A Little Help From My Friends by John Lennon and Paul McCartney). Friends are your most consistent and reliable emotional investments. Friends are always there. Friends are forever. You can count on your friends. Friends understand you and like you. You can talk to your friend and share what's going on and he/she will support you. Of course I am talking here about good friends. I am not talking about "fair weather" friends. And I am also talking about friends with a relatively high degree of maturity, whose advice and counsel you can trust. You don't want friends who say, "Give it time," when there is not really chemistry, and therefore no long-term potential. Nor do you want friends who say, "Give it up," when the chemistry is there and the issue is maturity which could perhaps be helped with counseling.

I have more to say about friendship in Chapter 8.

3. Sex.

This topic was covered in some detail in the last chapter. Depending on your particular solution to overcoming deprivation, one or more of your friends may also be a sex partner. Or you may decide to rely on professional sex (you may have to go to Nevada if you want to avoid legal risks). The key is to have a reliable source of sexual fulfillment in case the primary relationship does not include sex or evaporates. One-night stands, reviving past loves, or finding a new love/sex partner may help, but are hardly "reliable sources" of sexual fulfillment. The key is to have a source or sources of fulfillment with whom you can be honest and who you know you can rely on. You don't want to go without water for too long! (Also, I can't emphasize often enough the importance of using safe sex procedures—see Appendix 4.)

4. Prospects.

If you are looking for and have not yet found a very high chemistry, emotionally stable, full-fledged soulmate relationship, it's good to have several prospects in the wings. This is part of the diversification strategy. If you are in the middle of the search then you will be turning up new prospects all the time. On the other hand, if you are in the middle of a long wait for a primary soulmate prospect that is not yet secure then it's important to have several secondary prospects. There is even a diversification among these prospects:

a. High Potential Prospects.

If there appears to be mutually very high chemistry but the maturity is not yet known or there is still a lot of growth required, you have a "high potential" prospect. These are important because if you have a primary prospect and he or she leaves then you have other prospects of approximately equal value.

With a high potential prospect your chemistry feeling will be very high (a ⚃). The interesting feature about any relationship like this is that it doesn't matter what the other person ever does, you will always love them, just because "that's the way it is" (chemistry never changes).

b. Medium Potential Prospects.

It is hard to find soulmate prospects. A ⚃ or a ⚄ on the chemistry scale is nothing to be frowned at. "If you can't be with the one you love, love the one you're with" is often good advice. A short to medium term non-committed love relationship where the chemistry is a ⚃ or a ⚄ can be reasonably rewarding. It may eventually lead to a strong friendship. It may help with sexual fulfillment. If definitely helps with self-esteem. It may fade away. Or it may lead to a ⚄⚅ (good love relationship). Most people would feel very lucky to have this, and even those searching for a soulmate may decide that this is better than continuing the search. No matter what transpires in the long run, it can help fill a void in the short to medium term.

c. Prospects with Unknown Potential.

These are prospects who have just appeared on your radar screen but you are not yet clear about either the chemistry or the maturity. These need to be given time to reveal themselves and get sorted out. But unless your emotional investment portfolio is already very full, it is good to continue to investigate new potential investments.

5. Home/Family/Children.

Family responsibilities can be both fun and time consuming. As such they qualify as distractions, even though they may also be a predominant feature of one's life. To be involved in the soulmate search means balancing work, family, and social life, keeping them all in perspective. One can be a distraction for the other!

6. Work.

Work is very often a primary activity and a distraction. It may even be a sufficient distraction. But sometimes your work can suffer if you are too obsessed with what's going on (or not going on) with your most significant soulmate prospect. Using other distractions from the list above can reduce your obsession and free up mental energy so you can be more productive at work.

One should never underestimate the value of his or her prospects even though any particular one may not be "#1" right now. The leader at the beginning of a race is not always the winner at the end. It frequently happens that #1 right now is not capable of finishing, in which case #2 becomes #1, and so on. The position can change with time. A leader that appears very fast around the final turn may fade in the home stretch and finish last. And in real life any participant could disappear suddenly into another "committed" relationship.

Although real life is not a game or a race, the analogy is interesting because it suggests that being #2 can be a "good thing." #2 sometimes ascends to #1. #3 sometimes ascends to #1. #8 can sometimes ascend to #1. Therefore I personally am happy to be anywhere on someone's list where there is high chemistry; I do not require that I be #1.

I often hear people say, "For me it's all or nothing." "If I can't be #1 I don't want any part of him/her." This seems shortsighted. How do you jump from obscurity to being #1? First you have to show up on the radar screen (#8). Then you have to make a good impression of some kind (jump to #5). Then you have to hang in there for a while (move up to #3). Then you have to prove yourself worthy of further investment (edge up to #2). Then your friend has to decide (as do you) where his or her heart really is, and you may or may not ascend to #1. Most people want to know right away if they are #1. But it's not going to happen overnight. If it does, it probably means both people are very lonely, and bears no relationship whatsoever to the ultimate validity of the relationship. More than likely this process will take months or years. So I say be happy with position #2 or #3! It is so much better than not being there at all. You will have more strength to go on if you accept that being #2 or #3 is a good thing.

Remember that there may be no clear order of #2, #3, #4, etc. The only thing that's clear is #1. There can be only one #1 at any given moment. New Year's Eve, Valentine's Day, etc. cannot be conveniently divided. But after #1 it could be a dead heat among #2, #3, and #4. Time will show the staying power of any given relationship.

If all of this is too much for you, that's OK. You have a lot of company. The majority of those desiring love want it to happen the way it is "supposed" to happen, as depicted in the movies and on TV. Go out with a few people, fall in love, get married, and live happily ever after. Statistics of course show this isn't what happens, but we all tend to think statistics are about "the other guy." This book is for those who have come to the realization that the old way doesn't work (if you want a quality love relationship) and who have the courage to consider something new.

It is important to note that this concept of diversifying your emotional investments is appropriate for the "search" phase, and as such can possibly take years. However, as trust builds with the #1 soulmate or quality love prospect, the emotional investment in him or her can and should gradually increase, and the emotional investment in others will naturally decrease. Picture your heart supported by a slender sapling—you might want four or five of them underneath you to keep you safe. But when one of them grows into a strong tree trunk, then you can put your faith there and be safe. Ultimately the investment with your primary love partner will be twenty times more than your investment with anyone else.

To recapitulate, what is the purpose of distractions? In the last chapter I indicated that "The highest purpose of sex is emotional closeness." Now we have:

The purpose of distractions is emotional stability

Suppose you meet Pam on Tuesday and there is soulmate chemistry. Should you marry her on Saturday? Clearly not. Should you push for a committed relationship on Saturday? Probably not.

So now your dilemma is—do you continue to go out with anyone else? Or just wait for Pam?

The answer is probably simple when it has only been a week. But what about a month? What about a year? Maybe Pam is married. Or maybe she needs to mature a lot. Maybe it will take ten years. What then?

If you have other irons in the fire you will not be as likely to pressure Pam. You will not feel as insecure. Several points of support make for improved stability, as in the proverbial "three legged stool." Some of your other irons in the fire may provide sex, so you won't have to push Pam for sex. Others may provide communication so you will not have to talk everything out with Pam, who has limited time. Another may one day turn out to be the soulmate connection you thought you might have attained with Pam. It's nice to know that if it doesn't work out with Pam that you have something to fall back on. If it fails you will not fall off the cliff and die 2000 feet below. You will land in some safety net of friends/sex/other prospects. And the knowledge that this safety net exists allows you to safely stand even closer to the edge of the cliff than you otherwise might. And it is only by standing at the edge that you will ever be able to reach Pam. This is because she, too, is standing on her own cliff and doesn't want to get too close to the edge.

So you have to work your way right to the edge and then lean over the abyss and hold out your hand and keep it extended for years while she decides if it's safe. Your distractions are like ropes that keep you tied back to a not-so-risky place.

But what would Pam say if she knew you regularly have sex with Dana? Or that you frequently have dinner with Ann? What would the rest of society say? More than likely both Pam and society would feel that you don't really care as much as you say you do.

But they would be wrong. Dana is a stopgap until Pam is ready sexually. Ann is a fallback in case Pam runs away. You can wait a long time (seventeen years?) for Pam if you have a safety net. If you do not focus too much on her, you will not put demands on her. If you don't put demands on her she can relax and enjoy your company.

Here are some stories that illustrate the power of distractions.

THE STORY OF TREVOR AND MELANIE

Trevor was a friend of Steve (Chapter 6). Trevor was searching for a soulmate relationship and his #1 prospect was Maria. But

Maria was immature and not ready for a quality love relationship and they had just broken up.

One day Steve said to Trevor, "Rachel has a friend she thinks you'd like."

Trevor replied, "I could use a distraction."

So Melanie came over to Trevor's house. She was blond, sweet, soft. Her laugh tinkled like a bell—Trevor was in love. His feelings for Melanie were a 270, or a 🎲 . But Melanie was a professional, so he was probably #25 on her list.

But it didn't matter. Making love with Melanie was wonderful. She would surrender herself and be so wide open and he could feel it deep inside her and it would go on for a long time until he couldn't stand it any longer and then everything went blue and red and yellow and the lights went out.

Melanie started as a distraction. Sex is a great distraction. But it soon became more than sex. The chemistry was there and she enjoyed it too and their relationship grew into a friendship as well as sex.

She went to his house before Christmas and they decorated the tree together. "I love decorating trees," she said. It must have been true, because she could as easily have stayed home preparing for her 5 A.M. "business trip" flight the next morning.

Then they lay down to make love. They cuddled, lying next to each other.

Melanie: "Lick me, baby."

And so he did, lightly for a while, in the right place, then harder. She told him how it felt and he could feel her body moving and her breathing getting harder and she came in his mouth. Then he entered her and it felt so good and she whispered, "Make love to me," and he said, "I love you like crazy," as she moved with him and they rocked back and forth together and the excitement was overpowering. He felt her getting more and more wide open. Then she slowed down and they stopped.

It felt so good just cuddling and talking with her. He told her he felt it would be better not to try to push it—the pressure would just make it worse. She said, "You can come twice next time!" They discussed their mutual wonder at people's hang-ups over masturbation, especially married couple's hang-ups over it. Neither of them could understand why a couple would eliminate one possible source of pleasure just because of some outdated moral standard. They discussed the number of customers she had that were married men. She could see from her experience the lack of communication in many marriages. And there they were, cuddling and communicating. It felt good. Almost better than coming! Eye to eye. Skin to skin. Laughter to laughter. She was a woman with a lot of experience with men. He was a man with a lot of experience with women. They both believed in love. They recognized sex as emotional closeness. He told her that the cuddling and talking was worth just as much as the coming. She said, "I like that." He felt a glow for days after, even though he was suffering from his temporary breakup with Maria.

One day Melanie announced that she was "going out of business." He didn't think that would really affect him because by that time she was a friend. She had moved from nowhere on his radar screen to a "distraction" to "#2 prospect." But Melanie wasn't ready for a quality love relationship. She didn't yet have the maturity that, for instance, Rachel had. Someday she would no doubt be a wonderful partner, but it was not destined to be with Trevor. Nevertheless, the relationship was fantastic for the time that it existed, and a great distraction for Trevor.

I would assess the relationship between Trevor and Melanie as follows:

Trevor Melanie

Trevor's chemistry for Melanie was very high
Melanie's chemistry for Trevor was high
Trevor's maturity was high
Melanie's maturity was medium

Did Trevor spend much time thinking about Maria during all this time? Of course he did. But did he get upset over it? No. Did he try to pressure her? No. Did he survive a breakup and getting back together? Yes. Melanie was a terrific distraction.

THE STORY OF FRED AND MARGIE

Margie was hoping for a soulmate relationship with Adam, but he couldn't make a commitment. As time went along, the relationship seemed to stagnate.

Margie went with a friend to a party. She was in need of a distraction.

At the party Margie met Fred. Fred was separated from his wife, in the process of getting a divorce. Fred and Margie dated for four months, then Margie learned that Fred was still living at home with his wife! Margie knew then and there that she could never marry Fred, because he had lied to her.

But she needed the distraction, and he needed the chemistry, the companionship, and the sex. Fred promised to move out from his wife, and did. Margie was lonely and needed some security. So she and her daughter moved in with Fred. He offered it as "an experiment" for a year, and the timing was right for Margie.

Fred was going through his divorce, a naturally unstable time. And he drank a lot, something that had seemed fun at the party but wasn't so much fun at home. Margie's father had been an alcoholic, so she really didn't like Fred's drinking.

And, she didn't trust him. After all, he'd lied to her about being separated. And he had been unfaithful to both his first wife and his second wife, so "why not with Margie?" She saw him as unstable. And, she wasn't really that much in love with him. It was a "cover," a "distraction."

He wanted to marry her. But Fred didn't get along with Margie's daughter. She couldn't see living another ten years (until her daughter turned eighteen) with two people who made each other unhappy.

Fred said if Margie didn't marry him, he was going to move out and live by himself.

That was enough for Margie. She moved out on Fred. Fred tried to apologize. He told her he didn't really mean it. But the time had come for Margie to move on. Her need for a distraction had dissipated.

My assessment:

Fred Margie

> Fred's chemistry for Margie was very high
> Margie's chemistry for Fred was medium
> Fred's maturity was medium
> Margie's maturity was high

This was neither a "quality love relationship" nor a "diamond in the rough." But Margie's relationship with Adam was not progressing, and the relationship with Fred served as a good distraction.

SOURCES OF DISTRACTIONS

Where can you find a distraction when you need one? The sources are many, and you already know most of them. But repetition is sometimes helpful and maybe I'll mention something you hadn't thought of before. Work, church, social organizations, friends of friends and bars are obvious starting places. Personal ads and video dating services can be very productive, especially if you see them as distractions and not as the source for the one-and-only-forever-soulmate-guaranteed relationship (although that could happen). Adult education classes of one sort or another can be fun and who knows what else? Travel to exotic worlds can take your mind off the present. Flying, skiing, scuba diving, dancing, and a host of other activities are distractions in and of themselves as well as possible sources of friends or prospects. These sources of distractions are actually the same sources that may be tapped when looking for a quality love partner. The difference is that a "distraction" typically refers to an activity taking place when you already have a diamond in the rough on your radar screen but it's too soon to take any definitive action.

SUMMARY

I believe that individuals as well as society somehow need to recognize and value the importance of distractions. Distractions are necessary to the success of a long-term search for a quality love relationship because they help to stabilize your emotions. They can save you if you fall, allow you to enjoy the search, and keep your mind off the dangers of failure. And, any one distraction could suddenly turn out to be a quality love relationship. Enjoying distractions is not a matter of using others. It is a matter of everyone helping everyone search, maybe find, and being reasonably happy along the way.

Therefore:

> Build a strong safety net.
>
> Get on the high wire—relax—enjoy—play.
>
> De-focus your mind.
>
> Use distractions so you do not put pressure on yourself or on #1.
>
> Remember that being #2, #3, or #4 is a good thing (for you as well as for others).

ASSIGNMENT

Write down the names of everyone in your safety net. Do you have a diverse mix of friends, sex, and prospects, as well as family and work? Do you have enough of each to be sure the net will hold up if something goes wrong with one of them?

The next chapter contains more tips on building a network of value.

Secret 8

LOOK FOR A RAINBOW OF VALUES

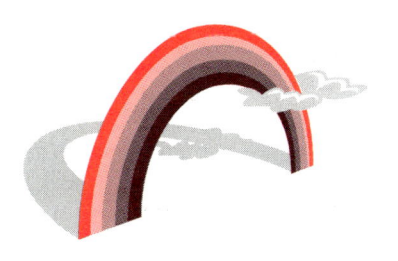

Friendship Plus

"I get by with a little help from my friends"
From the song "With A Little Help From My Friends"
By John Lennon and Paul McCartney

Let's capsulize what we've learned so far. Finding a quality love relationship means finding someone with mutual high chemistry and mutual high maturity. This is not easy because the odds are stacked against you. To counter the odds you need to interview and/or kiss a lot of frogs. And you need to keep your eye out for a diamond in the rough. Doing all this will take geologic time, so you will need food and water (emotional fulfillment and sex). And you will also find yourself out on a limb, so you will need a safety net (distractions). If you are patient and persistent you may find a quality love relationship. If you are not patient, not persistent, or you are unlucky or your standards are too high or you are unwilling to compromise, you may not.

Let's consider my statement that you "may not" find your quality love. If you think of the search for a quality love relationship as an all or nothing game, then it's true that you "may not." But remember the warning of the love goddess:

Love is not a game.

The search for a quality love relationship is *not* "all or nothing." Such a win/lose proposition is antithetical to love. This chapter is about expanding the definition of the search.

To begin with, "mutuality" must be at the heart of this search. Everything I have mentioned involves mutuality. The concept of a quality love relationship is by definition something mutual. Sex is mutual. Emotional support is mutual. "Safety network" is mutual.

While all relationships must involve mutuality, each person is unique. It becomes apparent after kissing enough frogs that there is a vast diversity of individual personalities, each with his or her own unique qualities. In fact, the more people you meet, the wider becomes your awareness of individual uniqueness.

You might start out looking for a quality love relationship with a black and white concept of "true love or bust." But then of necessity you broaden your concept to include "shades of gray" as you find value in the support of friends, in sexual fulfillment, and in your safety net. But neither "black and white" nor "shades of gray" come close to describing the "rainbow of colors" that begins to emerge over time. This "rainbow of colors" has every imaginable shade and degree of every conceivable color. And the opportunities that exist to expand the fullness and richness of your life by sharing these colors are indeed limitless. You just need to get out there and be aware and open to new possibilities.

The trouble is that often we get so focused on one objective (soulmate, sex, business, etc.) that we are unable to see and appreciate something else that may be right in front of us. Or we may be so overtaken by guilt, "I don't think I could ever marry him so I'd better not see him," or fear, "She's out of my league," or social pressure, "He's too old for me," that we fail to retain those other aspects of a potential relationship that could be of value. Often, if we are open to it, we find something other than what we are originally looking for, and that turns out to be of value.

Here is a very short list of possible "values" that can be found along the way in the search for a quality love relationship. This just happens to be my list, values that have been important to me. But for you this list could be entirely different depending on your interests.

POSSIBLE VALUES

Friendship.

Finding someone you like and respect and who likes you and supports you and enjoys doing things with you is high on my "value" list. Such a friend need not have mutual very high chemistry nor even very high maturity, but there needs to be a moderate level of each, enough to hold the enjoyment of each other's company together. An important element of friendship is that it allows for the freedom of each person while also spending time together. Here I quote from Thomas Moore's book *Soul Mates*:

> *Friendship entails a paradoxical blending of intimacy and individuality. Friends, unlike families, have no claim on each other to live in certain ways. They enjoy an element of distance in that regard that sustains their necessary*

individuality, and given that distance, friends can choose to be close. In families, and in other structured relationships, we could foster deep friendship by easing up on power issues inherent in those structures and by giving more attention to the ways of freely chosen friendship.

Chemistry.

As was thoroughly discussed in Chapters 1 and 5, high chemistry is a rare jewel of great value. It may or may not be accompanied by emotional maturity and it may or may not be reciprocated. Yet it remains a value. If it is mutually very high and accompanied by very high maturity, you have found your soulmate! Treasure him/her. If chemistry is mutually very high but maturity is medium, you have found a "diamond in the rough." Treasure him/her if you can. If the chemistry is high for you but only medium for him/her, you are likely to feel frustrated and/or rejected. This is really a symptom of insecurity and immaturity. Overcome it if you can. If you are able to hold on to such a relationship it may provide you with several benefits: (1) It can help you to remember what true chemistry feels like. Some people have never experienced true chemistry, and even for those that have, its rarity makes it hard to hold onto the memory of the feeling. So a relationship that reminds you of that feeling provides a template for your search. (2) It is good practice to maintain a relationship and not try to make it into something that it isn't. (3) To maintain the relationship there must be "something of value" for the other person. It is good practice to identify what that is and then to determine if the value to you is worth the cost to you and whether the value to him/her is worth the cost and if so to work out a healthy and mutually rewarding balance.

One-way chemistry is OK if it's recognized and accepted for what it is.

Teacher *(Maturity)*.

To find someone with very high maturity (possibly higher than your own) is a great value, even if there is not high chemistry. This is a person you can learn from. This is a person who can provide realistic support, not just societal rules and platitudes. You may have to resist your feeling of being inferior. It is natural for us to seek the company of those who are more or less our equals. But this does little to improve our capabilities. A good teacher speeds up learning. If you have such a teacher available among your family and/or friends, count yourself lucky and do all you can to cultivate and learn from the relationship.

If you do not have such a teacher among family or friends, it is advisable to find one among professionals: psychologist, psychiatrist, counselor, social worker, or others (author?) where you can trade value for value and gain access to their insights. This is not an admission of failure. It is an intelligent thing to do. You wouldn't dream of going off by yourself to fly an airplane without hiring a flight instructor. Why on earth would you consider walking the high wire of love without a high wire love instructor?

Student *(Learning)*.

No matter what your own maturity level, it is bound to be higher than some and lower than others. Find a teacher among those who are above you. And if there happens to be someone who's maturity level has not yet reached yours but who would like to be your "student," give strong consideration to the value of such a relationship. It's not just of value to the student. It is of value to you. "The teacher learns from the student." In your effort to be the best possible teacher you will expand your own knowledge and understanding.

Activity Partner.

For some, having a dance partner is important. For others it may be a partner in golf or stamp collecting or reading or some other pursuit. It could be a friend, or you could pay a professional. There are a billion different activities and combinations of "colors" that can provide value to you and the other person if you are alert to their possibilities. And it doesn't have to be a direct trade of "dance partner for dance partner." Perhaps it can be "dance partner for skiing partner" or "scuba diving instructor for maturity guide" or "jogging partner for chemistry connection." The possibilities are endless. The *value* is what's important.

Sex.

One needs water in the desert. One needs sex during the soulmate search. A moderate amount of mutual chemistry and maturity makes the sex even better. Stay away from "poisoned water" (immature partners) if you can. And please use safe sex techniques (see Appendix 4.)

As discussed in Chapter 6, this sexual fulfillment could come from a friend or from a professional. In either case it is a value for value relationship. Whatever the combination is that works, nurture it.

And keep in mind that just as with friends and activity partners, there can be a rainbow of sexual values. With friends you can have one for golf, another for shopping, another for talking. So it is with sex. Consider values such as understanding, soft touch, anal sex, etc. You don't have to drink only plain water in the desert. Enjoy lemonade, coconut milk, and coffee if they're available!

Emotional Support.

Just as sex is the "water," emotional support is the "food" that is necessary during the long search for a quality love relationship. In Chapter 6 this was the second option for overcoming deprivation: "Establish Emotionally Fulfilling Friendships." Emotional support is that unique combination of friendship, chemistry, and maturity where you feel deeply cared about for the person you are, especially when it is coming from someone of the opposite sex.

Intelligence.

All of these colors may be overlapping of course. Intelligence may be found among friends or among sexual partners or in your teacher/maturity guide. But I feel it is worth its own category. Perhaps you meet someone who is especially well versed in computers and you are interested in computers. Or maybe you are trying to learn a foreign language and you meet someone who is already fluent in it. Or maybe you both happen to enjoy discussing global economics. Whatever the "intelligence connection" might be, value it, and keep it if it is mutually beneficial.

Good with Children.

Especially if you have children of your own, finding a friend who likes children and/or family and is good with them could certainly be of value.

Roommate.

If you are single it can be valuable to have a roommate. Maybe not all the time, but sometimes. Roommates can provide companionship as well as sharing of expenses. They can be a "distraction." Who knows what other values there may be. I have had roommates on and off most of my unmarried life. Most of them have been women, and this has helped me to understand the often-strange viewpoints of the fairer sex. I have found that male/female roommate combinations have a very high value for the support and sharing opportunities that they offer. There tends to be a "balance" that is valuable. Contrary to popular opinion in such cases, I have never had sex with any of my roommates, although I remember one with whom I would have dearly loved to!

Association through Work.

If you meet someone who can contribute to your knowledge or performance on the job, whether met at work, at a conference, or in the midst of searching for your quality love, take note of the value. Maybe it's in marketing, accounting, production, or any of the thousands of work related areas of interest; your rainbow can be even brighter by valuing such relationships.

The list could go on.

I have suggested but a few. Again, the array of values is as varied as the rainbow. The search for a quality love relationship is *not* a black and white affair!

Keep in mind some other dimensions to these values. Some may be long-term, some short-term, and some in between. Often you don't know at the outset how long the value will last. Sometimes the "value of the value" changes with time. Sometimes you don't have enough time/energy/money resources to keep all of the values you come across in your life. Therefore some existing ones will at times be edged out by newer, higher values. Sometimes the lesson has been learned from a given relationship, and the "value" has fulfilled its role. And other times the value turns out to be permanent. Acceptance of these shifting colors is important to the enjoyment of the rainbow.

Also remember the principle of mutuality. Just because something is of value to you doesn't mean there is a reciprocal value to the other person. You'd like her for a dance partner but she already has one. You offer her maturity in return for dancing, but she sees no value in maturity. You offer to pay for her time but she sees that as sleazy. If you can't find mutually agreeable values, then just let it go. It has to be mutual. But it's OK to be creative!

And…Don't give up a relationship without first considering the values. Don't give it up just because he's not your soulmate or because she won't provide sex or for all the other myriad reasons. Consider whether there is short-term or long-term value in skiing or learning a language or earning money or whatever. But if you can't find a reasonable place of mutuality, then let it go. Or if the previous value changes, and there is no longer a place of mutuality, let it go. But keep your rainbow bright by continuously cultivating value.

Especially focus on the value "niches" that are important to you. If a dance partner is important, find a way to fill that niche. If a dance partner is not important but scuba diving is, then find a way to fill that niche.

In any relationship, even if you have just met, there is almost always something of value. Your challenge is to determine what it is, and then determine if there is a value for the other person and what that is, and then determine if the mutuality and values are high enough and sufficiently in balance to warrant further expenditure of your time, energy, and resources. If so, keep working on it. If not, let it go.

Be careful of the popular notion that mutual interests are the natural basis for successful love relationships. I have too often seen this notion fail.

Mutual interests are of course a value as I have just described, and should be treasured. They may also be a vehicle for bringing people together, and may provide something to hold on to during the early phases of a relationship.

But the keys, as we have discussed many times, are chemistry and maturity. No mutual interests can create chemistry if it is not already there. And mutual interests can not counter immaturity.

In fact, just the opposite is true. Chemistry and maturity can counter a lack of mutual interests. If both chemistry and maturity are there, mutual interests can be cultivated, and the lucky couple that has both will enjoy doing so. If chemistry and maturity are there, diverse interests can not only be tolerated, but actually enjoyed as an added dimension to the relationship. Just remember: chemistry and maturity can create mutual interests. Mutual interests can not create chemistry or maturity.

Some readers may argue that if there are "billions of colors" in the rainbow of values, then my use of the Love Dice as an analogy is a gross oversimplification. This would be a misinterpretation of my message. The Love Dice relate to chemistry and maturity, the two essential ingredients in a soulmate relationship. They are not intended to relate to the rainbow of values that can include mutual interests, work relationships, and others. Certainly the six-point scale of the dice is an oversimplification, and for more gradations I would again refer you to the 300-point scales created by Dr. Bessell and discussed in Chapters 1 and 2. I find the six-point scale, albeit an oversimplification, more fun as well as easier to work with in describing general concepts. As it is, even with the dice, there are 1,296 different combinations!

It is also important to remember that one ⚅ ⚅ relationship is not going to be identical to another ⚅ ⚅ relationship. Every relationship has its unique chemical "feel" as well as its other "values."

Here is a story about the value of friendship.

THE STORY OF CHAD AND KATIE

I have placed "friendship" at the top of my list of values. It is not there by accident. True friendship is one of the few things that can last forever. And depending on the nature of the individuals it can provide a safety net, or an activity partner, or sex, or a distraction, or any number of other values.

Chad met Katie at an upscale cocktail lounge. Live music for dancing during happy hour on Thursday, Friday, and Saturday nights, and a good atmosphere were an unbeatable combination. You could relax, drink, talk, dance, meet people, and be home in bed (for sleep or sex) by 10:00 PM!

Chad saw an attractive lady dancing with another partner. She was obviously enjoying herself. Chad wished he could be the one dancing with her…

As he danced with others he noticed that she was not always dancing with the same person. That meant either she was there with a group, or she was there on her own. It seemed interminably long, waiting until she sat out for a dance and seemed potentially approachable. But the moment eventually arrived and he asked her to dance. Later she agreed to trade business cards and the next week she agreed to go out to dinner. Maybe this was his soulmate!

At dinner he learned that she was divorced and had two children. She learned that he was divorced and had one child. She said she was not interested in marriage. He was, but was also interested in her.

On their second date they went to a movie and then went back to her house for a drink. It was clear she wanted to make love, and so did he. He couldn't believe his eyes as he took her clothes off. This was what he had always wanted!

Actually their lovemaking didn't turn out well the first time. And not even the second time. But as they learned to know each other it improved. The open honest communication which they were developing made it even better. It was clear she loved sex just as much as she loved dancing, maybe even as much as he loved sex!

After a couple months they went for a walk in the park. It was a romantic evening and he was enjoying her company. She said she wanted him to know that she had met someone who she was really attracted to and wanted to get to know better. She didn't want to hurt Chad and hoped they could still be friends.

In spite of her well-intentioned hopes, Chad was hurt. But not as much as he would have expected. He was only slowly learning what she already knew—there wasn't really strong chemistry between them.

Chad surprised her by remaining her friend. Usually the end of a sexual relationship is the end of the relationship. And she surprised him by continuing the affection. "Friends plus"! Although she had a new boyfriend, she would lie in bed with Chad and cuddle and talk. If nothing else it was a humane way to wind down what had been a sexual relationship. The standard "sharp cutoff" is really inhumane. Gradual start-up and gradual letdown seems far better psychologically.

Chad saw Katie through all the ups and downs of her new relationship. Katie saw Chad through the anxiety of kissing a lot of new frogs. Katie moved in with her new lover. Chad was still single, still searching, and jealous that she was having sex every night and he only once a month.

It was harder for Chad to see his friend Katie when she was living with someone. He couldn't call her at home. She had to call him. They couldn't go out in the evening. Dancing, movies, cuddling, sex were out. Love has a way of becoming a prison. But they still talked once in a while. And as the relationship between Katie and her new boyfriend wore thin and the arguments got worse and the sex became less frequent Chad began to think that maybe his sexual encounters with professionals once a month free of strings and problems were a good thing after all…

When Katie's relationship ended Chad was again able to spend time with her as friends. He supported her in trying to deal with the breakup. She supported him in his quest to find a soulmate.

Chad moved away to another state. Katie met Ron and six months later announced that she was getting married. Chad was glad for her although sorry for the fact that jealousy always seems to insert itself between friends. And again he was depressed that she was getting so much sex and he was not.

Then a month after the marriage she said, "I'm married but I'm not happy. He doesn't allow me to fix up the house the way I want and he treats me like a tax exemption instead of a wife." So now Chad was back to supporting her and being happy he was single even if a little thirsty. And she tells him, "Don't ever get married."

She came full circle from "not interested in marriage" to "marriage is my goal" to "I am married" to "don't ever get married."

He seemingly has gone nowhere (if marriage is the goal). But he has found a variety of relationships of value and has grown in the process. Katie is still an anchor in his safety net, and he in hers.

William Blake said: "*Opposition is true friendship.*" If that's the case, Katie and Chad were true friends. She listened to his ideas and often did not agree but then she would laugh and tell him her opinion. She was not threatened by other beliefs, nor was he. As her life came crashing down on a periodic basis she tried to understand why. As his search continued he tried to understand why it took so long. They did not always see eye to eye, but they were always a stable force in each other's life. He was a consistent friend to her, and she to him. They learned a lot from each other.

I would assess Chad and Katie's relationship as follows:

Chad Katie

Originally

Chad's chemistry for Katie was medium
Katie's chemistry for Chad was medium
Chad's maturity was medium
Katie's maturity was medium

Now

Chad's chemistry for Katie remained medium
Katie's chemistry for Chad remained medium
Chad's maturity grew to be very high
Katie's maturity grew to be very high

This assessment again highlights several of the essential secrets of the Love Dice:

1. Chemistry never changes.

2. Maturity can increase.

3. Good friends are extremely valuable.

"Good" friends are valuable not only as activity partners and safety network support but are valuable in helping you grow as a person.

PERFECT FRIENDS

This combination of all around medium chemistry and maturity is what I call the "perfect friend" combination. The chemistry is high enough to like and enjoy the other person but not high enough for romantic love. Because the chemistry is equal, there is balance. If it were a relationship then there would be a degree of imbalance, one partner may always be hoping for more, the maturity may not be enough to stabilize the imbalance, and the friendship may fall apart.

But a does not have this imbalance, hence although the maturity may not be high initially, the friends can remain friends "through thick and thin" and help each other grow. That is why I call the [🎲🎲] template "perfect friends" and consider it to be a very important template, a rare and special value. And with time "perfect friends" can become "even better friends" ([🎲🎲]) as shown by the story of Chad and Katie.

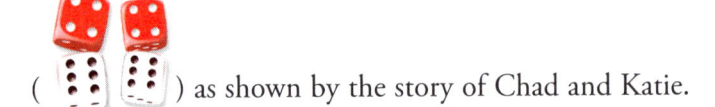

Maybe while discussing the "perfect friends" template it might be instructive to review just a few of the most important Love Dice templates we have already discussed and that have heretofore been well kept secrets:

[🎲🎲] **"Soulmates"**

[🎲🎲] **"Good Love Relationship"**

[🎲🎲] **"Perfect Friends"**

[🎲🎲] **"Diamond in the Rough"**

Chad learned a lot from Katie and vice versa. She valued the support he gave her over the years, and he valued hers. Each knew that the other would be there as a part of his or her safety net. It stood the test of time. This example shows that friends can fill a variety of niches—understanding and support, dance partner/activity partner, sex/semi-sex/emotional closeness partner, and growth catalyst, to name a few.

A NEW MODEL FOR DATING

> *"The bird a nest, the spider a web, man friendship."*
> William Blake

I'd like to synthesize what we have discussed in the last two chapters with a new model for dating. Perhaps it is not new, just underutilized.

I call my model the "value network" model of dating. I envision a future civilization where this is the standard approach to the search for a quality love relationship. The difference between that future and now is the manner and attitude of searching. People of the future know what they are looking for (mutual chemistry and mutual maturity) and know how to search (value network). They are not shackled by the ancient dating rituals (serial one-on-one relationships with little understanding of chemistry and maturity).

I suppose I could call this the "friendship" model of dating, but in my definition of things, "value" is more inclusive than friendship. And "network" brings in the concepts of safety net and distractions from the last chapter.

The "value network" model of dating is an alternative to "serial one-on-one relationships," the norm in today's world. The value network model is a healthier alternative in my opinion because it reduces the extreme ups and downs and takes the pressure off the parties involved. It is a more rewarding alternative in that it is based on growth and values. It is a more realistic alternative because it recognizes the difficulty of finding suitable partners and avoids the popular shortcut strategies that jump to "commitment" so quickly but turn out to be a waste of time in the end.

In the value network model, everyone is striving for a variety of relationships, searching for the individual value in each one. Maybe it's friendship, maybe it's sex, maybe it's chemistry or maturity or whatever. From this variety will come stability and connection, even "interconnection."

So the search for a quality love relationship becomes a "search for value."

All who are involved in this type of search will find fulfilling connections on a variety of levels.

And somewhere along the way many will also find love connections. With knowledge, and depending on individual standards and persistence, some will find "good love relationships," and a few will find their "soulmate."

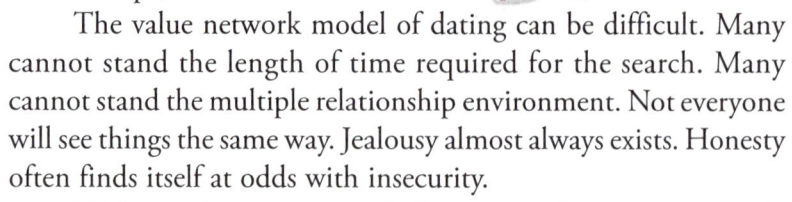

The value network model of dating can be difficult. Many cannot stand the length of time required for the search. Many cannot stand the multiple relationship environment. Not everyone will see things the same way. Jealousy almost always exists. Honesty often finds itself at odds with insecurity.

We have a long way to go before we can become completely comfortable with this model. But maybe we can make small changes in this direction.

It's hard to change our attitudes. Can we embrace the value network model? How long will it take?

The ability to change attitudes depends a lot on how much our fear causes us to hold on to our current beliefs. The next chapter deals with fear.

SUMMARY

Find and maintain relationships that have mutual value, whether the values are friendship, chemistry, sex, or something else. A network of value-oriented relationships can provide a variety of fulfilling connections while searching for your quality love.

ASSIGNMENT

Answer ten personal ads. Or run an ad yourself and meet ten of the respondents. I know we did personal ads at the end of Chapter 3. But kissing frogs is an ongoing effort. This time look for the values that might be mutual, keeping an open mind to many values, not just a love relationship. Find out what you may have of value to the other person and see if there is mutuality or "value for value." See if the other person is even aware enough to have a discussion such as this—often they are not! Remember that every contact has some value. Start by identifying what that value is. Then determine if there are others, and if the values are high enough and mutual enough to warrant continued exploration.

Notes

Secret 9

WITHOUT FEAR THERE WOULD BE NO COURAGE

Fear Means It's Real

"I want to hold you 'til the fear in me subsides"
From the song "Sometimes When We Touch"
By D. Hill and B. Mann

The dragon lives! Love has its enemy. It is fear.

Searching means encountering fear.

Not searching means avoiding fear.

"I'm not afraid of searching." This is what people say, but then they go on to say, "But I don't like bars," or, "But I'm presently involved in a relationship," or, "But I think if it is right it will happen on its own."

They say they have no fear, but what they have is no courage.

If there were no fear, there would be no courage.

If there were no fear, love would be only a game, and there would be no need for this book.

If there were no fear, no one would have kept the secrets from you that the Love Dice now expose.

Why have these things been kept secret? Why have we been led to believe that "love fades" and "people never change" and "love will grow," all of which are only half-truths?

Is there a sinister plot to prevent us all from finding a quality love relationship?

No. There is no sinister plot. That is the most sinister thing of all—we don't even know there is a villain to be found. We simply believe what "everyone" believes—marriage is the goal and serial one- on-one relationships are the path to the goal.

These beliefs are so ingrained they go without being seriously questioned. And that's not all bad. The resulting marriages provide a degree of security for children and a degree of relief from loneliness for adults.

So what's my point?

My point is that we can increase fulfillment, add meaning to life, and maybe even find a soulmate if we come to grips with our fears, both seen and unseen. Coming to grips with our fears so we can find a new and better way requires courage. Doing this sensibly requires knowledge.

This book is about gaining knowledge to better understand quality love relationships and the search to find them. But gaining knowledge is not easy. Especially when there is a war going on—in this case the war between desire and fear. Here I offer you words from *The Teachings of Don Juan: a Yaqui Way of Knowledge* by Carlos Casteneda:

> *A man goes to knowledge as he goes to war, wide awake, with fear, with respect, and with absolute assurance. Going*

to knowledge or going to war in any other manner is a mistake, and whoever makes it will live to regret his steps.

When a man starts to learn, he is never clear about his objectives. His purpose is faulty; his intent is vague. He hopes for rewards that will never materialize for he knows nothing of the hardships of learning.

He slowly begins to learn—bit by bit at first, then in big chunks. And his thoughts soon clash. What he learns is never what he pictured, or imagined, and so he begins to be afraid. Learning is never what one expects. Every step of learning is a new task, and the fear the man is experiencing begins to mount mercilessly, unyieldingly. His purpose becomes a battlefield.

And thus he has stumbled upon the first of his natural enemies: Fear! A terrible enemy—treacherous, and difficult to overcome. It remains concealed at every turn of the way, prowling, waiting. And if the man, terrified in its presence, runs away, his enemy will have put an end to his quest.

What will happen to the man if he runs away in fear?

Nothing happens to him except that he will never learn. He will never become a man of knowledge. He will perhaps be a bully, or a harmless, scared man; at any rate he will be a defeated man. His first enemy will have put an end to his cravings.

And what can he do to overcome fear?

The answer is very simple. He must not run away. He must defy his fear, and in spite of it he must take the next step in learning, and the next, and the next. He must be fully afraid, and yet he must not stop. That is the rule! And a moment will come when his first enemy retreats. The man begins to feel sure of himself. His intent becomes stronger. Learning is no longer a terrifying task.

When this joyful moment comes, the man can say without hesitation that he has defeated his first natural enemy.

And so it is in learning the secrets of the Love Dice. If you run away in fear, you will not likely find a quality love relationship.

STORIES OF FEAR

Let's go through some of the stories from earlier chapters and name some of the fears. Naming them does not make them go away. But at least it shines the light of day on them and if they are visible they are more easily dealt with. The secrets of the Love Dice help light a path through the fear.

MIKE AND LORI REVISITED (Chapter 1)

When Mike first met Lori working in the restaurant, he didn't yet understand that he should have a **fear of immaturity**. The magic chemistry between them blinded him to the fact that she was a ⚀ on the maturity scale. It is probably a good idea to fear immaturity. Although many people may not be able to define immaturity exactly, they know they've been treated poorly and they know they were hurt and they know they don't want to repeat that. So they fear and stay away from immaturity.

But reality is not so black and white. Immaturity is a matter of degree, not just "mature" or "immature." And immaturity can possibly be outgrown with patience, time, proper guidance, and luck. Fear prevents us from providing support and guidance. It may be right to fear immaturity, but that does not mean we should always stay away from it. Courage can overcome fear.

Worse yet is that many people have a **fear of maturity**! "Accept me the way I am" means "I am afraid to grow." Associating with a more mature person exposes one's weaknesses. The result can be a feeling of inferiority. The more mature person does not see it this way, but the less mature person does. So they avoid mature people because of their **fear of feeling inferior.** Furthermore, the mature person's greater flexibility, willingness to experiment, and broader range of experience can be perceived as threatening. "I would never try *that!*" (**fear of experimentation**).

The result is that people tend to stick to their own kind. They avoid those who are either less mature or more mature than themselves.

"Stick to your own kind" provides a feeling of stability and comfort by limiting risk. But it is not true stability. A weathervane may appear stable if the wind never changes direction. But it is not really stable. If you can control the wind you can maintain the stability of the weathervane. For this reason many people try to control their environment and others around them so that nothing intrudes on their own comfort zone. As long as they are successful with such control they seem stable.

But true stability does not require controlling the wind or other people. True stability involves letting go of control. True stability accepts the wind and others and their ability to change. True stability allows one to travel out of his or her own small comfort zone with relative calm. True maturity supports others and provides guidance. It is not necessary to fear maturity.

Maturity is having the courage to overcome fear. Immaturity is fear without courage.

RICK AND JACKIE REVISITED (Chapter 2)

Why did Rick hold on to Rudi for dear life instead of giving her up in favor of Jackie where there was more chemistry and more maturity? Because he had a **fear of abandonment**. He had been emotionally abandoned by his mother, and so could not trust another woman. Fear of abandonment is the mirror image of the **fear of commitment**. It is the fear that commitment isn't real (which often it is not). Fear of abandonment is often not recognized as such, but it is pervasive in our culture. Children have been physically abandoned by parents who die or divorce. Children have been emotionally abandoned by parents who lack the maturity to give them emotional support, whether they live under the same roof or not. As adolescents, our girlfriend/boyfriend breaks up with us. As adults our spouse/parents/children die or leave. We have experienced "abandonment" at every stage of life, and we come to expect it just around the next corner. Therefore we are careful not to invest too much, because we know the likely outcome is abandonment. Even once we are married we don't invest fully because down deep somewhere we know that it is not as secure as it seems. Of course limiting our investment limits the potential returns. So fear of abandonment, while based on reality, needs to be recognized and overcome gradually, based on increasing trust.

During the relationship with Rick, Jackie encountered **fear of second best**. Everyone wants to be #1. Jackie didn't like being #2. She thought, as do most, that if you are #2 you are more likely to be hurt than if you are #1. Of course divorce statistics argue that #1 is the one most likely to get hurt! **Fear of emotional closeness** and **fear of commitment** are paramount when you are #1 (and explain why so many relationships break up). Jackie learned that being #2 may actually be a safer position! But she still had to deal with her **fear of loss** and **fear of being alone**. However, she learned that by eliminating her expectations of ascending to the #1 spot and accepting her role as #2 she could have a fulfilling (if partial) relationship with Rick. For that matter, she found it possible to have several fulfilling (partially) relationships. And several partially fulfilling relationships can be better than a single unfulfilling one. So it's OK to have some distractions, and to be someone else's distraction. But you may have to overcome your **fear of distractions**.

NATE AND SHARI REVISITED (Chapter 3)

High school sweethearts reunited to become the perfect family, but their marriage didn't work. Why? Because something was missing. Nate thought it was sex, but really it was chemistry. Shari thought it was maturity, and that was also a part of the problem. The lack of chemistry would have been a good reason for ending the marriage and beginning the search for a quality relationship. But instead Nate and Shari stayed married. Why? Because of fear. **Fear of the unknown. Fear of being alone. Fear of being hurt. Fear of hurting someone. Fear of loss. Fear of unfulfillment. Fear of rejection.**

Why would they fear rejection?? They were both caring, clean, intelligent, and reasonably good looking. But rejection is a very real fear. People don't like to extend themselves only to be slapped down. And if anyone else is watching, it is even worse (**fear of humiliation**). And if you spend time and get to know each other and then get rejected, it's worse still!

But keep in mind that rejection happens for one of two primary reasons: (1) The other person does not feel the chemistry that you feel. (2) The other person is too immature to recognize chemistry (has a lot of his or her own fears). Either way the result is the same—"rejection." But neither reason has anything to do with your worth as a person. Your self-esteem is not determined by any one person's interest or non-interest, rather by your own knowledge that you treat people with caring and respect.

Most likely, 5 out of 6 people (random probability) will not feel chemistry for you, and 5 out of 6 of those that do will be immature. So the overwhelming probability is that you will be "rejected." But if you see rejection as the natural result of probability statistics, you will not take it personally.

BRUCE AND KAREN REVISITED (Chapter 3)

Karen and Bruce were very much in love and their affair lasted for twelve years. So why did Karen stay married for seven of these years? Did she say to herself "I'm a fearful person and lack courage"? No. She said, "I don't want to hurt my husband or my children." And there was truth in that. But not the whole truth.

There was **fear of chemistry.** This is very basic. Chemistry is the power engine of soulmate relationships. Therefore we should want it, not be afraid of it. In fact we both want it and are afraid of it. It's natural to be afraid of it because it can give us joy but it can also give us pain. From what I hear, more people have experienced pain from chemistry than have experienced joy. When this happens it is typically caused by immaturity.

It has often been said, "There is no growth without pain." Or more concisely, "No pain, no gain." And oh, how true it is! We know the sayings but we still try to avoid the pain (no courage).

Of course there was also the **fear that the chemistry won't last.** Bruce also had this fear, along with the **fear of misjudging it.** If either one of them misjudged it then there was also the **fear of never finding it again.** They were both afraid of losing what they already had. She was afraid of being alone. He was afraid of the unknown. She convinced herself that Bruce was only "sex" and her husband and family were "love." That was the safe way.

And then, finally, Karen and Bruce were together. But it blew up in their faces with her new affair, proving once again that you shouldn't believe in love or chemistry or soulmates or anything like that. Right? Enough bad experiences and "fear of loss" becomes an ingrained way of life—"no investment, no loss" (no courage).

Why did Karen blow up this love relationship with Bruce? Was it for the economic security that millionaire Charles could offer? It would appear that way. She chose money over love, that's the simplistic answer. But we know how everyone hungers for love, so why would she choose money? Because she had a **fear of vulnerability** that is natural and can also be expressed as a **fear of emotional closeness**. She was afraid that her weaknesses would be seen and not accepted. When she made love with Bruce she was higher than she'd ever been in her life. But she couldn't trust it. Fear of loss. Fear that the chemistry wouldn't last. Fear of rejection. And…

Fear of commitment. As long as Karen had her eggs in more than one basket, she couldn't lose them all in a single blow. This is a curious paradox to Chapter 7 where I advocated distractions, or a "portfolio of investments." But in the evolution of a love relationship there comes a time when the one primary bond is strong enough and has been tested enough to know that this single bond is in fact stronger than all the other multiple points of support. Multiple points of support are better when they are relatively untested. But a single tested bond is better if it has been shown to be strong. However, if a person has not learned to trust, they cannot make a commitment. And since many people have never experienced such a strong bond themselves and have never seen it in others, there really is no role model and no basis for trust. Trust can not be based on shallow evidence. It needs to be based on solid experience and testing to be sure that "this particular relationship is in fact really good." Meaning (1) there is real and mutual high chemistry, and (2) there is high and mutual maturity. With the right experience and knowledge, "trust" can overcome "fear of commitment." But until a 🎲🎲 (or maybe a 🎲🎲) relationship is found, "commitment" will often lead to disaster (or at least disappointment), thus reinforcing the "fear of commitment."

BARRY AND LINDA REVISITED (Chapter 5)

Linda never had an affair with Barry, but why did she hold on to her marriage when her husband was an alcoholic and the chemistry wasn't there? Of course there were the "shoulds" heaped upon us from childhood by our parents and society (I suggest reading Karen Horney's *Neurosis and Human Growth* for a full explanation of "The Tyranny of the Shoulds"):

She should be a good wife.
She should be a good mother.
She should uphold her marriage vows.
She should be able to deal with this.

No one likes to put their children or their husband or themselves through pain. Unless they know for sure that it will be better on the other side. And she didn't know for sure. **Fear that the chemistry won't be real. Fear that she'll misjudge it**. And since no one can ever know the future for sure, **fear of the unknown.** And of course if her children are hurt she feels hurt so there is **fear of hurting others** and **fear of being hurt**. And if it doesn't work out with Barry, there is **fear of loss**. So she was stuck. Paralyzed. Paralyzed by fear.

All of these fears are real. None of them are to be discounted. What is necessary is the knowledge to recognize true chemistry (the kind that doesn't fade) and to recognize true maturity (the kind that doesn't blow up in your face). Linda was still afraid and lacked the knowledge. She thereby instilled her own fears into her children, who by example learned "don't take chances," "stick it out," "don't trust," "don't believe in true love," "don't make the effort to understand chemistry and maturity." All these "beliefs" are really just reflections of their mother's fears (which in turn are reflections of society's fears).

Barry was more mature than Linda, but he had his fears also. Because he was single and trying to meet people he had the **fear of kissing frogs.** He knew that to find his soulmate he was going to have to kiss a lot of frogs and that meant he would have to deal with the **fear of rejection**. But he was not as prepared for the **fear of disapproval.** Barry respected the fact that Linda was married. But he was afraid no one else would understand his relationship with her. Monogamy is the only recognized game in town, and it was likely that others would not see his friendship with Linda as appropriate. However, love is not a game. And though monogamy is consistent with quality love relationships once you find him or her, it is inconsistent with the "search" phase. Unfortunately our culture does not distinguish very readily between these two phases. A relatively short and limited search is expected and OK. A long period of monogamy is OK. Divorce (serial monogamy) is OK (once or twice). But an extended, widespread search is seen as "playing the field" or "playboy" or "promiscuous." These attitudes reflect the fears people have individually and hence collectively as a culture: **Fear of rejection** (don't try too many encounters). **Fear of loss** (hold on to him/her for dear life). **Fear of being alone** (find him/her fast). **Fear that the chemistry won't be real** (if he or she marries me it must be real). All of these fears get molded into a cultural value system that discourages "searching," encourages "settling," and keeps bad marriages together. "Settling" is a fear-based culture. A "courage-based" culture would provide the support system needed for real searching over a long period of time. That is to say it would provide emotional support, make sex more readily available, and give credibility to distractions and to value oriented connections among people.

MARIO AND ELISE REVISITED (Chapter 5)

In order to have the patience to deal with Mario's glacial pace of growth and development, Elise had to overcome her **fear of waiting**. Waiting for your diamond in the rough feels like rejection. It feels like you're alone. You are afraid of losing him or her (or losing the potential that you see). These are very real fears.

Therefore patience is a form of courage, and the necessary one while waiting through geologic time.

As an analogy, picture a prospector looking for diamonds. In his lifetime he has found a variety of diamonds, most of them small. He finds a large rock with a bright speck on one side. He chips away and the bright speck grows. He chips a little more and it grows some more. He chips a little more and suddenly realizes that he may be looking at one of the largest diamonds in the world. Adrenalin shot! It's hard to contain his excitement! He wants to know how big it really is. He wants to run and show everyone. He wants to crack it open in one blow. But he needs to overcome his **fear of not knowing** and be patient. Chip away at the same speed. Maybe even slower. Be very careful. Do nothing to hurt it. He could probably find 100 small diamonds in the time it will take to slowly find out what's inside this big rock. He needs to overcome his fear of loss and take it slow.

Why did Mario insist on his freedom and not want to be tied down? Because he needed to be in control. He had a **fear of being controlled**. He had been controlled before and had been hurt in the process. He was not going to put himself in the control of a woman again. Did he say, "I'm afraid"? No. He said, "I'm strong." "I just want to have fun." "Just accept me the way I am." And who can argue with him? A life at 70 percent happiness is immensely better than a life without happiness! Was he afraid to win? Probably not. But he was afraid to lose. Therefore his solution was to "not play," i.e. if you don't play the game of love, you can't lose. And you can have a reasonably good life (70 percent happiness). Just don't allow yourself to feel. Maintain control at all times. But love is not a game…

The male preoccupation with sex arises in part from the female **fear of being controlled**. Regardless of women's liberation, power in our culture is still largely male dominated. The male sets up "things" as status symbols (cars, houses, clothes). Then, through marketing, he gets others (women) to believe in this value system. As long as the man has control over these "things" (i.e. monetary superiority) he controls the power, and he controls the women. But of course women don't want to be controlled, inasmuch as their major life experience is one of being controlled. They want the power, they are afraid of being controlled, and so they control the sex. In this way they control the men. The desire for control stems mainly from their **fear of being controlled.**

Closely related is the **fear of losing control.** It is necessary to lose control to have good sex. Therefore a corollary is **fear of sex.** Sex is good. Sex is natural. People like sex. But sex is held in limited supply. People fear sex. People fear sex because they have a **fear of emotional closeness** or a **fear of vulnerability** or a **fear of rejection** or a **fear of commitment** or a **fear of investment** or a **fear of loss** or a **fear of losing self.**

When a person is in intimate contact with another there is both a desire to share all and a fear that in so sharing their inner self will be exposed and subsequently rejected. And rejected at precisely the time that they are most vulnerable.

Thomas Moore, in *Soul Mates* says:

> *It isn't easy to expose your soul to another, to risk such vulnerability, hoping that the other person will be able to tolerate your own irrationality. It may also be difficult, no matter how open-minded you are, to be receptive as another reveals her soul to you. Yet this mutual vulnerability is one of the great gifts of love: giving the other sufficient emotional space in which to live and express her soul, with its reasonable and unreasonable ways, and then to risk revealing your own soul, complete with its own absurdities.*

One common solution to the fear of emotional closeness and fear of vulnerability is to relegate sex to a purely physical act. Most men and many women enjoy sex in this way. And it is enjoyable. But the greatest joy is denied them by the fear of emotional closeness. Another solution is to avoid sex altogether (more frequently the solution of women than men). This of course denies both the physical *and* emotional joy.

STEVE AND RACHEL REVISITED (Chapter 6)

The male preoccupation with sex, regardless of its causes, stems from a **fear of deprivation.** This is the opposite of "fear of sex." It's the "fear of not getting enough sex." Fear of sex (for whatever reasons) keeps sex in limited supply, giving rise to fear of deprivation and thereby limiting the possibility of finding a quality love relationship. Rachel helped Steve overcome his fear of deprivation by providing an availability of sexual fulfillment untainted by cultural hang-ups.

OTHER FEARS

Fear of change.

If we are to move into the future and create a better environment for people to find quality love, it will be necessary to change basic attitudes and beliefs. This is usually very difficult to do because people are afraid of change, especially change in attitudes and beliefs. They are comfortable with their current way of life, and even though it isn't everything they would like it to be, they would rather keep it the same than change it.

Fear of values.

"I am not afraid. I live within my values and there is nothing to fear." This is the codification of fear. Set limits and call them "values." Find a good reason to not go outside your comfort zone…

Fear of the law.

Society takes collective values and translates them into "laws." Most laws are good of course, but some are not. Fear of the law is good also. But some laws need to be changed, as do some values.

Fear of God.

"These are not my values, these are God's values. Therefore I am not only safe within my limits, I am good." OK. You win. Don't change. Don't grow!

Fear of misunderstanding.

It is easy to misunderstand an emotionally mature person. They are different. They are spiritually advanced. It would be easy to misunderstand them and think that they are against values, or the law, or God. But they are not against these things—only against those aspects that inhibit growth. If advanced beings from a future century were transported backward in time, they would fear being misunderstood by us because they would not share our cultural norms.

Fear is so prevalent that it is covered up by all manners of rationalization. "I'm not interested in love." "I don't want to get married." Can't you just hear Mario or Katie speaking? Such philosophies create a "safe" environment where one does not have to deal with one's fears.

In my experience there seems to be an exponential relationship between fear and chemistry. It's not just "the higher the chemistry the higher the fear," but "as chemistry increases fear skyrockets out of sight!"

If I had to put numbers on it, it would look like this:

Chemistry	⚀	⚁	⚂	⚃	⚄	⚅
Fear	none	none	none	25%	95%	1,000%

When you have more to gain, you have more to lose. At 1,000% you can become paralyzed by fear. You may be afraid to approach her because of fear of rejection. Or afraid to invest in him because of fear of vulnerability. You may become possessive because of fear of loss. You may be afraid to trust because of fear of getting hurt. (This latter fear leads to the paradoxical result that "You trust least those that you love most.") Fear causes you to become "stuck" wherever you are.

And so a person's tolerance for fear becomes a deciding factor in the quality of a relationship they are willing to search for. In my experience most people can only handle about 50% fear, so I see most settling for a chemistry level of about " ⚃ 1/2."

The antidote for fear is, of course, courage. In his book *The Road Less Traveled*, Dr. M. Scott Peck discusses "the courage of love":

> *When we extend ourselves, our self enters new and unfamiliar territory, so to speak. Our self becomes a new and different self. We do things we are not accustomed to do. We change. The experience of change, of unaccustomed activity, of being on unfamiliar ground, or doing things differently is frightening. It always was and always will be. People handle their fear of change in different ways, but the fear is inescapable if they are in fact to change. Courage is not the absence of fear; it is the making of action in spite of fear, the moving out against the resistance engendered by fear into the unknown and into the future.*

Without fear there would be no courage!

Here is another story full of fear:

THE STORY OF PETE AND INGA

Fear of never finding it. Fear of being alone. These are powerful forces that often spell a precipitous end to the search for a quality love relationship.

These fears drove Inga and Pete together and ended Inga's search for a soulmate. He had just gone through a painful divorce. Her various relationships had all ended in disaster.

Pete and Inga were a "marriage waiting to happen." He was wealthy but felt lonely in his big house. Time alone on business trips didn't help. She was tired of the search and ready for a stable relationship. "I've finally found the right man," she thought. After a year they were married. She was elated. Her life goal had at last been reached.

She moved into the big house in the exclusive neighborhood. She started to give it her woman's touch. She had a flair for decorating.

But Pete would have none of it. Everything in the kitchen was "just the way he wanted it." In the living room he liked his furniture "just the way it was." She was not allowed to add any personal touches.

Her feelings were, "I'm just there to make his life comfortable. I'm there to help him with his house, his needs; I pay for half the household expenses. I pay for the upkeep on his assets with my money and time. What a great deal for him! But what's in it for me?"

He controls her every move. She screams back at him. He blames her.

When they're not arguing or when he's not being selfish, there are occasional times when it's "nice" or "pleasant." He says he's in love with her, but it's not spontaneous, not flexible. "It's harder to live with Pete than anyone else I've ever known," she says.

"Why did you marry him?" I ask.

"I was hoping it would be OK."

Inga's so confused in this situation that she can't really assess it accurately.

Here's my assessment along with a few comments based on my discussion with her.

Pete Inga

Note 1   Note 2

Note 3   Note 4

Pete's chemistry for Inga was high.
Inga's chemistry for Pete was medium.
Pete's maturity was medium low.
Inga's maturity was high.

Note 1. At first Inga told me she thought Pete's chemistry for her was a ⚄. "He says he's in love with me." Then she revised her assessment and told me maybe it was only a ⚂. "He just wants someone to take care of him." My own opinion is that it's hard to tell for sure, with all the immaturity going on. It could be a ⚄, a ⚄, or a ⚄. My guess, as noted above, is a ⚄. I think his **"fear of emotional closeness"** (among others) is driving his irrational behavior. But it's only a guess…

Note 2. She said her feeling for him "started out as a ⚄ but now is just a ⚄." Again, it's hard to say whether it is "infatuation fading to reality" or whether it is "true chemistry tarnished by immaturity." Her assessment of "nice" and "pleasant" when they're not fighting sounds like a ⚄ to me.

Note 3. Inga first graded Pete as a ⚁ on the maturity scale. Perhaps because of his age. But age is not the issue. Upon further questioning and observance of his childish, controlling, infantile behavior, she revised her assessment of his maturity downward to a ⚁. I think her initial assessment of ⚄ was a reflection that her hopes had triumphed over reality. (She calls it "female *libido*"— women's romantic notions about family, security, nice house, etc.)

Note 4. Inga has matured into a quality, caring person. But she is not yet perfect. She should obviously have paid more attention to the "**fear of misjudging it**." And in this relationship with Pete, she found herself being dragged back down to his level. So although in terms of growth and maturity one can gain ground, one can also lose ground, especially under the bad influence of an extremely immature person. However, Inga is a strong person. She will regain her perspective, and along with it her maturity.

SUMMARY

Let me repeat the list of fears, since it is so long:

Fear of immaturity
Fear of maturity
Fear of feeling inferior
Fear of experimentation
Fear of abandonment
Fear of commitment
Fear of second best
Fear of emotional closeness
Fear of loss
Fear of being alone
Fear of distractions
Fear of unfulfillment
Fear of the unknown
Fear of being hurt

- **Fear of hurting someone**
- **Fear of rejection**
- **Fear of humiliation**
- **Fear of chemistry**
- **Fear that the chemistry won't be real**
- **Fear that the chemistry won't last**
- **Fear of misjudging it**
- **Fear of never finding it again**
- **Fear of vulnerability**
- **Fear of kissing frogs**
- **Fear of disapproval**
- **Fear of waiting**
- **Fear of not knowing**
- **Fear of being controlled**
- **Fear of losing control**
- **Fear of sex**
- **Fear of investment**
- **Fear of losing self**
- **Fear of deprivation**
- **Fear of values**
- **Fear of the law**
- **Fear of God**
- **Fear of misunderstanding**

I'm sure this is not a complete list. You can certainly add your own fears!

Fear limits knowledge and understanding. Fear keeps people from searching. Fear creates barriers between people. Fear creates a culture that does not support the search for a quality love relationship.

Fear is pervasive. It starts in childhood and is perpetuated by parents, society, and the media. Fear hides behind names like "values" and "religion."

Fear can be overcome by knowledge and experience. You would be afraid if you were being launched on a space voyage without any training. But astronauts have been trained and have practiced and have the confidence to deal with their mission. You would be afraid to walk out on a high wire alone with nothing beneath you. But high wire performing artists have trained and practiced to do this. This book is intended to supply you with knowledge and information that will help you feel comfortable in the search for quality love. The assignments at the end of each chapter are intended to build confidence and reduce fear.

In the end there will still be fear. It will be your courage that determines how far you can go in your search for a quality love relationship.

ASSIGNMENT

Here's an assignment to challenge your fear of the unknown, fear of experimentation, fear of sex, fear of laws, fear of God, fear of changing your attitudes, and maybe some other fears.

In Chapter 6, as one solution to sexual deprivation, I suggested the option of increasing the availability of professional sex. Therefore the assignment here is to search out and have a conversation with a professional sex worker. I'm not talking about a street prostitute. And I don't want you to do anything illegal, so please don't offer money for sex!

I won't tell you exactly where to find a professional sex worker, that's part of the assignment. You might start with the yellow pages or personal ads or the Internet for clues. The challenge is to move yourself out of your comfort zone and find out what reality is like in their world.

I can't predict what you will find. In my experience there are many intelligent, caring, understanding professional sex workers. But there are also some that are not so wholesome. Therefore please take precautions to ensure your personal safety.

I would like to see you challenge yourself to do this and to gain the insight that might come from a face-to-face conversation with a professional sex worker. However, I understand that this may arouse just too many fears for some, so I am offering an alternate assignment. Unfortunately I know that most readers will take the easy way if there is one. However, in this case I feel I must offer an alternative, although it is not as productive as personal interaction. The alternative is to visit the Prostitutes' Education Network website on the Internet at www.bayswan.org. This website provides comprehensive information about sex worker rights and issues, and is very informative on a variety of subjects.

Whichever route you take on this assignment, I hope you will remain open to unexpected revelations about not only sex but about emotional closeness and love. And most importantly that you experience the enjoyment of doing something outside your comfort zone.

Notes

Secret 10

IF YOU'RE TRYING TO RELAX, DON'T ASK QUESTIONS

Let It Be

If you're trying to relax
Don't ask questions
That will surely tax you
Later on you'll have your answers.

From the song "Since I Met You"
By W. Stergis and S. Stills

I just met Jan. Sparks fly from her eyes when we're together. Her smile lights up my soul. I hang on her every word, every move, every act. We dance—she is stunning! She doesn't insist on "just friends," but I want to go slow, so we do "Friends Plus." She cuddles up with me and rests her head on my shoulder. We lay down and I hold her while she sleeps. No sex. This is *my* rule (believe it or not).

The chemistry is so high. My fear is out of sight! I can feel it like a vise around my chest, tightening.

I asked for the first two dates. She asked for the third. I like that. I've been honest with her from the start and she with me. I've known many women and she's known many men. I have other female friends and she has other male friends. Being honest like this is consistent with my values.

The connection is there. I can feel it. The experience of holding her in my arms is wonderful.

Today as she left my house I cried. The relationship is still new. I'm afraid of losing her. I'm very vulnerable. I'm not afraid of being alone, but I'm afraid of not ever finding my soulmate. And I'm afraid of misjudging it. I'm afraid of immaturity. There hasn't been enough time to assess hers. She's given enough already that I'm past fear of rejection and into fear of abandonment.

She said she'd call and let me know her plans for the weekend. But she seemed hurt to know I have other female friends. I'm afraid she will misunderstand me. She is clearly first in my mind but I'm afraid that she doesn't believe it and that she is afraid of being just one of many.

> Will she call?
> When will she call?
> Should I call her?
> When should I call her?
> Was she hurt by my disclosures?
> Is it a permanent barrier?
> When will I see her again?
> What are her feelings for me?
> Will she open up further?
> Where is this leading?
> Can I accept her smoking?

> *When I find myself in times of trouble*
> *Mother Mary comes to me*
> *Speaking words of wisdom*
> *Let it be*
> *Let it be*
> *Let it be*
> *Let it be*
> *Let it be*
> *Whisper words of wisdom*
> *Let it be.*
>
> From the song "Let It Be"
By John Lennon and Paul McCartney

I can see why "Let it be" needs to be repeated so many times in the song. Because the questions go 'round and 'round so many times in my head. And so many questions!

I dig into my brain for the answers. I wrack my memory for every word she's spoken and every move she's made trying to determine what will happen. I want a crystal ball in the worst way.

I could call her right now and ask her point blank. That might calm my nerves and get me the answers to my questions. I think I will call her. No, maybe I won't. Should I?

If I call her, I'll never know if she'd have called me or when.

The phone rings!

Maybe it's her!

It's not. Disappointment!

If I ask her if she was hurt, she'll say, "No." If I ask her if she'll open up, she'll say, "What are you talking about?" If I ask her where this is leading, she'll say, "I don't know."

So I don't ask questions. Or if I do (and I do in my mind) I answer them like this:

Will she call? — Time will tell.
When will she call? — You'll know when she calls.
Should I call her? — Not yet.
When should I call? — After you've given her enough time.

The phone rings!
It is her!! Thank God!

Four questions are answered in the one second it takes me to recognize her voice. And a fifth when she says she'll see me tonight.

But six questions remain unanswered. And there will no doubt be thousands more as the relationship progresses (will it progress?).

At dinner tonight I am still tense. What are her true feelings? It would help me to know. So I open up with her and tell her that my feelings for her are a 🎲 . I ask her, "What are your feelings for me?" She says they are a 🎲 . Knife to the heart! But what is the truth? I still really don't know. Perhaps her feelings are only a 🎲 . But perhaps they are a 🎲 and she is still protecting herself. Her answer did nothing to relieve my tension. Asking the question did not help me to relax.

The mindset that I tried to develop was:

1. Be her friend.
2. Support her in her life.
3. Enjoy the wonder of her company.
4. Don't push for anything.
5. Take things as they come.
6. Accept my vulnerability.
7. Stay open and real with her.
8. Find other things to occupy the rest of my time.

If You're Trying to Relax, Don't Ask Questions

This was not easy for an action-oriented person like me! And there were so many more questions:

Does she love me?
When will I know?
Will she want to try making love?
When?
Does she feel pressured?
What should I do differently?
What should I say?
Will she be upset by my other relationships?
What will she do?
Should I forget about the others?
What if it falls through?
Am I making a fool of myself over her?
Could I spend my time more productively elsewhere?
Where?
When will she want to go out again?
Should I push her?

I cannot relax with all these questions going around in my brain. I *should* be able to answer them! But I can't.
"Let it be."
Each answer will come it its own time.

If you're trying to relax, don't ask questions.
That will surely tax you.
Later on you'll have your answers.

If I try to force the questions, hoping to stop my mental turmoil, I will get half-baked answers. These could be worse than waiting.

Only one of these questions has a realistic answer now. "No, don't push her!" Just enjoy her company. Later on I'll have the rest of my answers.

Of course telling myself to stop asking questions and actually stopping are two completely different things! I know better than to ask all these questions. But they just pop into my mind, unwanted.

My solution is distractions. Refer to the list in Chapter 7. Find something powerful. Maybe a powerful distraction won't force these questions out of my mind 100 percent, but if it can force them out 80 percent, that is major progress.

I think I'll invite Mandy to go dancing on Saturday. She is #2 on my list and a contender for #1. A good distraction. Mandy is not yet ready for sex, so I think I'll call Tara and see if she's available on Sunday. If so, we'll make love. Tara is a professional, and we are also friends; we like and respect each other.

I'm trying to keep the pressure off Jan, and it's working. The vise is loosening its grip. I still feel the tension but it's easing off. I have written my questions in my journal. That has helped because now they are off my mind and on to paper but not loaded on Jan.

The questions are still there. But I am accepting that the answers will come in their own time. And I want to just enjoy Jan. I don't want her to feel pressure. I'm afraid I have already applied too much pressure. Have I?

I'm trying to relax. So I do not ask questions. Later on I'll have my answers.

I once had a friend who always used to say, "Time will tell." She was right.

Let it be.

Let it be.

SUMMARY

When it comes to strong emotional involvement, we often want to know quickly where things are headed in order to avoid pain. But exactly because of the strong emotions, people often don't know for sure or are reluctant to say where it is going because of their own fears. Premature questions can feel like pressure to the other person, and often the verbal answers aren't reliable. Only behavioral answers are reliable, and answers to questions about long-term stability can only be answered by observing long-term behavioral patterns. If you're trying to relax, don't ask questions! Later on you'll have your answers.

ASSIGNMENT

Start a journal. It doesn't have to be anything fancy. It could even be just a file or a box into which you throw scraps of papers on which you've written your thoughts. You needn't write something every day (this is not a diary). Only write when you feel stressed or depressed or when you have questions that you don't know the answers to. Write the questions and your fears about the answers and how much you want to know the answers right now. Ask yourself "What is the truth of this situation?" Then write the reasons for not asking questions and what you think the truth of the situation is and when you think would be the right time to know the answer. Keep writing until you don't feel like writing anymore, then quit. That may be one minute or a half-hour.

Writing can be cathartic. It can help get your questions out without burdening your soul-friend (or anyone else for that matter). Keep these "notes to yourself" totally private so that you can feel comfortable in writing anything that comes to mind, in whatever language (including *libido* language) without fear that anyone else will ever read it. This is one of the best ways to get in touch with your emotions, and to identify what the insecurities are that drive you to want to know the answer to a question before its time.

I know that many men and some women think journal writing is only for young girls or budding authors. I'm not suggesting either keeping a diary or writing a book. I'm suggesting that you can be your own best friend by having a conversation with yourself on paper. Your other friends probably don't have very good information to guide you, so you are better off having this conversation with yourself. Just thinking it through in your head usually does not get to the bottom of the matter. No matter where you are, you can usually find some paper (it doesn't have to be a bound "journal") and write down what's bothering you. Keep writing until either it doesn't bother you anymore (because you understand it) or until you run out of time (in which case you'll find out later if it's still really bothering you). Write until you feel good about your course of action, even if the action is to "wait," or to "write more later."

I have found it interesting to look back on these notes after weeks, months, or even years to see what was important then and what's important now. But it is not necessary to save your journal entries. Burn them if you want. The important thing is to get your feelings out and down on paper where you can see them objectively. The mere process of getting them out and down on paper will often be enough to relieve whatever stress you may be feeling, even if you don't yet have the answers you want.

If you really want to have fun, write down your sexual fantasies and then read on in the next chapter!

Secret 11

DISCOVER THE TRUE MEANING OF FANTASIES

Genuine Acceptance

*I've always been crazy
But it's kept me from going insane.*
From the song "I've Always Been Crazy"
By Waylon Jennings

MAKING LOVE FUN

Emotional closeness in a quality love relationship requires a genuine acceptance of the other person. Sharing deep feelings is essential to such acceptance as described by Dr. Marie Robinson:

> One important thing that husbands and wives must learn to do is to share their deeper thoughts, problems, and feelings with one another. Over the years the general withdrawal of both partners [makes] communication of any

kind most superficial, and hope of any important contact through conversation has been abandoned almost entirely.

Everything may be discussed in such conversations, although one should avoid any recrimination or "confessions" that would hurt the other. Conversation about one's emotional or reality difficulties, about one's loneliness, plans, successes, fears, and hopes are deeply moving...

An individual's fears and hopes may be as mundane as a fear that the family picnic will be rained out on Sunday, or as fantastic as the hope of winning a $10 million lottery. Whether your partner fantasizes about living in a mansion overlooking the ocean or about being president of the United States, he or she hopes that you will listen and understand.

The difficulty is that it's not the fantasy itself that's important, but what's behind the fantasy. The fantasy is a symbol of an unmet need. The person who wants to be president may have felt powerless as a child and fantasizes about having ultimate power and control. The person who wants to live in a mansion may have grown up in poverty and to them the mansion symbolizes financial security.

To be close in a quality love relationship, a couple must share their fantasies. And the ability to share requires a high degree of trust that the other person will not close off or put you down.

Understanding fantasies implies understanding that they may never be fulfilled in reality. Not very many people will actually become president. Only a few will live in a mansion overlooking the ocean. But it's FUN to dream, FUN to talk, FUN to plan, and whether you get there or not will be relatively unimportant if you sincerely feel that your partner is listening to you and is right there with you every step of the way.

Fantasies are very, very common, and cover a wide range of subjects. Some represent serious desires and some represent the emotional system making up for past deprivations.

Perhaps the ultimate test for the participants in a quality love relationship is the ability to understand and accept their partner's wildest sexual fantasies. This is especially difficult for women, because they are afraid that the male's sexual fantasies are a sign of their own inadequacy as a woman, instead of recognizing them as a symbol of the man's past deprivation.

Sexual fantasies are not a game, although they can be fun. In sexual fantasies, as with any fantasies, it's important to see what's behind the surface, what the real meaning is. Is the real meaning of the man's sexual fantasy

1. His partner isn't good enough, or
2. He's a perverted lunatic, or
3. He's compensating for a lifelong deprivation of sex?

The willingness to listen to fantasies and to not miss the point is an important ability for partners in a love relationship. If a child says to his mother, "I'm going to kill you," the mother knows the real meaning to be, "I'm extremely angry with you." The mother does not dwell on the words, "I'm going to kill you," but on the meaning behind the words. Lovers need to be able to do the same thing with each other, even (or especially) as regards sexual fantasies.

Most people have an easier time dealing with the fantasy of, "I want a mansion overlooking the ocean," than with the fantasy of, "I'd like to make love with two women at one time." But because affection and sex and emotional closeness are so important to quality love relationships, I want to focus the remainder of this chapter on the aspect of sexual fantasies.

Sexual Fantasies…Why are they important? How far can you go? How much can you share? Why are we so inhibited? Why do we have to hold so much inside? When will we be able to be open and honest with our partners? Is it different for soulmates than for other quality love relationships?

My thesis is that partners in a quality love relationship need to understand, accept, and enjoy each other's fantasies, including sexual fantasies. This may mean exploring territory previously considered taboo. "*The road of excess leads to the palace of wisdom.*" (William Blake)

My desire is for men and women to have more fulfilling love relationships (and more fulfilling sex) by understanding the role of fantasies, exploring fantasies, and having a wide range of "OK" sexual fantasies. I would like to see love partners enjoy each other, overcome deprivation, and grow together without always running up against barriers, blocks, or taboos.

Understanding, of course, begins with knowledge. Knowledge does not always come easy (see Chapter 9 quote from Carlos Casteneda regarding a "man of knowledge"). But I never said the search for a quality love relationship was easy…

WHY ARE SEXUAL FANTASIES IMPORTANT?

Here's what various authors have to say:

In the "Foreword" to *My Secret Garden* (women's sexual fantasies by Nancy Friday), "J" (author of *The Sensuous Woman*) says:

> *You won't really know your lover until you have unearthed his or her hidden desires. Nor will you have achieved complete trust and intimacy until you have been*

able to share your fantasies with each other and have them accepted. Perhaps this book (My Secret Garden) will break the barrier of silence.

Thomas Moore puts sexual fantasies in perspective of the soul:

Sexual intimacy begins with the acknowledgement of and respect for the mystery and madness of the other's sexuality, for it is only in mystery and madness that soul is revealed…At times we may have to protect ourselves from another's sexual confusion and acting out, but if we want an intimate relationship, we will have to find it in ourselves to create a place for the other's sexual fantasy. (From the book Soul Mates.)

And Nancy Friday (author of *My Secret Garden*) sums it up concisely:

No man can be really free in bed with a woman who is not.

The importance of fantasies is in building emotional closeness. Remember (Chapter 6) "The highest purpose of sex is emotional closeness."

Emotional barriers block emotional closeness and ultimately break down the enjoyment of sex, undermining the fulfillment of love. Sexual fantasies often create barriers and restrict intimacy because they exist but are not disclosed.

WHERE DO SEXUAL FANTASIES COME FROM?

It is important to recognize the emotional meaning of sexual fantasies. Fantasies spring from deprivation. Deprivation was discussed at length in Chapter 6 (remember the analogy of a man's obsession with water after being stranded for years in the desert). It may be worthwhile for you to go back and review some of the material from Chapter 6 before proceeding with this discussion of fantasies.

The following quote from Nancy Friday in *My Secret Garden* summarizes the connection between deprivation and fantasies (famine and dreams) quite well:

> *I think the violence and alienation in some of these women's fantasies is a measure of how much the human being will rage against sexual famine. The well fed diner will idly choose between this dessert and that; the starving person will dream of "eating a horse."*

Fantasies may take myriad forms, but they all trace their roots back to deprivation. Understand deprivation and you understand fantasies. Just like dreams, fantasies "happen." Fantasies do not accede to our culturally inbred limits. As a result they often involve subjects that are taboo, either for society as a whole or for the individual in particular. Fantasies have a childlike playfulness—anything is OK.

Partners often fear that "If you fantasize about someone else that must mean you don't love me." But it may or may not mean that. It is essential to uncover the real meaning. It could be (1) I don't really love you so I fantasize about others to get off; or (2) I love you so much I'm afraid I'll lose you if I invest too much, so I fantasize about others to remind me not to go too far out on a limb; or (3) I love you and I want to try anything and everything with you, or (4) I saw a very sexy girl today and given my lifelong deprivation I can't help but wish I could have her, and this is totally unrelated to my love or non-love for you. Remember that the origin of fantasies is deprivation so all of the above sprout from never having had enough chemistry or emotional support or sex. Therefore fantasies about having other women and/or men are the emotional system trying to rectify past deprivation and should not be taken personally.

What's important is spending time together sharing feelings, getting to know the other person, and building trust, security, and acceptance.

Laugh at the craziness of the fantasies.

Be serious about dealing with the underlying deprivation.

WHY IS IT SO HARD TO ACCEPT SEXUAL FANTASIES?

Unfortunately, sexual fantasies are not readily accepted by many. In *My Secret Garden* (female fantasies), Nancy Friday says:

> *I told my first lover about my fantasies. He abruptly got out of bed, put on his pants, and went home. There were other lovers, and other fantasies. But I never introduced the two again. Until I met my husband. Bill brought my fantasies back into the open again from those depths where I had prudently decided they must live, never to be spoken again. I realized how much he loved me, and in loving me, loved anything that gave me more abundant life.*

It is precisely because fantasies spring from such a deep emotional source (deprivation), that they don't respect cultural limits and therefore are not accepted. In fact, the deprivation was *created* by cultural limits, so it is natural that cultural limits will do their best to keep us from accepting the fantasies.

Thomas Moore writes about cultural taboos and sensibilities:

> *From the erotic point of view,...our culture's fear of sex and our anxious controls on sex are at bottom due to a mistrust of the soul. Soul is a generator of life, spilling imagination into a world that tries to keep itself stable and secure. Sex is always making new connections, filling fantasy with new possibilities for intimacy, unfamiliar and exciting emotions and sensations, and new ways of experiencing life. Our literalistic attitudes and our reductionistic narrow readings of sex try to bridle it, attempting to halt its threat to the status quo by squelching it at the physical level.*

WHAT HAPPENS IF WE DON'T ACCEPT SEXUAL FANTASIES?

Blocking off some part of ourselves emotionally creates an inner rage (as if it weren't there already!). This rage will come out somewhere. If the relationship is incapable of providing an escape valve for these pent-up emotions, they will find an outlet in affairs, abuse, neglect, indifference, or some other dysfunction.

Fantasies can be an escape valve and therefore lie near the heart of the emotional closeness issue.

CAN SEXUAL FANTASIES HURT YOU?

The wonderful thing about sexual fantasies is that they typically are not physically harmful. There are exceptions, of course: rape, physical abuse to the point of injury, etc. But the "harm" associated with most sexual fantasies is simply the breaking of taboos—harming one's "sensibilities," so to speak. The narrower one's sensibility limits, the more likely they are to be "harmed," and the less likely they are to listen to, accept, and have fun with fantasies. Such a narrow limit person will therefore less likely be able to support their partner in emotional growth.

So it is our fears that are more likely to hurt us than our fantasies.

Sharing sexual fantasies with our partner taps into the **fear of emotional closeness.** The fear of emotional closeness is one of the most pervasive and elusive of the fears listed in Chapter 9. Most people could benefit from a better understanding of emotional closeness and its relationship to sex and love.

The more intimate the relationship the deeper the emotional closeness, or at least the opportunity for such closeness. But as the intimacy increases, the fear increases. "What if my lover doesn't like the way I look? Or the way I dance? Or the way I cook, or the way I think about politics or religion, or my particular sexual fantasies? Will he/she still like me? Can he/she accept this? How much can I share without being rejected? This person is important to me. I don't want to be rejected; I don't want to lose him/her. Therefore I'd better not share."

So many fears lie hidden beneath the surface. **Fear of Disapproval. Fear of Misunderstanding. Fear of Rejection. Fear of Loss. Fear of Emotional Closeness.** Can't we ever get rid of these fears and just be human?

This is the fundamental dilemma in emotional closeness: we want to share but we are afraid to share. If the relationship is supportive at a deep level, gradual sharing can take place. "I'd better not share" can be replaced by "I'd better use judgment in what I share; once mutual security is established I will be able to share more." If the relationship is not supportive at such a deep level (unfortunately the majority of relationships), closeness is followed by rejection which is followed by fear, and the cycle repeats itself until the fear predominates, sharing subsides, and an inner loneliness takes over.

With regard to sexual fantasies, sharing should be distinguished from acting out. Fantasies can range from murder to rape to oral sex. Nearly everyone would abhor acting out fantasies of murder or rape. Only a few would object to oral sex. There are a million possibilities in between, a whole spectrum of fantasies that are acceptable, not acceptable, or acceptable "depending." But I can't control the fantasies any more than I can control the emotions that give rise to them. What I can control is what I do about them (if anything).

In sharing fantasies, it is important to acknowledge the following:
1. Fantasies are OK.
2. Any and all fantasies are OK.
3. Let fantasies be fun.
4. Have as wide a range as possible of things that are "OK to act out."

Sharing fantasies about murder or rape is OK. But if your partner demands to act out a murder or rape fantasy, call the police!

Sometimes it is difficult to distinguish between "sharing" and a "demand" to act something out. Fears or expectations may condition us to think our partner wants to act out a fantasy when he or she only wants to talk. Dr. Bessell once gave me a very interesting analogy:

> *If you go into a delicatessen and say, "I want a ham and cheese sandwich," they will probably make one for you. You then say, "Why did you make me a sandwich? I was just expressing a desire. Yes I want a sandwich, but I didn't ask you to make one! I'm sorry but I can't pay for it. If I had wanted you to make one, I'd have said, 'please make me a ham and cheese sandwich.'"*

Their expectation created a false interpretation of the original statement, "I want a ham and cheese sandwich." Although their interpretation was false, it was certainly very understandable!

So be careful what you say to your partner. If you say, "I want to have two women at once," she may jump to the conclusion that you are making a serious proposal for action, and she may not be able to accept it (or you). But if you say, "From time to time I've thought about having sex with you and someone else at the same time but I'm not sure how you'd feel about it," your communication will be clearer and (hopefully) better received. So be careful about sharing being misinterpreted as a serious proposal to act something out. A great deal of misunderstanding is possible.

It is up to each individual couple to decide which fantasies can or should be shared and which ones acted out. Thomas Moore says:

In extreme instances we may decide that we can't tolerate a particular erotic world, or we may realize that some sexual thoughts are dangerous for us. In most cases, though, we may want to try to stretch our imaginations and sensitivities, acknowledging that the soul shows itself in each of us differently, and particularly in the precise directions of sexual fantasy.

Oral sex, anal sex, water sports, S&M without physical injury could all be considered to be in the realm of "OK to act out"; i.e. if it's within the one-on-one relationship and not physically harmful, "Why not?!" But two-on-one or any other involvement with others outside the relationship should be approached with extreme caution. You involve not only your own levels of chemistry and maturity but someone else's as well. They may not be able to handle it even if you are. And their fantasy may or may not be exactly the same as your fantasy expectation. I'm not saying avoid such acting out, I'm saying discuss it thoroughly with your partner before deciding, and realistically assess the ability of all participants to handle the particular situation, given everyone's chemical attractions and maturity levels. The templates given later in this chapter can be used as a guide.

Caution is always advisable, of course.

Here's what Nancy Friday has to say about caution:

> *Sexual fantasies release powerful, unpredictable energies. Once the imp is let out of the bottle, once fantasies are told to someone else, they pass out of your control. The ideas may never be forgiven or forgotten.*
>
> *Being rejected by a beautiful girl you don't know doesn't cost much. You didn't have anything to begin with. Deciding to act out a fantasy with someone you love risks forever scarring a relationship that means a great deal.*
>
> *I am aware that perhaps the pitfalls of sharing and/or living out fantasies has been belabored to the near exclusion of describing the excitement—even exaltation—that comes from asking one's lover into the secret confines of the erotic imagination.*
>
> *If you decide to go ahead, note that in the most happily played out fantasies, ...coercion plays no role. The ideas are discussed, and agreement is voluntary, with no threats of "Well, if you won't, I'll leave you and find someone who will."*
>
> *A step-by-step approach is always safest.*

I agree with her that a step-by-step approach is safest. Assess your relationship in terms of chemistry and maturity using the templates given below to determine how fast and how far you can go.

HOW WELL CAN DIFFERENT TYPES OF RELATIONSHIPS ACCEPT SEXUAL FANTASIES?

The ability to share and act out fantasies (sexual or otherwise) depends on the quality of the relationship and its capabilities. Soulmates have the strongest relationships and the highest capabilities.

The Love Dice hold the secret to the capabilities of various relationships to handle sexual fantasies:

Soulmate Relationship.
Very high mutual chemistry and very high mutual maturity.

Soulmates, by definition, are connected at a deep, soul level. There is a *desire* for a natural free-flow of emotions and understanding, which of course includes sexual fantasies. True chemistry creates this desire. There is also an *ability* to free-flow, which is created by mutual high maturity. Although in most other couples the free-flow of emotions usually stalls out or is avoided because of fear, soulmates have such free-flow and are able to go a long way toward sharing sexual fantasies. They have the chemical connection and the maturity to handle it. Soulmates want no barriers. Soulmates want to support each other's emotional growth. They want to help each other live down deprivations and rectify injustices. Therefore they want to share fantasies. And they have the maturity to do so.

Very Good Love Relationship.
High mutual chemistry and very high mutual maturity.

Although they do not quite have soulmate chemistry, couples like this have the maturity to handle sharing sexual fantasies. In building this relationship, whether in a marriage or as "friends plus," they will probably enjoy the added dimension that sharing sexual fantasies brings. Sharing fantasies as "friends plus"? Why not?!?

Good Love Relationship.
High mutual chemistry and high mutual maturity.

Couples like this don't quite have the maturity to handle everything in sexual fantasies, and don't quite have soulmate chemistry. In building this relationship, whether in a marriage or as "friends plus," experimentation with sexual fantasies can and probably should occur, but the partners should proceed with caution and lots of communication.

Diamond in the Rough.
Very high mutual chemistry but medium maturity.

This relationship has the potential to go all the way to being soulmates, so the couple needs to be careful. They have soulmate chemistry but they may not yet have the maturity to handle much in the way of sexual fantasies. Their first focus should probably be on keeping the relationship together while building maturity and trust. Some of the material in this chapter on sexual fantasies may be helpful now, but much of it should possibly wait until they are better able to handle it.

Typical Relationship.
Mixed bag of medium to high chemistry with low to medium maturity.

In this typical (and not so good) relationship (can we really call it love?), a little playing with sexual fantasies may be fun, but more than that is probably playing with fire. The couple does not have sufficient maturity to handle it, and doesn't appear to have the chemistry to hold it together when things go wrong. On the other hand, there's not much here to be lost, so "what the hell?"

As shown in these examples, the nature of the love relationship is directly related to the ability to accept the other's fantasies. I therefore disagree with Nancy Friday's statement that accepting fantasies has nothing to do with love:

> *There is a kind of child's blackmail here ["If you love me, you will accept these bizarre erotic ideas of mine, and not get hurt or angry or stop loving me."]. Whether your partner can or cannot accept your fantasies has nothing to do with love.*

As indicated above, whether your partner can or cannot accept your fantasies has *everything* to do with love. It has to do with maturity (the capability to understand) and chemistry (the desire to understand). High maturity plus high chemistry equals "love" and therefore equals the ability to accept fantasies.

The templates given above can help you determine how far and how fast you can approach the questions of sharing and/or acting out sexual fantasies with your partner.

CAN FANTASIES CLASH?

"Crossed fantasies" can be a serious (and often unknown) source of unfulfillment in sex and relationships. To my knowledge they have not been discussed in any other book.

Up until now we've talked generally about fantasies and how important it is to understand and share them (after considering the qualifiers above). But there is a dynamic that occurs when two people are making love that has not as yet been discussed.

If both partners are sharing the same fantasy, or if the sex is routine, each in his/her own separate fantasy world, everything is OK.

But suppose I want to play "dominant" and I want you to play "submissive." But you want to be dominant and want me to be submissive. Or you may be turned off by the concept of submissiveness. We then have crossed fantasies.

I get hard fantasizing about your impending submission. Then I try to get you to submit. You fight back, resisting submission or wanting me to submit. I lose my erection because you are not playing along with my fantasy. You think you aren't doing things right so you try to play with it to make it hard. I try to switch to a fantasy about you playing with it, but my emotions won't let me switch. My subconscious or maybe my conscious remembers your refusal to submit. I am secretly angry with you. I can't get hard. You try harder, then get frustrated—"Why won't it get hard?" You finally flop down beside me and we both feel unfulfilled. But we don't talk, because sex is to be enjoyed, not analyzed (or so many think).

I want you to submit because of the rage I feel over lifelong deprivation. You want to dominate because you rebel against male control. We don't talk, we just "do it." Or fail.

Sharing fantasies can improve your sex life not only by increasing emotional closeness but also by avoiding crossed fantasies. If you share your fantasies you can get on the same wavelength and achieve synergistic fulfillment instead of experiencing frustration. But to have genuine acceptance it is important that you discover the true meaning of the fantasy.

This example also underscores the importance of the "surrender" role of the female in sex as described in books by Dr. Robinson and Dr. Eichenlaub (see Chapter 6). If the fantasies clash, it is the male that loses the erection. The female is able to go on. But both end up frustrated. The male loses his erection because there is not the emotional closeness that is desired. One could say that the male should change his fantasy to be more in line with that of the woman. And this is always worth a try. But in the end both will be frustrated if the male cannot sustain an erection, so it is in the best interest of the woman to follow the man's fantasy. If she can get with it, so much the better. But even if she doesn't get high on his fantasy, she can get high on her ability to satisfy him. And next time maybe he can get high on her fantasy.

Keep in mind that fantasies, like emotions, come and go, slip and slide, fade and rush. Soulmate couples know this, share the flow, sometimes in words, sometimes in actions. For mature soulmates, anything one-on-one is OK, so there is not likely to be resistance. Mature soulmates know that if there is any doubt the woman should follow the man to ensure fulfillment for both. Other quality love relationships need to follow the soulmate lead to the degree that it is possible for them to do so.

Crossed fantasies are most likely to occur in the early phases of a relationship while the two partners are still getting to know each other. Along with general tension and anxiety, crossed fantasies may account for much of the failure that occurs during the first few sexual encounters with a new lover. And crossed fantasies can occur at any time with immature partners who have a limited range of ability to share and a limited range of willingness to experiment.

Crossed fantasies are not likely to occur in mature soulmate relationships. However, as discussed elsewhere in this book, soulmate relationships are extremely rare. Any relationship can benefit from an awareness of crossed fantasies and increase mutual fulfillment by working to avoid them.

ARE FANTASIES THE TRIUMPH OF LOVE OVER RAGE?

The subtitle of Nancy Friday's book *Men In Love* (male sexual fantasies) is "The Triumph of Love Over Rage." She has this to say about men's love for women and the role of fantasies:

> *[Writing] this book* [Men in Love] *has persuaded me that men want women more than the other way around. Toward satisfying their love, need, desire, lust, men will give up more than women will. …the majority of men still dream of sex with a loving woman. Men love women at any price, love women even though, beginning in childhood, it is the female sex which makes the male feel guilty about what he desires most from them.*
>
> *Men may resist, but in the end most do marry because they want women more than anything else; if responsibilities, mortgages, ulcers, childcare, and monogamy are part of the package they must buy to get women, they'll do it. The thesis of this book [*"Men in Love"*] is that men's love*

of women is filled with rage. Observation shows that in the end love wins out over rage.
Fantasies are the triumph of love over rage.

Nancy Friday's observation is that in the end love wins out over rage, and that "fantasies are the triumph of love over rage." My interpretation of her words is that men desire women so much they will marry them even though they are filled with rage against them, and then they will use fantasies to augment their love lives. I don't think this is a "triumph." As I see it, this means the rage continues; it is only contained!

In bringing us so much understanding not only of the specifics of men's fantasies but of their origin, she has helped us to get over societal induced ignorance, superstition, and inhibition. This is an important first step. And she has left a door open for me to bring you this book, with its concepts wherein the rage can actually be reduced, not just contained. My view is *not* "Fantasies are the triumph of love over rage," but that "Fantasies are a *vehicle* for love to triumph over rage." But first there needs to be love.

What I mean, of course, is that there must be both chemistry and maturity. That is the fundamental basis of this book, of soulmate relationships in particular, and love relationships in general. A love relationship without chemistry cannot reduce the rage because the emotional need for connection goes unfulfilled. A love relationship without maturity cannot reduce the rage because the likelihood is that the lovers will hurt each other (and increase the rage).

SUMMARY

Sharing fantasies can increase emotional closeness by increasing understanding and decreasing emotional barriers. Knowledge of deprivation, chemistry, maturity, and the interaction of these factors with fantasies and emotional closeness can improve your ability to understand and genuinely accept your partner.

Sharing fantasies also raises a myriad of fears, such as fear of disapproval. Therefore sharing fantasies should be approached with caution and opened up gradually. The higher the maturity and the higher the chemistry, the better able lovers are to share fantasies and maximize emotional closeness and sexual fulfillment.

Sexual fantasies are often the most difficult to understand and accept, because of societal induced taboos. Most sexual fantasies are not physically harmful, but may harm someone's sensibilities. Experimentation and experience can reduce these fears and feelings.

Sharing fantasies and acting on them are different. Sharing is often sufficient to break down emotional barriers and allow free flow of emotions. Acting may or may not be necessary or appropriate depending on the nature of the fantasy, the depth of deprivation, and the ability of the couple to handle it.

In the end, with time, sharing fantasies can, for the chemically bonded and mature couple, overcome rage with love. It is not the fantasies that overcome the rage, but the sharing and the love.

Such emotional closeness at a deep level can lead to a state of excitement and contentment, two states that seem mutually exclusive. Sharing fantasies is exciting as new frontiers are explored. Experiencing emotional growth together brings contentment when you have a high degree of trust. Contentment and excitement is hard to beat!

STORIES

Hopefully you've been enjoying the stories I've used to illustrate my points throughout this book. I don't want to let you down in a chapter as interesting as this! And, rather than reinvent the wheel when Nancy Friday has collected so many exciting sexual fantasies, I have chosen to condense a variety of her stories and include them in an appendix (Appendix 5). The language in many of these stories is very explicit, but I include them to encourage readers to expand their limits, increase their opportunity for emotional closeness, and enhance their chances of success in the search for a quality love relationship. As William Blake says: "The road of excess leads to the palace of wisdom" (in this case the palace of wholehearted, genuine acceptance based on a foundation of true chemistry, high maturity, and knowledge).

How well can YOU accept sexual fantasies?

ASSIGNMENT

The assignment for this chapter is to read Appendix 5, the condensed sexual fantasies from Nancy Friday's collection. Read them with an open mind, listening to Nancy Friday's explanations. Keep in mind what you have already learned about sexual deprivation, chemical connection, emotional closeness, and emotional maturity.

True soulmates (🎲🎲) can enjoy these fantasies without judgmental inhibitions.

Are you prepared to be a soulmate lover? If these fantasies turn you off, the answer is probably "No." Why are you allowing yourself to be controlled by taboos, fears, and cultural limits? Does the language offend you? Why? They're only words! It's a cultural taboo thing. Quality lovers and soulmates know they must get rid of taboos so they can love and enjoy each other fully.

I'm not urging you to get over your taboos unless you want to find a quality love relationship. If you do, then get yourself out there on the "Road of Excess" and start exploring and experiencing! (I said at the outset that quality love was not for the fainthearted…) If you've come this far you've shown that you've got a lot of stamina, so go ahead and push yourself over the top! I encourage all readers to purchase and read the full text of Nancy Friday's books *Men In Love* and *My Secret Garden*.

Question: Do you know how your sexuality fits into your spirituality? If you can't answer this question, read the next (and final) chapter.

Secret 12

TRUST THE RIVER

Spirituality

Let your love bind you
To all living things

From the song "Let Your Love Flow"
By L. E. Williams

It seems like quite a jump from "sexual fantasies" to "spirituality." Perhaps polar opposites unfortunately juxtaposed. Or are they so opposite?

Most people know exactly how their car fits into their garage. But few know how their sexuality fits into their spirituality. How would *you* describe your sexuality in relation to your spirituality?

SEX AND SPIRITUALITY

For me, I think sex leads directly to spirituality. Here's my view:

Sex is a God-given energy that is a manifestation of the basic life force. Sex by its nature seeks connection and creates new life. The desire for physical connection soon translates to a desire for emotional connection. Emotional connection can occur when two people have mutual chemistry, something that is god-given. The desire for emotional connection translates to a desire for emotional closeness. But emotional closeness cannot effectively occur between immature people; therefore the life force (sex combined with life experiences) drives people toward emotional growth. Emotional growth in turn results in increased levels of emotional maturity, which is the same as advanced spirituality, something that is god-like.

What I am describing here is a "path." A path toward spirituality. It is the path of love. Although many proclaim to be on this path, most are not. It is not an easy path. The odds deter most people. Maybe saying that sex leads "directly" to spirituality was a slight exaggeration…

This book is about the search for meaning in love relationships. The search for a quality love relationship or maybe even a soulmate. The search for a relationship that is not a game. This search may not be the only path toward higher spirituality, but it is a natural path. It is a path aligned with higher forces that give us sex, chemistry, the capacity for connection, and the capacity for growth.

Let's elaborate briefly on each step of this path, and then describe the type of person that it leads one to be.

Sex as a manifestation of the life force.

Thomas Moore in *Soul Mates* devotes a section of his book to the "Holiness of Sex." He says:

> *It would help if we would stop thinking of sex as in the slightest way medical or biological. The whole sphere of sex—emotion, body, fantasy, and relationship—falls within the domain of the soul.*
>
> *As long as we think of sex in a limited way, as a biological function or even as only a means of communication or intimacy, we will be mystified by its unexpected turns. It would be better to recognize from the beginning that sex is a profound, far-reaching aspect of the soul, bringing together body, emotion, and imagination in an intense experience that can touch every branch of feeling and meaning, yet one we may never fully understand. It is by nature mysterious.*

The poet William Blake says:

> *Man has no Body distinct from his soul*
> *Energy is the only life, and is from the Body*
> *Energy is Eternal Delight*

Few would dispute the pervasive worldwide interest in sex. And clearly it is natural. Sex drives us to seek connection. Whether you use it just for fun or use it to drive you along the path toward spirituality is up to you.

Connection as spirituality.

I believe connection is the basis of spirituality. "Let your love bind you to all living things." I want to feel connected.

Everyone wants to feel connected. We are all connected. The higher forces of the universe are acting through these connections.

Dr. M. Scott Peck, in his book *The Road Less Traveled*, puts it this way:

> ...the more and longer we extend ourselves, the more we love, the more blurred becomes the distinction between the self and the world. We become identified with the world.
>
> A "mystical union" with the entire world may be established.

He uses the term *"oneness with the universe."*

Thomas Moore in *Soul Mates* says:

> *The family the soul wants is a felt network of...interconnection that grounds, roots, and nestles.*

There are many types of connections, and we've already discussed them in earlier chapters so I will briefly summarize:

Chemistry is the "greased connection." If the chemistry is very high, soul knows soul in a natural flow. Chemistry can not be manufactured or destroyed. It is either there or not there. It is outside of our control. It comes in degrees. Very high chemistry connects us naturally to the heart of the universe.

Other connections (i.e. less chemistry) are also valuable and help us create a network. The network can include friends, sex partners, and value-oriented relationships. This network both supports and teaches us.

Emotional closeness as deeper connection.

There is a connection with everyone in our network. But the depth of the connection varies from one person to another.

Mutual chemistry, when it exists at a high level between two people, greases the path to deeper connection and emotional closeness. Sex is an engine that pushes us along this path. Sexual fantasies are a vehicle for increasing emotional closeness. Greater emotional closeness means greater understanding between two individuals. I must extend myself to understand you, and you must extend yourself to understand me. (I must also extend myself to understand me, so that you can then understand me.)

Dr. Peck provides a particular definition of "love" to describe this process of extending oneself:

> [Love is] the will to extend one's self for the purpose of nurturing one's own or another's spiritual growth.

While I have used a different definition of "love" for this book (mutual high chemistry combined with mutual high maturity), I support Dr. Peck's definition. There are many facets to love. Therefore it is important not to use the term "love" indiscriminately, but to define it in context, as I have done and as Dr. Peck has done. I would interpret his definition as "brotherly love" whereas this book is oriented toward "romantic love." They are both aspects of the multifaceted concept of love.

Emotional growth as the spiritual path.

Up till now we've been having fun. Sex is fun. Connection is fun. Emotional closeness seems like it will be fun.

But here is where the "fun" ends. We come face to face with our true nature and our fears. We're not so sure we like who we are, and we're afraid our partner won't like us either. So we pretend to be someone we're not. Or we pretend to like the person we are. But we know the truth about ourselves, so we create distance. We don't want to change. Maybe we can just have fun and not work on growth. "If only your hang-ups were the same as mine, we would get along famously!"

I like to think of the emotional makeup of two individuals as being similar to a set of two gears as shown below. The larger diameter, smoother parts of each gear represent the fully developed and mature parts of the individual's emotional structure. The smaller, irregularly shaped parts represent the as yet undeveloped, narrow, fearful aspects of their emotional structure.

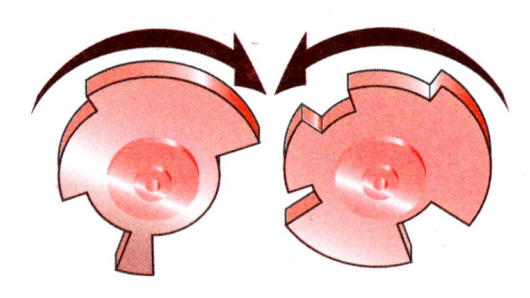

Typical Relationship.
The clashing, banging painful relationship
of an emotionally underdeveloped couple.

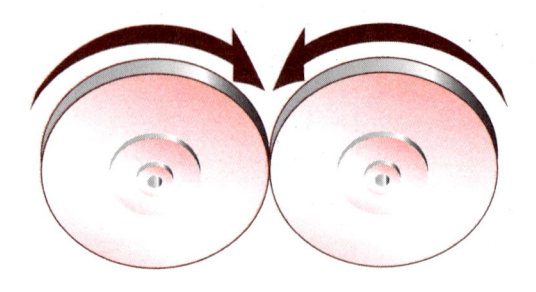

Soulmates.
The smooth-running harmonious relationship
of an emotionally mature couple.

When you bring two emotionally mature people together, their fully developed emotional structures mesh together as smoothly as would two wheels, resulting in an harmonious relationship.

But when you bring two immature people together, instead of smooth "wheels" you get unevenly developed "gears." You can't really expect them to mesh, and they don't. They clash and they tear each other up. So they back away to avoid the pain. Sex, chemistry, the desire for connection/closeness pushes them back together. They grind each other up a little more and back away. Sooner or later they back away permanently until they (hopefully) are able to grow emotionally.

Emotional growth is the process of developing all aspects of the emotional structure into a full, smooth circle so that when two people "engage" one another they will have a smooth-running relationship.

But emotional growth is not easy. Dr. Peck describes the difficulties this way:

> *We have spoken in various ways about how difficult it is to grow up. A very few march unambivalently and unhesitatingly into adulthood, ever eager for new and greater responsibilities. Most drag their feet and in fact never become more than partial adults, always shrinking from the demands of total adulthood.*
>
> *Spiritual competence may increase (<u>although it usually does not</u>) until the moment of death in advanced old age.* (I added the underlining to emphasize his point that "it usually does not.")

Maturity as spirituality.

Spiritual growth and emotional growth are the same thing.

Dr. Peck says: *"...spiritual growth...is inseparable from the process of psychological maturation."*

He further elaborates on the goal of spiritual growth as follows:

> *If we postulate that our capacity to love, this urge to grow and evolve, is somehow 'breathed into' us by God, then we must ask to what end. Why does God want us to grow? What are we growing toward? Where is the end point, the goal of evolution? What is it that God wants of us? ... all of us who postulate a loving God and really think about it eventually come to a single terrifying idea: God wants us to become Himself (or Herself or Itself). We are growing toward godhood. God is the goal of evolution. It is God who is the source of the evolutionary force and God who is the destination.*
>
> *When I said that this is a terrifying idea I was speaking mildly. It's a very old idea, but, by the millions, we run away from it in sheer panic. For no idea ever came to the mind of man which places upon us such a burden. It is the single most demanding idea in the history of mankind. Not because it is difficult to conceive; to the contrary, it is the essence of simplicity. But because if we believe it, it then demands from us all that we can possibly give, all that we have. It is one thing to believe in a nice old God who will take good care of us from a lofty position of power which we ourselves could never begin to attain. It is quite another to believe in a God who has it in mind for us precisely that we should attain His position, His power, His wisdom, His identity.*

> *But we do not want this obligation. We don't want to have to work that hard. We don't want God's responsibility. As long as we can believe that godhood is an impossible attainment for ourselves, we don't have to worry about our spiritual growth, we don't have to push ourselves to higher and higher levels of consciousness and loving activity; we can relax and just be human.*
>
> *The idea that god is actively nurturing us so that we might grow up to be like him brings us face to face with our own laziness.*

Whatever path you are taking toward spirituality, the theoretical (never completely reached) end state is the same: the capacity to understand, forgive, be patient, love, etc. i.e. emotional maturity. No one is perfect, but those seeking spiritual growth strive to be always better than before.

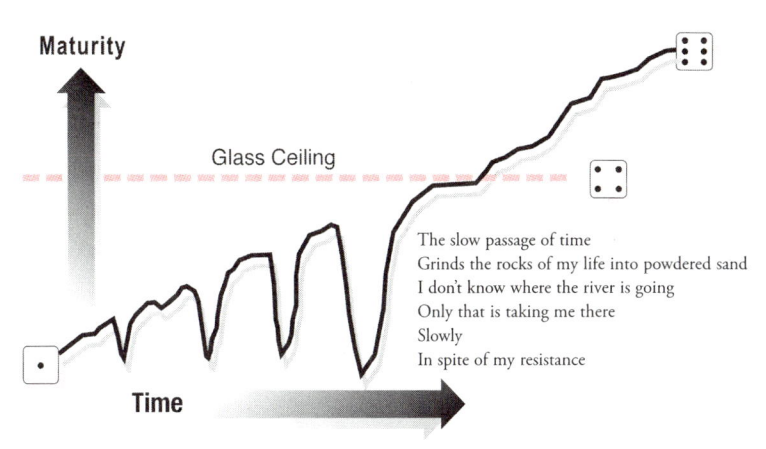

The slow passage of time
Grinds the rocks of my life into powdered sand
I don't know where the river is going
Only that is taking me there
Slowly
In spite of my resistance

The path toward maturity is not a straight line. For me it has been anything but a straight line. Above is a graph and text showing how I see my own spiritual growth. With all the mistakes, pain, and disillusionment of my early relationships it would have been easy to stop growing at about a ⚁ . Only with the help and intervention of Dr. Bessell was I able to move beyond this "glass ceiling" of medium maturity. Hopefully I am now worthy of the ⚄ I have awarded myself, and hopefully I have not stopped growing.

Your path will no doubt be different, but do not expect it to be easy!

THE SPIRITUALLY ADVANCED PERSON

> *"With our brothers we will share*
> *All the secrets of our mountain…"*
> From the song "One Tin Soldier"
> by D. Lambert and B. Potter

As we said earlier, "spiritually advanced" means the same thing as "emotionally mature" so I will use these two terms interchangeably.

Although spiritually advanced people look the same as everyone else, they are not the same. If you observe them for a long time you will be able to note the following characteristics. Spiritually advanced (emotionally mature) people are:

Open
Caring
Patient
Flexible
Stable
Forgiving
Understanding
Sexual
Realistic
Cautious
Courageous

Honest
Reliable
Spontaneous
Warm
Responsive
Experimental
Tuned in
Gentle
Strong
Insightful

They know themselves.
They value friendship.
They recognize the importance of sex to emotional closeness.
They recognize the power of chemistry.
They value the stability of maturity.
They communicate on a deep emotional level.
They enjoy sharing fantasies.
They are good listeners.
They work to advance their understanding.
They recognize their own fallibility.
They are able to deal with uncertainty.
They value their freedom.
They value the freedom of others.
They do not abandon their friends.
They are slow to make commitments.
They do not make commitments they cannot keep.
They make and keep commitments.

This is not a complete list.

This is what the young lady in our "Prequel" should have been looking for, in addition to romantic chemistry. Her search was limited to "skyrockets," and she stayed far away from the "Saturn Spacecraft." In other words, she did not recognize the value of emotional maturity (coupled with strong romantic chemistry). She failed at love as a result, and passed her values along to her daughter who will most likely suffer the same fate. Unless, of course, she happens to read this book.

Before you conclude from the above list that emotionally mature people are "perfect," I should qualify the list by saying that emotionally mature people reflect these attributes at a level ⁜. In other words, at a level of 85 percent or above.

And even though "85 percent" may not be perfect, it's very good, very hard to find, and a goal worth striving for.

The list of attributes is the same for males, females, heterosexuals, homosexuals, bisexuals, transgenders and anyone else.

Many of these attributes of the emotionally mature person have been dealt with already (chemistry, maturity, patience, courage, fantasies). To deal with all of these desirable attributes in detail would take another book. But there are a few that deserve special attention here because they are central to the concept of spirituality in the context of the search for a quality love relationship. These are Stability, Freedom, Flexibility, Forgiveness, and Faith.

STABILITY

Stability is a prerequisite to emotional closeness and spirituality. It is a prerequisite to making and keeping friends on any but a superficial level. It is a prerequisite to togetherness, teamwork, and partnership.

You can't make close friends if you're unstable. They will want to stay distant from your ups and downs. No one can trust you if you're unstable and if they don't know day to day where you'll be coming from. People like fair and consistent treatment. They like people who listen and understand.

How does one become stable? Through experience and guidance. If you don't have much experience you cannot be very understanding. If you have a lot of experience but poor or no guidance you will likely interpret your experience incorrectly, and your understanding will be flawed. If you have had only bad experiences you will not likely have good stability. To grow straight and true a tree needs both sun and rain, and not too much wind.

Experience brings knowledge, but it is useful to have an emotionally mature person as a friend to help you interpret experience into a coherent set of skills and knowledge. Without such guidance it is possible to build "knowledge" that is incoherent and gives rise to inner conflicts as well as conflicts with others.

Everyone has bad experiences in their lives. And the natural tendency is to build defenses against further hurt. These defenses are usually at least moderately successful, so people hold on to them for dear life. These defenses usually have an outward appearance of something "good." Karen Horney (*Neurosis and Human Growth*) defines three basic personality types associated with the nature of the defense system that each personality type has constructed (see Footnote 1 at the end of this chapter). Although a gross oversimplification of her extensive work, the following types are *not* spiritually advanced or emotionally mature:

Type 1: The "Pseudo-Strong" Person.

Individuals in this category believe they should be able to master all situations and all people. They are expansive without limits. They have high perfectionistic standards. They are self-confident and proud. But underneath, they are angry and vindictive. This may manifest itself as irritability, sulking, making others feel guilty, even open rages. An unfortunate childhood has caused a "hardening process," a need to deny positive feelings, and a drive for a triumphant mastery of life.

And in a society that emphasizes aggression, the "angry" person can come off as "strong." Being angry at the hurts we have received is understandable. But it is not strong. It is the child that doesn't get its own way throwing a tantrum. It is an effort at control. It is rigid. This is not the same as stable. Emotionally mature people are not angry. They recognize the hurts they've received and the deprivations and the rage so engendered. But in recognizing it and dealing with it and understanding it they are no longer controlled by it.

Type 2: The "Pseudo-Loving" Person.

This person believes he/she should be the ultimate of helpfulness, generosity, consideration, understanding, sympathy. He or she should sacrifice everything for love. This type of person leans over backward to avoid anything which feels arrogant, conceited, or presumptuous. But underneath this person is suffering and feels helpless. This may manifest itself in attempts to elicit reassurance by being apologetic, or by emphasizing his or her helplessness. Or it may lead to a clinging dependency. A precarious childhood has caused a "shrinking process," a need for approval, and a need to deny any attempts toward triumph or superiority.

Suffering from the hurts we have received is understandable. But it is not love. The self-righteous martyr may not show their inner hurt too much, but their "givingness" is their "wall." They feel they are not getting back as much love as they are giving or deserve. So they suffer even more. You can't get inside their wall because they are not really happy with themselves and don't want you to know. Dr. Peck says: *"...dependency may appear to be love because it is a force that causes people to fiercely attach themselves to one another. But in actuality it is not love; it is a form of antilove."*

Emotional closeness with the "pseudo-love" type person seems like it should be possible but it is not. On the other hand, emotional closeness is possible with a spiritually advanced person. They approach love as a give and take, an emotional communication among equals. They may have experienced suffering, and they value love, but they do not cling. They are helpful and understanding, but they are not helpless. They have become more emotionally mature as a result of their suffering.

Type 3: The "Pseudo-Stable" Person.

These people believe they should be self-sufficient, independent, free from desires and passions, stoic, and fair. They are careful not to impinge on the rights of others. They have an essential sincerity and integrity. But underneath this person is afraid. The fear manifests itself in a desire to maintain emotional distance, a hypersensitivity to pressure, and an aversion to change. Any stronger attachments would curtail this person's freedom. He or she wants to be free and hence will not tolerate pressure. A demanding childhood caused a process of "detachment," a need to avoid friction, and a determination to not become emotionally involved with others. This person intends to defend his freedom to the last ditch.

This person has solved their hurts by turning off the depths of their emotions. They are not angry. They are not suffering. They are just shallow. This is not immediately apparent, because they are frequently charming, fun-loving, active people. But spiritually advanced people will observe their lack of genuine caring, the unwillingness to allow emotional closeness. Because pseudo-stable people are neither prone to outbursts of anger nor to clinging dependency, they can appear stable. And if you mean "unchangeable," they probably are. But "stable" they are not.

Emotionally mature people also value freedom. But it is the "freedom to grow," not the "freedom from interference."

In summary, inexperience, or bad experience coupled with little or poor guidance causes people to limit their potential and adopt "pseudo" real personalities as defenses against further hurt. Their defenses deny access to spiritual forces, forces that enhance emotional growth. Often these pseudo-persons are "religious," and their defenses are bolstered by their particular religious and/or cultural beliefs—beliefs that reinforce the "good" attributes of their defense system but fail to recognize the "evil" associated with fear, laziness, and narrow living, which inhibits their real spiritual advancement.

In contrast to the spiritually underdeveloped, angry, suffering, or shallow person, emotionally mature people are calm, stable and deep. They believe in the potential of others to grow. They are willing to provide guidance, share experiences, and offer interpretations. They encourage, but do not push.

The inexperienced person may misinterpret someone who is emotionally mature as "demanding." Because the more mature person is interested in the emotional/spiritual growth of the other, and sees areas where growth is possible, the immature person's fearful self may interpret this as a demand to change. But it is not. The "demand" is only a reflection/projection of the immature person's own inner knowledge that they actually should grow in this regard. Because they don't like what they see, they throw away the mirror!

Emotional closeness is possible with a spiritually advanced person. They are connected to the higher forces of the universe.

FREEDOM

Because I am stable you are free. You can drift in and out of my life and I will love you as you are. I have no need to control you (as does the "pseudo-strong" person) or cling to you (the "pseudo-loving" person) or avoid you emotionally (the "pseudo-stable" person). I will never hurt you. I will not force you. I will just be here for you.

> *He who binds to himself a joy*
> *Does the winged life destroy*
> *But he who kisses the joy as it flies*
> *Lives in eternity's sunrise.*
>
> William Blake

You are free.   BUT…
You may be free to flit and fly about, but you are not yet free from feeling alone.

You are not yet free from searching.

You are not free to safely share your fantasies.

You are not free to feel safely connected at a soul level.

Something paradoxical is happening here. It's related to the popular notion that "love" and "freedom" are conflicting terms. People want freedom. They want love. They think they have to give up freedom to have love.

But the reverse is true. True freedom requires love, requires commitment. When you trust the chemical bond between you then you can use it to connect to the universe. True love is freedom!

Here's an analogy. Suppose you want to be an artist on the flying trapeze. "Fly through the air with the greatest of ease." This is certainly an ultimate in freedom! And, wanting to be the best (or you wouldn't be reading this book) you want to do a "triple"

(triple somersault in the air before being caught by your partner on the other trapeze). Now you're not likely to try this with any stranger, at least not without a net. You want a partner you can trust. Someone who is capable of catching you. Someone who is on your wavelength and will be there at the right time. And you still start with a safety net. And you still start with basic hand-to-hand passes. And you do lots of them before you try your first "single." And then you slowly build trust, gradually build understanding. You let time show the ability, you don't rush, don't push, you keep talking, keep practicing. Finally there comes a time when you both say, "I trust you more than anyone else to be my trapeze partner. I am willing to work with you for as long as it takes to get however good we can be. We don't know how good we can get, but our *commitment* is to work together to keep getting better." And through this commitment you build the freedom to attempt a "triple." But it takes mutual desire (chemistry), mutual capability (maturity) and commitment. Genuine trust based on actual experience provides real safety.

Freedom and commitment are closely intertwined. The ultimate in freedom requires commitment. In the absence of commitment I am still free to connect to the universe. It just takes more effort. I am regenerated by my friends and the chemical connections I do have. I am a part of life. I am one with the force. I float in the river of life. I play in the river. The river connects me.

But if I have a commitment in, let's say, a soulmate relationship, the chemistry will connect me directly into the river. Her maturity supports my friendships, my interconnections. She loves, respects, values, and supports my freedom. I love, respect, value, and support her freedom. Neither of us will take advantage of the other because we always maintain a sense of balance. Our commitment is to each other's fulfillment and growth. Dr. Peck uses these words:

> *"Genuine love not only respects the individuality of the other but actually seeks to cultivate it, even at the risk of separation or loss." Also, "A good marriage can exist only between two strong and independent people."*

"Commitment" in this sense is a commitment that goes beyond sex. Sex is a manifestation of the desire for connection. But the real connection is our very high chemistry, and it is maintained by our caring treatment of each other. It is not maintained by artificial "exclusivity." Exclusivity is not the same as commitment. Exclusivity is the manifestation of jealousy, of fear. It represents a *break* in the connection. Jealousy restricts, closes in, creates alienation, frustration, anger. On the other hand, true commitment is a manifestation of true chemistry (a god-given quality) and high maturity (a god-like quality). True commitment therefore represents *stability* in the connection. I know you will meet other people with whom you feel chemistry, because 'chemistry happens.' But I am not worried about it because (1) our chemistry is so high, (2) we have the maturity to handle it, and (3) neither of us want to lose it (who would leave a "295" for a "297" on Dr. Bessell's scale?). Our connection may be the center of the universe, but it is not the entire universe, nor does it cut us off from the rest of the universe.

It should be clear that I am not talking about the "I do" commitment of typical marriages. The typical marriage is a product of society, and although often blessed by the church, often it is not a product of god. It is a product of man. The commitment exists on paper, and may be believed by the couple at the time, but it is not necessarily very real, deep, or permanent. Although some marriages may last for a long time, deep connection and fulfillment often are not there.

What I am talking about is the commitment that comes from mutual high chemistry and mutual high maturity. These are the marriages formed in accordance with the highest laws of the universe.

This is a commitment that will last because both partners know that the relationship is truly and outstandingly good for them.

The Love Dice hold the secret to commitment. Here is the quality of commitment you can expect from various relationships:

Soulmates.

The commitment in a soulmate relationship is the most reliable because there is nothing significant missing in either the chemistry or the maturity. Freedom will not likely result in finding another, better partner.

Quality Love Relationships.

The commitment in other quality love relationships is less reliable than in soulmates but is still pretty good because chemistry and maturity are high. Although freedom could possibly result in finding another, better partner, the odds are against it, and the maturity of the partners is enough to know that.

Typical Relationships.

The commitment in typical relationships is not very reliable because there is too much missing in the mixed bag of chemistry and maturity. This is where you really see jealousy in action. Here freedom results in fear based on jealousy, which creates a demand for exclusivity, which creates a break in the connection, which stunts further spiritual/emotional growth (even though it is desperately needed!).

Therapy Lover.

A word of caution is needed for this diamond in the rough relationship. As has been discussed at length, soulmate relationships don't usually start out as soulmates, but rather start as diamonds in the rough. In such a relationship a commitment to freedom needs to be tempered by the reality of the relationship. For instance, although the relationship shown has a lot of potential, it may be harmed by any outside sexual connection because the ⚁ partner is probably still in the grips of jealousy. The ⚄ partner may have to live with sexual exclusivity for some period of time while the relationship matures. The key for the less mature partner is, "Don't imprison your therapy lover's mind!" Share fantasies, allow non-sexual connections, work toward growth, have a fulfilling sexual union. The more mature partner can maintain sexual exclusivity for a long time, maybe forever, under such circumstances because the relationship is so important and he or she knows it.

Soulmates are the ultimate in connection. They support each other's freedom but keep everything in balance. They work together, re-energize each other, and radiate their energy outward into their network, re-energizing others. Other quality love relationships can take their cue from the soulmate model, but need to temper their activities in relation to the quality of their chemistry and maturity.

FLEXIBILITY

The spiritually advanced/emotionally mature person is stable because he or she is flexible. "Do you want a non-sexual relationship?" "OK." "Do you want a sexual relationship?" "OK." "Do you want an exclusive relationship?" "OK." "Do you want a non-exclusive relationship?" "OK."

There are many ways to connect with an emotionally mature person. Connection is more important than limits. Establish a relationship with such a person, and the relationship can continue and grow because there are always multiple solutions to the inevitable problems. Having multiple solutions means a greater likelihood of finding a mutually acceptable solution.

Take a problem as mundane as going out to a restaurant. If you each have twenty different restaurants that you like or accept, then you'll probably be able to find a match that you're both happy with. But if you have only one or two and your partner has only one or two then there's a high probability of no acceptable solution.

Unresolved problems breed distance, resentment, and anger.

Resolving problems together fosters emotional closeness and builds trust.

Flexibility increases problem solving ability.

Limits decrease problem solving ability.

You can't get close to someone who is inflexible or has narrow limits. You feel like you are walking on eggshells.

How about sex, the ultimate in the search for emotional closeness? The place where fantasies can be shared and maybe even acted out. Where inhibitions can be let go.

How flexible are you? Are you OK with oral sex, anal sex, water sports, S&M? Or only with conventional missionary or woman-on-top? Will I feel like you are my partner, who enjoys doing everything, or will you be my enemy, the one who keeps me from doing what I like? Will the emotions flow or be blocked off?

Sexual flexibility mirrors problem solving ability in other areas of your relationship because it reflects the degree to which options are limited by attitudes. Spiritually advanced people are the most flexible sexually and are usually the best problem solvers.

FORGIVENESS

No one is perfect. Everyone has made mistakes. I am not proud of my own mistakes. I hope the people I've hurt have forgiven me. I have grown and am now a better person. I hope those that know me see that.

To be imperfect is human. It may even be "soulful," as per the following passage from Thomas Moore in *Soul Mates*:

> *It isn't easy to live with the power and mystery of another's soulful personality. For one thing, you can't depend on what the person promises, since soul isn't willing to be chained to intentions or even to commitments...The only solution to this problem that I know is for both parties to respect soul, to acknowledge the mystery that is inescapably contained in the soulful life, and to come to treasure that very unpredictability. This may entail a radical shift in values. Ordinarily, without thinking about it, we honor commitments, promises, fidelities, and reliable habits. When these values are trespassed against, we become indignant and complain about a failure in relationship. If, on the other hand, we had a larger picture in mind and honored the tendency of the soul to move in mysterious ways, we might see that the unpredicted developments that come from the soul can have a positive effect on a relationship. They demand a great deal of adjustment and allowance, but they also offer continuous deepening of the connection and a grounding of the attachment in soul rather than in any one person's will. Besides, individual willfulness is usually laced with fear and manipulation, and is hardly solid ground for the building of intimacy.*

Whether you lay it at the feet of "soul" or attribute it to immaturity, most of us continue to make mistakes. Here is a story of hurt and forgiveness.

THE STORY OF JASON AND KELI

Jason and Keli met on the Internet. They corresponded by e-mail and telephone for six months. Jason fell in love with her voice and Keli fell in love with his soft-spoken manner. They traded photographs and were attracted to each other. By the time they decided to meet they were already very much involved with each other emotionally.

It turned out they lived in different states, so ultimately Jason took a trip to visit Keli. She met him at the airport dressed to kill and cute as a button. He looked a fright from a long trip.

Jason took an engagement ring with him. He was ready for a serious relationship and it seemed that Keli was also.

Jason turned out to be right about Keli's readiness. She stayed with him every night and lovemaking was their #1 priority every day. Jason was in heaven. Keli was in ecstasy. The third day he gave her the ring. It seemed the right thing to do given their enjoyment together. At the end of the first week he was entertaining some doubts, but she was cute and a really nice person, and he was still deprived, so "why not?" One doesn't have to get married just because one is engaged. After ten days he was pretty sure it wasn't the quality love relationship he had hoped for, and because of that he was somewhat disillusioned, but he still wanted the sex and she was still a good quality person.

Toward the end of their two weeks together her parents arranged an engagement party. When Jason realized that there were hundreds of guests and a master of ceremonies he panicked. He thought about calling it off, but the party was already underway. He rationalized that it was only an "engagement ceremony" even though it felt like more like a wedding. So they had the ceremony and had the party and everyone was happy for them, except Jason. He managed to keep up the front. And he liked the sex. They experimented a lot and had fun together.

Going back home on the plane his soul was in turmoil. What had he done? What was he to do? Forget her? Tell her he didn't love her? Bring her to visit his parents as they had discussed? Give it a further chance? Without very high chemistry, he just couldn't commit to marriage, even as a possibility. He just didn't know what to do. Keli could feel his distance, but kept hoping that it would work out.

He went to visit her a second time. He tried to love her but it wasn't really there. Sex was good, then just OK. He found himself looking at other women while he was with Keli. He did his best to explain his feelings.

She was terribly hurt. It caused her a lot of embarrassment with her family and friends. He felt terrible. He should probably have backed out on the "steps of the church" as it were. He did his best to explain and to make it up to her. He continued to be her friend. They continued sexual relations for a while in their newly based friendship ("friends plus"). For a while she harbored hopes that it would grow again into love. What she found instead was honest consistent friendship, which she reciprocated. Ultimately she was able to forgive him. Now they are good friends. She has grown stronger emotionally and now thanks him for being in her life. She outgrew her parents and her friends. She now values his friendship and he values hers.

This relationship must be assessed both before and after the growth period that both Jason and Keli experienced:

Jason Keli

Before

Jason's chemistry for Keli was medium low
Keli's chemistry for Jason was very high
Jason's maturity was medium
Keli's maturity was medium

After

Jason's chemistry for Keli remained medium low
Keli's chemistry for Jason remained very high
Jason's maturity increased to high
Keli's maturity increased to very high

Neither Jason nor Keli was very mature at the beginning of this relationship. They should not have jumped into something so quickly with little real time together. Jason jumped into it because he was sexually deprived. Keli jumped into it because she felt very strong chemistry. But as a result of this relationship they both grew emotionally and became more spiritually advanced. Keli grew more than Jason because she had a stronger motivation (her very high chemistry for Jason).

Jason and Keli are now good friends. He is thankful that she has forgiven him and he appreciates her as a terrific person. He attributes her substantial growth to the hard work she put into understanding herself as well as him.

Can Jason forgive himself? That is another question!

Here's a conversation I had with Jason some time after this event:

OK, Jason, why did this happen?
I was deprived.
Why were you deprived?
So many women have said "No."
Why do they say "No"?
They don't like me.
Really? You are a very likeable person.
OK. It's what they were brought up to say by their parents.
Why?
Their grandparents taught their parents.
Why?
The culture teaches everyone.
So you're not to blame for what happened to Keli!
Well, yes and no.
Well, is it "yes" or "no"?
It's "no" because I was set up for this by my parents and our culture. It's "yes" because I did nothing to change what happened.
So who should we blame, your parents?

No.
Your grandparents?
No.
Society in general?
Yes!!!
But that's futile.
I don't care! Society is to blame!
But hasn't "society" done anything good for you?
Of course it has.
What?
I've been fortunate to have good jobs, wonderful children, valuable connections, all in a clean and safe environment.
So you still want to blame society?
I guess not. It's not perfect either. It wouldn't do any good anyway.
So how about your parents?
Can't really blame them either.
So you've no one but yourself to blame.
No! It was *them*!
Who?
All of them!
Come on now…
OK. What do you want?
The truth.

To this Jason acknowledged that he was not fully mature in his way of handling this situation. He wishes he'd handled it better and he says he will not make this mistake again in the future. He recognizes that he can do nothing to change what has already happened. He sees that he is human, fallible like all others, and he has now forgiven himself for his weakness. He forgave himself because he now understands that he was not fully aware of or in control of his actions, and now he understands why, and that enables him to take responsibility for his future actions.

In my own life I have had relationships where I have been hurt and where I have hurt others. But now I have forgiven even those who hurt me the most. I have forgiven them partly because I was not perfect either. And I have forgiven them because I understand that they were the product of their parents, their culture. And I have forgiven them because I hope for their spiritual growth. Holding grudges does not help another's spiritual growth. Forgiveness does.

It's very easy to forgive someone when the chemistry is very high. I can think of one specific former lover who I have forgiven a thousand times. I've probably forgiven her when I should have confronted her. There needs to be a balance between forgiveness and supportive confrontation—they are not mutually exclusive.

There are also plenty of people who have hurt me where I did not feel that same kind of strong chemistry. Some bosses come to mind... But again, they were products of their personal pasts. I think they had a long way to go in their spiritual development, but they were programmed by our society, as I was.

Although I don't subscribe to any particular organized religion, many of them offer good insights. The following quotation from *The Bible* relates directly to the negative social programming most of us have received:

Father, forgive them, for they know not what they do.
(Luke 23:34)

I think that applied to my bosses!

The ability to forgive comes from the ability to know and understand. The ability to understand comes from digging deeply into the reasons behind the actions.

For instance, take a person who is angry.

Why are they angry?
> It's their defense mechanism.
>> Why?
>>> They've been hurt.
>>>> Why?
>>>>> Parents, friends, tend to hurt us.
>>>>>> Why?
>>>>>>> Our society and culture have not supported our highest level of development.

It is easy to want to fix "blame." But "blame" is not the issue. Can you blame the shoot for not being a flower? We are all growing into higher forms of being.

Anger is really a request for understanding, a cry for help. "Please understand that I have been hurt and don't want to be hurt again."

Keep asking "why?" and you keep getting back to the same answer. We are weak, fallible, imperfect not so much because we are human but because we come from a weak, fallible, imperfect culture.

But society is evolving. We are growing as individuals, and society as a whole grows along with us. Someday we will be flowers, and society will be a garden.

I like to think of a future culture that is more advanced than ours. It is more flexible, more stable, more understanding, more supportive. This future culture works to advance the emotional maturity of each person in its society. We need to learn as much as we can from such a vision of the future, and build our own spirituality and the spirituality of today's culture on such an advanced model.

Here is another story of forgiveness. It is also a story about spiritual growth.

THE STORY OF TED AND PAULA
(A Quality Love Relationship)

Paula met Ted at a book club. In was an unlikely match, Paula being a homebody and Ted being married. But he had an eye for women, and he noticed Paula. She had had several disastrous relationships and was ready to forget about men. He was not happy in his marriage, and was already involved in an extramarital affair with someone else. Things did not look good for either of them.

But when they talked a strange, calm, peacefulness surrounded them. For him it was dramatically different from other experiences, in a quiet way. For her it was as if their auras meshed. But she had no intention of having a sexual relationship with a married man. That was fine with him—he had his hands full already, and anyway he didn't believe in love.

But they hit it off, talking in a relaxed, natural way.

This relationship obviously had no future, so she went to South America on an archaeological dig. He remained in the U.S.

with his wife. Two years later he got a divorce. A year after that Paula and Ted met again at a party, unexpectedly. They were both surprised, and again found themselves experiencing the same pleasant sensations as before. The next day they met for coffee, went for a walk, and exchanged phone numbers. They genuinely *liked* each other. What bloomed for them at first was not so much romance or sex, as it was a good friendship.

They dated for four months. One night driving home from a party with some friends, Paula said, "Why doesn't everyone come to my house for a drink?" The friends said, "Sounds great!" Ted said, "I don't feel like it." She asked, "Why not? It will be fun." The friends said, "Yeah, what's with you, man?" Ted said, "I just don't feel like it, all right?"

So he dropped Paula off in a snit and went home. He was hurt that Paula didn't want alone time with him. The relationship hadn't deepened to the point that he was confident in her love. But neither was he ready to end it, so he went back the next day with flowers.

She said, "I was just trying to be friendly. I don't know if I want to continue this relationship if you're going to be so paranoid like that all the time!"

They walked from room to room talking and debating what a jerk he was, the dog following them everywhere. In the end they wound up on the sofa passionately kissing. She said, "The only reason you're still here is because you curl my toes."

He dated someone else for a short time, but there was no excitement. With Paula, once affection was added to the genuine friendship, the excitement grew for both of them. He liked the quiet sense of peace that it gave him. She felt an overwhelming mad passionate thrill.

They both valued the intellectual aspect of their relationship. She said, "You're the first guy I've gone out with that could talk about something other than sports!" She enjoyed discussing a wide range of subjects. He even enjoyed discussing her archaeology, and kept some of her artifacts in his office. It surprised her that he cared enough about her and her interests to display her treasures in his office.

After a golden late summer evening, Ted said, "I think we should get married." Paula said, "When?" Ted just about fell over in shock. He thought they should get married within six weeks because he didn't want to lose her. She thought they should wait another six months to be sure. She won, as usual.

Let's look at their relationship just prior to marriage using the Love Dice. I would assess it as follows:

Ted Paula

Ted's chemistry for Paula was high
Paula's chemistry for Ted was very high
Ted's maturity was medium
Paula's maturity was high

This is a "zirconia diamond in the rough." Ted's feelings of romantic attraction for Paula were high, but not *very* high (pleasant, peaceful affection). Paula, on the other hand felt *very* high romantic attraction for Ted ("you curl my toes"). He was still rough around the edges in the emotional maturity department (possessive), about as mature as the average adult. She was more emotionally mature than the average adult—she was honest, reliable, caring, optimistic, realistic, maybe a little shy—everyone liked her. But based on their emotional maturity I don't think you could say that either of them was "spiritually advanced" at this point.

Ted invested more and more of himself emotionally with Paula. He said, "I never used to believe in love, but now I do because you have loved me."

But as the wedding approached, Ted started to feel a knot in his stomach, a great fear like going into combat with no armor. He was experiencing the **fear of being vulnerable**. He was afraid he wouldn't be good enough for her. He was afraid she would be displeased with him. The knot in his stomach lasted for two years. But it finally went away with her unflagging devotion.

Her biggest problem was that at parties Ted would gravitate toward other women and start charming them. He was a big flirt, and this made her nervous. One day she brought this up to him, and thereafter he tried to flirt less, out of respect for her. She was slowly trying to increase his emotional maturity (she was his therapy lover).

They went out to dinner at a nice restaurant. He sat down and waited for her to sit also, but she remained standing. He said, "Why are you still standing up?" She said, "I wish I was married to a gentleman." He jumped up to hold her chair, and always did so thereafter. She was gentle and clever in helping him grow up.

They had to conceal from others how happy they were, because others were jealous.

Although their sex life was reasonably satisfactory, he wanted her to "surrender" completely. She resisted. He wanted to share sexual fantasies with her. She didn't understand. She might have been quite mature (a ⁚), but she was not yet very mature (a ⁞).

During the first half of their thirty-one year marriage, Ted had occasional outside sexual encounters. He was just proving he was lovable, making up for his deprivations. It had nothing to do with Paula; the affairs were meaningless and empty. It never dawned on him that it could have repercussions with Paula.

It was a disaster when Paula eventually found out. She was hurt and withdrew from him emotionally. She suggested he have his own apartment so he could play his little games and then he could come see her when he truly wanted to be with her. She thought the outside sex *did* have to do with her. It was an insult to her pride, a realization that Ted was not as totally invested in her as she had thought.

But they were committed friends. They liked and enjoyed each other. She didn't want a divorce and neither did he. Love was a reality for them, and the most important thing in their lives. They continued living together and working to improve the relationship. They were both committed to understanding what was going on and how to make it better. Nevertheless, the hurt and the mistrust between them lasted for a long time.

Paula talked to Ted. She talked to friends. She talked to a psychologist. She read books. She ultimately forgave him his indiscretions when she came to understand about male sexual deprivation and fantasies. She did not forgive him out of blind love, which could have had repercussions later; she forgave him out of true understanding. She came to understand the forces that were controlling him, even though he did not. ("Father forgive them for they know not what they do.") She grew to become a spiritually advanced person.

As for Ted, he learned that security in the home is a basic instinct in women, and he also learned that the loneliness he felt before he met Paula returned when she started to withdraw emotionally. The loneliness was worse than his unfulfilled impulses for sexual variety. Although the desire for outside sex continued lurking in the background, he learned that he could control it if his marriage provided an outlet for his fantasies.

They learned together that they could discuss all these things, play with them in their fantasy and sex life, and in so doing become closer than ever. She helped him with his work, he helped her with the children. They became better lovers. There were still areas in which he needed to grow up, and she helped him through them, more capably than ever before. What had started as a "zirconia diamond in the rough" became a good love relationship and ultimately a very good love relationship.

Their marriage ended tragically after thirty-one years when Paula was killed in an automobile accident. Ted was devastated. The loneliness rushed back in. Now, when it was too late, he realized fully that the love he had had with Paula was the best thing he had ever known, the only thing in his life that had real meaning. He had stumbled into the relationship by luck, and he stumbled through it with her support. He recognized with a rush how difficult he had been to deal with through the years. Yet he had loved her, and she had loved him. He had learned from her and grown. She had learned from him and grown. Here are the before and after snapshots of their relationship:

Ted   Paula

Before

Ted's chemistry for Paula was high
Paula's chemistry for Ted was very high
Ted's maturity was medium
Paula's maturity was high

After

Ted's chemistry for Paula remained high
Paula's chemistry for Ted remained very high
Ted's maturity increased to high
Paula's maturity increased to very high

Unfortunately, diamonds take a long time to grow. It took half their marriage for Ted to grow from the adult average ⚃ to a more mature ⚄ , and for Paula to grow from a mature ⚄ to a spiritually advanced ⚅ . She had grown, and he reaped the benefits of living with a goddess. But it took her death for him to grow ultimately to a spiritually advanced level (a ⚅ , not shown).

Although this relationship was not perfect, it was a quality love relationship. They genuinely enjoyed each other's company and affection. They were committed to working through all problems, however serious. They both grew in the process. He might have grown faster if his feelings of romantic chemistry for her had been higher. But as he felt more secure in her love and understanding, he ultimately felt more fulfilled and less lonely. She had to work hard to help him overcome his immaturities, but she valued the very high chemical connection that she felt, and that made it all worthwhile.

This relationship had high chemical connection coupled with emotional growth to high levels. This is the picture of quality love. The story of Ted and Paula is the only quality love relationship discussed in this book, because such relationships are rare. Barry/Linda and Mario/Elise in Chapter 5 had as much original potential as Ted and Paula, but they didn't make it. As discussed throughout this book, the odds against finding and/or building a quality love relationship are very difficult to overcome. Paula and Ted overcame them, and were rewarded with a fulfilling love life.

One reason they were able to overcome the odds was that they had faith in the ultimate value of what they had together. They had this faith even when things were not going well between them.

FAITH

I don't claim to be an expert on faith. Nor can I present anything comprehensive in one small section of a single chapter in one book. There have been centuries of thought given to this subject. What I can do is give you a summary of things that have been helpful to me.

I see faith as the belief that there are higher forces shaping our destiny and that these are the forces of good. If you like, we can call these forces "God," although we can also call them "Buddha" or "The Force" or "The River" or whatever appeals to you. These forces are not necessarily the same as the God we have been taught to follow. Dr. Peck says: *"...you do not know the mind of God. All you know is what you have been told about God. Much of what you have been told about God is wrong."* Whether what we have been told about God is right or wrong, clearly it is greatly subject to the interpretation of whomever it is that is telling us. Therefore we have to separate the wheat from the chaff based on our own experience. Hopefully our experience includes experimentation "outside the box" and not blind acceptance of another's dogma. ("The road of excess leads to the palace of wisdom.") Blind faith (otherwise known as conventional wisdom) can cause us to resist the true forces of the universe.

Faith comes when we give in to these true forces, and do not resist them, even though they may be unfamiliar. There are alternative ways to phrase this non-resistance: "Let go and let God"; Let go and let Good"; "May the Force be with you"; and "Trust the River."

What do I mean by "Trust the River"? I am referring to the metaphorical story in the book *Illusions* by Richard Bach. It is so good that I repeat it here:

The Master answered and said, "Once there lived a village of creatures along the bottom of a great crystal river. The current of the river swept silently over them all—young and old, rich and poor, good and evil, the current going its own way, knowing only its own crystal self.

Each creature in its own manner clung tightly to the twigs and rocks of the river bottom, for clinging was their way of life, and resisting the current what each had learned from birth.

But one creature said at last, "I am tired of clinging. Though I cannot see it with my eyes, I trust that the current knows where it is going. I shall let go, and let it take me where it will. Clinging, I shall die of boredom."

The other creatures laughed and said, "Fool! Let go, and that current you worship will throw you tumbled and smashed across the rocks, and you will die quicker than boredom!"

But the one heeded them not, and taking a breath did let go, and at once was tumbled and smashed by the current across the rocks.

Yet in time, as the creature refused to cling again, the current lifted him free from the bottom, and he was bruised and hurt no more.

And the creatures downstream, to whom he was a stranger, cried, "See a miracle! A creature like ourselves, yet he flies! See the Messiah, come to save us all!"

And the one carried in the current said, "I am no more Messiah than you. The river delights to lift us free, if only we dare let go. Our true work is this voyage, this adventure."

But they cried the more, "Saviour!" all the while clinging to the rocks, and when they looked again he was gone, and they were left alone making legends of a Saviour.

I have faith in the river. I trust the higher forces. I believe in the connection among all living things. My free will exits as one small part of the whole, operating in harmony with these connections and forces.
The river flows.
I flow with the river.
I give joy to be part of the river.
I praise the deep water and the shallow.
I have joy in my heart for the pain.
With my network of friends I will not have to cling to the sides of the river.

With my understanding I tap into the source of love.
With my adherence to the secrets contained in Io's Love Dice I find peace of mind.
I am connected to the heart of the universe.
My future lover is there, somewhere.
And I ask the river: "Not my will but thine be done."

When I can't sleep, anxious and tired from the search, I let the river take over my mind. I can feel it washing over me, soothing me. I can hear it, sometimes moving slowly, sometimes rushing forward. I let myself go into the current. I am comfortable that it knows where it is taking me. It has brought you to me and me to you. We are connected. We can never be separated. The River will always be there binding us together. It is taking me toward my destiny, and you toward yours. I fall asleep whispering

"Trust the River."
"Trust the River"
"trust the river"
"trust…

And tomorrow I will awaken ready to continue the search for my quality love relationship. I recognize how hard it is to find mutual high chemistry and mutual high maturity, how hard it is to overcome deprivation, how little understanding and support there is for honest communication about fantasies, and how difficult it is to change the world. But it is easier knowing you, my friends and readers. You are the stars of the universe and I have enjoyed spending this time with you. Your energy gives me strength. And the river will bring us all to a higher destiny.

"Larger voices callin'…"

SUMMARY

Higher forces act in our lives, regardless of what we call them, and we need to learn to trust them. These forces include, in particular, romantic chemistry and the inner drive toward emotional growth. When we align ourselves with these forces, we are on the path of quality love relationships. Stability, freedom, flexibility, and faith are but a few of the attributes that lovers should develop in themselves and should seek and support in others if they want to travel this path.

ASSIGNMENT

Evaluate your goals to determine if finding a quality love relationship is important to you.

Evaluate your emotional maturity to determine if you are prepared to search for such a relationship.

Evaluate your knowledge to determine if you understand the secrets of the Love Dice.

Evaluate your attitudes to determine if they help make the world a better place for quality love relationships.

Do your part to help the world of today become a better world in the future.

Footnote 1. Neurosis and Human Growth by Karen Horney. These personality types are described in detail in the following chapters: Chapter 8 "The expansive solutions: the appeal of mastery." Chapter 9 "The self-effacing solution: the appeal of love." Chapter 11 "Resignation: the appeal of freedom." Her descriptions are thorough and excellent, and you will recognize many of your friends and/or lovers. I highly recommend reading her book to gain a better understanding of the people in your life.

LOVE IS NOT A GAME

Summary and Checklist

Here is a brief summary of the Secrets of the Love Dice. Use it as a checklist of questions to ask yourself periodically to determine whether or not you are on track with your search for a quality love relationship. This checklist can also be used when talking with a friend about his or her search. If you need further explanation about any of the material in this summary, refer back to the appropriate chapter.

1. Power and Magic.
    What is the degree of **romantic chemistry**?
    Yours? His/Hers?

2. Gyro Stabilization.
    What is the degree of **emotional maturity**?
    Yours? His/Hers?

3. Kissing Frogs.
    Are you meeting enough people?
    Do you **know the odds**?

4. The Spaceship.
    Does it all work together?
    Are **all systems "go"**?

5. Diamonds Take a Long Time to Grow.
    Do you have a patient attitude about waiting through **geologic time**?

6. **Sex is Like Water.**
    Do you have enough sex and emotional support
    (**water and food**) to cross the desert?

7. **Enjoy Sweet Distractions.**
    How strong is your **safety net**?
    How diverse is your portfolio?

8. **Look for the Rainbow of Values.**
    Do you find and keep **value-oriented**
    relationships in your network?

9. **Without Fear there would be no Courage.**
    Can you push outside your comfort zone
    to gain **knowledge**?

10. **If You're Trying to Relax, Don't Ask Questions.**
    Have you learned to "**let it be**" until the right time?

11. **Discover the True Meaning of Fantasies.**
    Have you traveled the "road of excess"
    to the palace of **genuine acceptance**?

12. **Trust the River.**
    Are you able to **let go** and let higher forces
    (even though unfamiliar) guide your life?

TO WRITE A POEM

Writing a poem
Is difficult indeed,
a clever imagination
is what you need.
A bubbling fountain
spouting and
tumbling
over and
out.
To visualize
without a
doubt.
To write a poem
is hard to do
unless you just
write
    true
        to
            you.

By Christy Hurlburt
Age 13

Notes

APPENDIX 1

From *The Love Test*
By Harold Bessell, Ph.D.

INFATUATION OR TRUE ROMANTIC CHEMISTRY? SIMILARITIES AND DIFFERENCES

Infatuation	True Romantic Attraction
Similarities	
Initially strong feelings of pleasurable excitement	Initially strong feelings of pleasurable excitement
Strong desire to be with that person	Strong desire to be with that person
You may or may not like, trust, or respect this person	You may or may not like, trust, or respect this person
High scores on Romantic Attraction Questionnaire	High scores on Romantic Attraction Questionnaire
Not related to emotional maturity of either person	Not related to emotional maturity of either person
Differences	
Based on limited time and real association	Lasts more than three or four months, usually indefinitely
A fantasy trip based on your wishes	Reality, based on genuine attraction and long-continuing satisfaction with the companionship of this person
The sexual interest weakens	The sexual interest persists
Real and frequent contact breaks the spell	Real and frequent contact reinforces the "chemical" attraction whether you like, trust, and respect the person or not
When the relationship ends, it is over forever, and you feel enlightened, relieved	The attraction of the other person's personality usually lasts indefinitely, whether or not you like, trust, or respect this person
The desire for association ends, a case of "mistaken identity"	The desire for association remains indefinitely
Strong emotion triggered by wish-fulfilling fantasy	Strong emotion as a normal positive biopsychological sense of excitement that is an intrinsic response not based upon or continued by fantasy
Almost always starts immediately, and ends soon	Though often starts immediately, sometimes it grows and blossoms with more frequent contact
Feelings die	Feelings persist

SEX OR TRUE ROMANTIC CHEMISTRY? SIMILARITIES AND DIFFERENCES

Sex	True Romantic Chemistry
Similarities	
Very pleasurable	Very pleasurable
Differences	
A great many people can enjoy it with each other	Experienced with fewer people
Enjoy each other in a physical way	Enjoy each other in many different ways
Can be bored with partner when sex is over	Continued interest in partner after sex
Variable to weak interest in permanent relationship	Very strong desire for permanent relationship
Focus of enjoyment is physical	Focus of enjoyment is in the other person's personality
May or may not include true romantic chemistry	Almost always includes strong sexual interest and satisfaction
May or may not be a strong interest in the other person's pleasure and well-being	There is a strong interest in the other person's pleasure and well-being
Relationship may end quickly when difficulties arise	Strong interest in continuing relationship despite difficulties
Desire is for physical pleasure	Desire is for lifelong relationship
Provides a temporary sense of well-being	Provides a lasting feeling of belonging
There may or may not be a strong protective interest toward the partner	There is a strong protective interest toward the partner

COMPARISON OF SEX, INFATUATION, ROMANTIC ATTRACTION, AND EMOTIONAL MATURITY

Sex	Infatuation	Romantic Attraction	Emotional Maturity
Biological urge	Wish-fulfillment, fantasy trip that ends as reality impacts, showing the fantasy to be a false indicator of true romantic attraction; the false belief is that the romantic partner has been found	A biopsychological attraction to another person's personality, a sense of pleasurable excitement, desire for intimate association, and the desire to be very much desired by the other person	The degree to which a person has developed coping ability in terms of having insight into one's self, to relate constructively in social relationships, to be able to solve life's problems, to have self-discipline, and to behave with high ethical standards.
Gives temporary satisfaction	Gives temporary thrill of having found an exciting and fulfilling companion	Gives very long-term satisfaction when the attraction and pleasure are mutual	Gives steadily increasing ability to cope realistically and effectively with the demands and challenges of life. Embodies the capacity to treat another person with respect and dignity and caring. Brings out the best in other people.
Interest can be one way or mutual	Can be one way or mutual, but always ends, usually quite soon	Can be one way or mutual. Once beyond the infatuation period, it typically lasts a lifetime. If it is there, we don't know how to make it go away. If it isn't there, we don't know how to bring it about.	Anyone who wishes can become more mature by practicing more mature behavior. Everyone can grow up emotionally, if the desire, determination, and efforts are strong enough.
Can be very boring if not accompanied by romantic attraction	Sequence is pleasure, followed by disappointment, disinterest	There is, when mutual, great satisfaction, fulfillment, with sex, companionship. When not mutual, is very frustrating, difficult to be together.	When present, builds strong relationships; when absent, destroys relationships, even if there is strong romantic interest
Purpose: procreation, via pleasure	Purpose: the wish to have found the lover	Can hold two people together forever, if enough maturity is present	Assure successful adjustment to life

APPENDIX 2

From *The Love Test*
By Harold Bessell, Ph.D.

ROMANTIC ATTRACTION QUESTIONNAIRE

Instructions: Rate how strongly you feel toward your partner/lover/spouse on each of the following sixty statements. Circle one of the five numbers to the right of each statement, with 5 indicating the strongest feeling and 1 indicating the weakest. *Circle one number for each statement.* Each statement must be rated; if you are unsure of an answer or do not understand the statement, circle 3.

Each partner should fill out a Romantic Attraction Questionnaire. Each partner can retest at a future date on the original questionnaire by using a different-colored ink.

Date_____ Rater_____
Total Score _____ Partner_____

	Low			High	
1. I feel very lucky to know this person.	1	2	3	4	5
2. It felt like there was something unusual and very special between us at our very first meeting.	1	2	3	4	5
3. We often have a very good time even when we are not doing anything special.	1	2	3	4	5
4. I miss this person a great deal when we are apart.	1	2	3	4	5
5. This person's approval is very important to me.	1	2	3	4	5
6. I get a thrill from just looking at this person.	1	2	3	4	5
7. I want this relationship to be permanent.	1	2	3	4	5
8. I am happiest when we are together.	1	2	3	4	5
9. Being with this person is far more important to me than where we are or what we are doing.	1	2	3	4	5
10. I enjoy this person in many ways other than just sharing affection.	1	2	3	4	5
11. I feel that we were meant for each other.	1	2	3	4	5
12. My friend is a beautiful person.	1	2	3	4	5
13. I enjoy planning things that we will be doing together.	1	2	3	4	5
14. I am curious about why and how much this person is interested in me.	1	2	3	4	5
15. I want our attraction to be mutual.	1	2	3	4	5
16. I am no longer looking for another romantic partner.	1	2	3	4	5
17. I get something very special from this person that I do not experience with anyone else.	1	2	3	4	5

		Low			High	
18.	I am willing to keep this relationship even if my friend makes no changes.	1	2	3	4	5
19.	I love to surprise this person with a card or gift.	1	2	3	4	5
20.	I can forgive this person almost instantly.	1	2	3	4	5
21.	I have a feeling of excitement when we are together.	1	2	3	4	5
22.	I want to be very special in this person's life.	1	2	3	4	5
23.	I would have to search for a long time to find someone I enjoy so much and so consistently.	1	2	3	4	5
24.	Physical affection with this person is something very different and very special.	1	2	3	4	5
25.	This person is a great companion.	1	2	3	4	5
26.	My friend has an attractive personality.	1	2	3	4	5
27.	I like doing things for this person.	1	2	3	4	5
28.	Our relationship has something that is splendid and very hard to find.	1	2	3	4	5
29.	This person is often on my mind.	1	2	3	4	5
30.	There is something almost mystical in our eye-to-eye contact.	1	2	3	4	5
31.	I experience unusual and pleasantly exciting feelings when I am with this person.	1	2	3	4	5
32.	I am very willing to continue this relationship in spite of all the unpleasantness.	1	2	3	4	5
33.	When there are tasks to be done, I prefer that we do them together.	1	2	3	4	5
34.	I have made efforts to change in order to be more pleasing to my friend.	1	2	3	4	5
35.	I enjoy discussing a wide variety of subjects with this person.	1	2	3	4	5
36.	This is my most favorite person to be with.	1	2	3	4	5
37.	We have something that could be described as spiritual intimacy.	1	2	3	4	5
38.	I get a very pleasant sensation when I meet this person unexpectedly.	1	2	3	4	5
39.	I would feel jealous if my friend became strongly interested in another person.	1	2	3	4	5
40.	I am, or could easily become, totally committed to this relationship.	1	2	3	4	5

	Low			*High*	
41. I enjoy being with this person even when we are silent.	1	2	3	4	5
42. I want this person to respect me for my abilities.	1	2	3	4	5
43. When things are going well between us I have a feeling of completeness and well-being.	1	2	3	4	5
44. It means a lot to me when my friend does something special for me.	1	2	3	4	5
45. At times I wish my friend would know me and accept me completely.	1	2	3	4	5
46. I would like to know what my friend finds attractive about me.	1	2	3	4	5
47. I like to touch and be touched by this person.	1	2	3	4	5
48. I am attracted in a way that others do not understand.	1	2	3	4	5
49. There are so many things I wish we could do together, if only there was enough time.	1	2	3	4	5
50. If criticized by others, I would defend my friend.	1	2	3	4	5
51. I am quite willing to do things for my friend without having to know the reason why.	1	2	3	4	5
52. I have a protective interest about my friend's well-being.	1	2	3	4	5
53. The pleasure I get from this relationship is well worth the price I pay.	1	2	3	4	5
54. This person has a great deal of influence over me.	1	2	3	4	5
55. I often wonder what my friend is thinking.	1	2	3	4	5
56. It's hard for me to say no to this person.	1	2	3	4	5
57. I like to think up special surprises for my friend.	1	2	3	4	5
58. I am happy when this person is pleased with me.	1	2	3	4	5
59. This relationship is my strongest interest in life.	1	2	3	4	5
60. This is the person with whom I would prefer to grow old.	1	2	3	4	5

APPENDIX 3

From *The Love Test*
By Harold Bessell, Ph.D.

EMOTIONAL MATURITY RATING FORM

Instructions: Rate your partner/lover/spouse on each of these sixty-three behavioral traits in terms of how often this behavior is observed by you, almost never (*an*); sometimes (*s*); moderately often (*mo*); often (*o*); very often (*vo*). When possible, rate this person's behavior when with you or relating to you. Every item must be rated. Circle the letter code which most accurately describes your partner's behavior. If you do not understand the statement, circle *mo*. Add up the number of ratings that you circled on the left-hand side of the stripe. These low scores should be totaled in each of the four major areas of maturity. Enter these scores on the lines below. Each of these low ratings show a probable area of immaturity.

Date_____ Rater_____
Maturity Scores_____ Partner_____
Number of Low Awareness Scores _____
Number of Low Relating Scores   _____
Number of Low Competence Scores _____
Number of Low Integrity Scores _____

Awareness

	almost never	sometimes	moderately often	often	very often
1. *Knowing your own feelings* — My friend is aware of and able to report his or her own feelings with accuracy.	an	s	mo	o	vo
2. *Knowing the feelings of others* — My friend is sensitive to and can accurately describe the feelings other people have.	an	s	mo	o	vo
3. *Being spontaneously expressive* — My friend is emotionally expressive in a natural and immediate way.	an	s	mo	o	vo
4. *Ability to discuss personal feelings* — My friend is able to discuss personal feelings with accuracy and is willing to do so.	an	s	mo	o	vo
5. *Coping with mixed feelings* — My friend accepts the inevitability of having mixed feelings and copes effectively with them.	an	s	mo	o	vo
6. *Curiosity* — My friend's behavior is inquisitive and investigative.	an	s	mo	o	vo
7. *Getting desires met constructively* — My friend's personal desires and needs are met in constructive ways.	an	s	mo	o	vo
8. *Coping with fear* — My friend is aware of his or her fearful feelings, but copes with the situation in effective ways.	an	s	mo	o	vo

Awareness (cont.)

9. *Coping with anger*
   My friend is aware of his or her feelings of anger, but copes with the situation in effective ways. an s mo o vo

10. *Accepting responsibility for failure*
    My friend undefensively recognizes and accepts his or her own limitations when they are the cause of failure. an s mo o vo

11. *Coping with frustration and discouragement*
    My friend is positive, persistent, and effective in resolving feelings of frustration and discouragement. an s mo o vo

12. *Accepting and approving of self*
    My friend freely acknowledges personal limitations and still feels acceptable and worthy. an s mo o vo

13. *Coping with uncertainty*
    My friend accepts some degree of uncertainty as inevitable and retains a positive and willing attitude about dealing with it. an s mo o vo

14. *Sorting out real and make-believe*
    My friend readily distinguishes reality, knowing clearly the difference between the real and make-believe. an s mo o vo

15. *Using imagination constructively*
    My friend displays a well-developed imagination and applies these ideas in constructive ways. an s mo o vo

Number of Low Awareness Scores _____

Relating

1. *Caring about others*
   My friend is sensitive and constructively responsive to the needs of others. an s mo o vo

2. *Getting attention constructively*
   My friend gets his or her needs for attention met in constructive ways. an s mo o vo

3. *Earning acceptance*
   My friend wins acceptance and inclusion by respecting the values of others. an s mo o vo

4. *Earning approval from others*
   My friend earns recognition and praise from others. an s mo o vo

Relating (cont.)

	almost never	sometimes	moderately often	often	very often
5. *Giving affectionate regard* My friend demonstrates warm personal interest in other people.	an	s	mo	o	vo
6. *Being socially responsible* My friend understands his or her ability to affect people for better or for worse and uses this power responsibly.	an	s	mo	o	vo
7. *Being considerate* My friend is aware of other people's feelings and deals with them in considerate ways.	an	s	mo	o	vo
8. *Making friends* My friend makes friends easily and keeps them.	an	s	mo	o	vo
9. *Coping with peer pressure* My friend is able to resist negative peer pressure.	an	s	mo	o	vo
10. *Expressing dissatisfaction constructively* My friend is able to express complaints or criticism in ways that are supportive of the other person.	an	s	mo	o	vo
11. *Reciprocating good treatment* My friend recognizes, appreciates, and voluntarily reciprocates good treatment.	an	s	mo	o	vo
12. *Sharing in decision making* My friend lives by the value of obtaining and giving others an equal voice in the decision-making process.	an	s	mo	o	vo
13. *Keeping promises* My friend keeps his or her promises.	an	s	mo	o	vo
14. *Resolving conflicts constructively* My friend, without sacrificing his or her own rights, uses peaceful and constructive means for resolving conflicts.	an	s	mo	o	vo
15. *Willingness to share* My friend willingly shares recognition and possessions.	an	s	mo	o	vo
16. *Becoming more likable* My friend appreciates and constructively uses criticism in order to become a more likable person.	an	s	mo	o	vo
17. *Coping with mixed feelings toward people* My friend recognizes, accepts, and deals constructively in disappointments and disagreements with other people.	an	s	mo	o	vo

Relating (cont.)

18. *Responding well to opposite sex*
    My friend is equally courteous to members of both sexes. — an | s | mo | o | vo

Number of Low Relating Scores _____

Competence

1. *Applying energy and effort*
   My friend is willing to apply energy and effort. — an | s | mo | o | vo
2. *Using knowledge and skills*
   My friend demonstrates that he or she has acquired knowledge and skills. — an | s | mo | o | vo
3. *Being planful*
   My friend behaves in planful and organized ways. — an | s | mo | o | vo
4. *Showing initiative*
   My friend initiates and implements ideas and projects. — an | s | mo | o | vo
5. *Showing creativity*
   My friend demonstrates original and inventive ways of doing things. — an | s | mo | o | vo
6. *Behaving with realistic expectations*
   My friend's expectations and goals are realistic. — an | s | mo | o | vo
7. *Showing self-reliance*
   My friend relies upon his or her own resources to meet objectives. — an | s | mo | o | vo
8. *Willingly takes on challenge*
   My friend is willing and eager to try his or her abilities with new tasks. — an | s | mo | o | vo
9. *Showing appropriate caution*
   My friend anticipates and avoids serious dangers. — an | s | mo | o | vo
10. *Showing self-confidence*
    My friend shows an attitude of assurance when coping with new situations. — an | s | mo | o | vo
11. *Being responsible*
    My friend, without being reminded, fulfills obligations. — an | s | mo | o | vo
12. *Being motivated to succeed*
    My friend shows interest in and motivation for success. — an | s | mo | o | vo

	almost never	sometimes	moderately often	often	very often

Competence (cont.)

13. *Being goal-directed*
    My friend has highly defined goals that are pursued constructively. — an s | mo o vo

14. *Showing high standards*
    My friend values and pursues high levels of accuracy and skill in his or her work. — an s | mo o vo

15. *Being cooperative*
    My friend combines his or her talents well with those of others to achieve a common benefit. — an s | mo o vo

16. *Showing flexibility*
    My friend is willing to consider new information and try new ways under changing circumstances in order to pursue the same original goal. — an s | mo o vo

17. *Developing personal interests*
    My friend has strong personal interests and pursues them. — an s | mo o vo

18. *Solving problems effectively*
    My friend is organized and effective in his or her problem-solving methods. — an s | mo o vo

Number of Low Competence Scores _____

Integrity

1. *Showing self-control*
   My friend's controls prevail over impulse. — an s | mo o vo

2. *Waiting willingly*
   My friend waits with a realistic and calm attitude. — an s | mo o vo

3. *Being truthful in statements*
   My friend is natural, spontaneous, and sincere when describing events. — an s | mo o vo

4. *Coping with unpleasantness*
   My friend shows a positive attitude about coping with unpleasantness, pain, or discomfort. — an s | mo o vo

5. *Being persevering*
   My friend finishes what is started. — an s | mo o vo

6. *Being fair*
   My friend gives equal consideration to the needs of self and others. — an s | mo o vo

Integrity (cont.)

	almost never	sometimes	moderately often	often	very often
7. *Being neat* My friend behaves in neat and orderly ways.	an	s	mo	o	vo
8. *Being reliable* My friend consistently fulfills his or her commitments.	an	s	mo	o	vo
9. *Being genuine in behavior* My friend's behavior is natural and sincere.	an	s	mo	o	vo
10. *Accepting blame when at fault* My friend undefensively recognizes and accepts responsibility for his or her own misconduct.	an	s	mo	o	vo
11. *Respecting property rights of others* My friend deals in respectful ways with the personal property rights of others.	an	s	mo	o	vo
12. *Willingly sharing in the work* My friend willingly carries his or her share of the work load.	an	s	mo	o	vo

Number of Low Integrity Scores _____

APPENDIX 4

SEXUALLY TRANSMITTED DISEASE INFORMATION

The following information was excerpted from the website of the Center for Disease Control (CDC), www.cdc.gov. The purpose of this appendix is to give a quick look at some of the more common sexually transmitted diseases, their prevention, symptoms, and treatment. More complete information is provided on the CDC website. Neither this appendix nor the CDC website are intended to substitute for professional medical advice (see disclaimer following the Table of Contents).

Excellent information is also available from the websites of Web MD, at www.webmd.com, and Planned Parenthood, at www.plannedparenthood.org.

Because new information is continuously being made available, these websites are frequently updated. Therefore the attached information is a snapshot of what was available in June, 2003, and the reader is encouraged to visit the referenced websites to obtain more recent information.

The CDC website includes the following disclaimer:

This fact sheet is for information only and is not meant to be used for self-diagnosis or as a substitute for consultation with a health care provider. If you have any questions about the diseases described below or think that you may have a sexually transmitted disease, consult a health care provider.

CHLAMYDIA

Chlamydia is a common sexually transmitted disease (STD) caused by *Chlamydia trachomatis*, a bacterium, which can damage a woman's reproductive organs. Because symptoms of chlamydia are mild or absent, serious complications that cause irreversible damage, including infertility, can occur "silently" before a woman ever recognizes a problem.

Chlamydia can be transmitted during vaginal, anal, or oral sex. Chlamydia can also be passed from an infected mother to her newborn during vaginal childbirth.

Chlamydia is the most frequently reported bacterial sexually transmitted infection in the United States.

Chlamydia is known as a "silent" disease because three quarters of infected women and half of infected men have no symptoms. The infection is frequently not diagnosed or treated until complications develop.

In women, the bacteria initially attack the cervix (opening to the uterus) and the urethra (urine canal). The few women with symptoms might have an abnormal vaginal discharge or a burning sensation when urinating. When the infection spreads from the cervix to the fallopian tubes, some women still have no signs or symptoms; others have lower abdominal pain, low back pain, nausea, fever, pain during intercourse, and bleeding between menstrual periods. Whenever the infection spreads past the cervix into the upper reproductive system, permanent and irreversible damage can occur.

Men with signs or symptoms might have a discharge from the penis and a burning sensation when urinating. Men might also have burning and itching around the opening of the penis or pain and swelling in the testicles, or both.

If symptoms do occur, they usually appear within 1 to 3 weeks of exposure.

Chlamydia can be easily treated and cured with antibiotics. A single dose of azithromycin or a week of doxycycline (twice daily) are the most commonly used treatments. All sex partners must also be treated.

Safe sexual behavior and seeking proper health care can help keep people from becoming infected or re-infected with chlamydia and from experiencing chlamydia complications.

- ✓ Use condoms correctly every time you have sex.

- ✓ Limit the number of sex partners, and do not go back and forth between partners.

- ✓ Get a screening test.

If you think you are infected, avoid sexual contact, and see a health care provider immediately.

If you are told you are infected, notify all your sex partners immediately.

GENITAL HERPES

Herpes is a sexually transmitted disease (STD) caused by the herpes simplex viruses type 1 (HSV-1) and type 2 (HSV-2). Most individuals have no or only minimal signs or symptoms from HSV-1 or HSV-2 infection. When signs do occur, they typically appear as one or more blisters on or around the genitals or rectum. The blisters break, leaving tender ulcers (sores) that may take two to four weeks to heal the first time they occur. Typically, another outbreak can appear weeks or months after the first, but it almost always is less severe and shorter than the first episode. Although the infection can stay in the body indefinitely, the number of outbreaks tends to go down over a period of years.

HSV-1 and HSV-2 can be found and released from the sores that the viruses cause, but they also are released between episodes from skin that does not appear to be broken or to have a sore. A person almost always gets HSV-2 infection during sexual contact with someone who has a genital HSV-2 infection. HSV-1 causes infections of the mouth and lips, so-called "fever blisters." A person can get HSV-1 by coming into contact with the saliva of an infected person. HSV-1 infection of the genitals almost always is caused by oral-genital sexual contact with a person who has the oral HSV-1 infection.

The signs and symptoms associated with HSV-2 can vary greatly. Health care providers can diagnose genital herpes by visual inspection if the outbreak is typical, and by taking a sample from the sore(s). HSV infections can be difficult to diagnose between outbreaks. Blood tests which detect HSV-1 or HSV-2 infection may be helpful, although the results are not always clear cut.

There is no treatment that can cure herpes, but antiviral medications can shorten and prevent outbreaks during the period of time the person takes the medication.

The consistent and correct use of latex condoms can help protect against infection. However, condoms do not provide complete protection because the condom may not cover the herpes sore(s), and viral shedding may nevertheless occur. If either you or your partner have genital herpes, it is best to abstain from sex when symptoms or signs are present, and to use latex condoms between outbreaks.

GONORRHEA

Gonorrhea is caused by *Neisseria gonorrhoeae*, a bacterium that can grow and multiply easily in mucous membranes of the body. Gonorrhea bacteria can grow in the warm, moist areas of the reproductive tract, including the cervix (opening to the womb), uterus (womb), and fallopian tubes (egg canals) in women, and in the urethra (urine canal) in women and men. The bacteria can also grow in the mouth, throat, and anus.

Gonorrhea is spread through sexual contact (vaginal, oral, or anal). This includes penis-to-vagina, penis-to-mouth, penis-to-anus, mouth-to-vagina, and mouth-to-anus contact. Ejaculation does not have to occur for gonorrhea to be transmitted or acquired. Gonorrhea can also be spread from mother to child during birth.

Gonorrhea infection can spread to other unlikely parts of the body. For example, a person can get an eye infection after touching infected genitals and then the eyes. Individuals who have had gonorrhea and received treatment may get infected again if they have sexual contact with persons infected with gonorrhea.

When initially infected, the majority of men have some signs or symptoms. Symptoms and signs include a burning sensation when urinating and a yellowish white discharge from the penis. Sometimes men with gonorrhea get painful or swollen testicles.

In women, the early symptoms of gonorrhea are often mild, and many women who are infected have no symptoms of infection. Even when a woman has symptoms, they can be so non-specific as to be mistaken for a bladder or vaginal infection. The initial symptoms and signs in women include a painful or burning sensation when urinating and a vaginal discharge that is yellow or occasionally bloody. Women with no or mild gonorrhea symptoms are still at risk of developing serious complications from the infection. Untreated gonorrhea in women can develop into pelvic inflammatory disease (PID).

Symptoms of rectal infection include discharge, anal itching, soreness, bleeding, and sometimes painful bowel movements. Infections in the throat cause few symptoms.

In males, symptoms usually appear 2 to 5 days after infection, but it can take as long as 30 days for symptoms to begin. Regardless of symptoms, once a person is infected with gonorrhea, he or she can spread the infection to others if condoms or other protective barriers are not used during sex.

Many of the currently used antibiotics can successfully cure gonorrhea in adolescents and adults. Penicillin is a common antibiotic that is no longer used to treat gonorrhea, because many strains of the gonorrhea bacterium have become resistant to penicillin. Because many people with gonorrhea also have chlamydia, antibiotics for both infections are usually given together. Persons with gonorrhea should also be screened for other STDs.

It is important to take all of the medication prescribed to cure gonorrhea, even if the symptoms or signs stop before all the medication is gone. Although medication will stop the infection, it will not repair any permanent damage done by the disease. Persons who have had gonorrhea and have been treated can also get the disease again if they have sexual contact with an infected person.

Gonorrhea can be prevented as follows:

✓ **Use latex condoms correctly every time you have sex.**

Persons who choose to engage in sexual behaviors that can place them at risk for STDs should use latex condoms every time they have sex. A condom put on the penis before starting sex and worn until the penis is withdrawn can help protect both the male and the female partner from gonorrhea. When a male condom cannot be used appropriately, sex partners should consider using a female condom.

Condoms do not provide complete protection from all STDs. Sores and lesions of other STDs on infected men and women may be present in areas not covered by the condom, resulting in transmission of infection to another person.

- ✓ Limit the number of sex partners, and do not go back and forth between partners.

- ✓ Practice sexual abstinence, or limit sexual contact to one uninfected partner.

- ✓ If you think you are infected, avoid sexual contact and see a health care provider immediately.

Any genital symptoms such as discharge or burning during urination or unusual sore or rash should be a signal to stop having sex and to consult a health care provider immediately. If you are told you have gonorrhea or any other STD and receive treatment, you should notify all of your recent sex partners so that they can see a health care provider and be treated. This will reduce the risk that your partners will develop serious complications from gonorrhea and will reduce your own risk of becoming reinfected.

HEPATITIS B

Hepatitis B is caused by the Hepatitis B virus (HBV). It occurs when blood or body fluids from an infected preson enters the body of a person who is not immune. HBV is spread through having sex with an infected person without using a condom (the efficacy of latex condoms in preventing infection with HBV is unkown, but their proper use may reduce transmission), sharing needles or "works" when "shooting" drugs, through needlesticks or sharps exposures on the job, or from an infected mother to her baby during birth. Consider the risks if you are thinking about getting a tattoo or body piercing. You might get infected if the tools have someone else's blood on them.

About 30% of persons with HBV have no signs or symptoms. Signs and symptoms are less common in children than adults. Some signs and symptoms include jaundice, fatigue, abdominal pain, loss of appetite, nausea, vomiting, and joint pain.

Hepatitis B vaccine is the best protection. Long-term chronic effects including death from chronic liver disease can occur without vaccination.

SYPHILIS

Syphilis is a complex sexually transmitted disease (STD) caused by the bacterium *Treponema pallidum*. It has often been called "the great imitator" because so many of the signs and symptoms are indistinguishable from those of other diseases.

Syphilis is passed from person to person through direct contact with a syphilis sore. Sores occur mainly on the external genitals, vagina, anus, or in the rectum. Sores also can occur on the lips and in the mouth. Transmission of the organism occurs during vaginal, anal, or oral sex. Pregnant women with the disease can pass it to the babies they are carrying. Syphilis cannot be spread by toilet seats, door knobs, swimming pools, hot tubs, bath tubs, shared clothing, or eating utensils. The signs and symptoms in adults are:

Primary Stage. The time between infection with syphilis and the start of the first symptom can range from 10-90 days (average 21 days). The primary stage of syphilis is usually marked by the appearance of a single sore (called a chancre), but there may be multiple sores. The chancre is usually firm, round, small, and painless. It appears at the spot where syphilis entered the body. The chancre lasts 3-6 weeks, and it will heal on its own. If adequate treatment is not administered, the infection progresses to the secondary stage.

Secondary Stage. The second stage starts when one or more areas of the skin break into a rash that usually does not itch. Rashes can appear as the chancre is fading or can be delayed for weeks. The rash often appears as rough, red or reddish brown spots both on the palms of the hands and on the bottoms of the feet. The rash also may also appear on other parts of the body with different characteristics, some of which resemble other diseases. Sometimes the rashes are so faint that they are not noticed. Even without treatment, rashes clear up on their own. In addition to rashes, second-stage symptoms can include fever, swollen lymph glands, sore throat, patchy hair loss, headaches, weight loss, muscle aches, and tiredness. A person can easily pass the disease to sex partners when primary or secondary stage signs or symptoms are present.

Late Syphilis. The latent (hidden) stage of syphilis begins when the secondary symptoms disappear. Without treatment, the infected person still has syphilis even though there are no signs or symptoms. It remains in the body, and it may begin to damage the internal organs, including the brain, nerves, eyes, heart, blood vessels, liver, bones, and joints. This internal damage may show up many years later in the late or tertiary stage of syphilis. Late stage signs and symptoms include not being able to coordinate muscle movements, paralysis, numbness, gradual blindness and dementia. This damage may be serious enough to cause death.

While the health problems caused by syphilis in adults and newborns are serious in their own right, it is now known that the genital sores caused by syphilis in adults also make it easier to transmit and acquire HIV infection sexually. There is a 2- to 5-fold increased risk of acquiring HIV infection when syphilis is present.

A single dose of penicillin, an antibiotic, will cure a person who has had syphilis for less than a year. Larger doses are needed to cure someone who has had it for longer than a year. For people who are allergic to penicillin, other antibiotics are available to treat syphilis. There are no home remedies or over- the-counter drugs that will cure syphilis. Penicillin treatment will kill the syphilis bacterium and prevent further damage, but it will not repair any damage already done. Persons who receive syphilis treatment must abstain from sexual contact with new partners until the syphilis sores are completely healed. Persons with syphilis must notify their sex partners so that they also can be tested, and, if necessary, receive treatment.

Having had syphilis does not protect a person from getting it again.

Two people who know that they are not infected and who have sex only with each other cannot contract syphilis. When someone's syphilis status is unknown, a good defense against becoming infected during sex is to use a latex condom before beginning sex and to keep it on until the penis is withdrawn. However, condoms do not provide complete protection because syphilis sores can sometimes be on areas not covered by a condom. This is equally important for other STDs, including HIV, as well. Only lab tests can confirm whether someone has syphilis. Because syphilis sores can be hidden in the vagina, rectum, or mouth, it may not be obvious that a sex partner has syphilis. Washing the genitals, urinating, or douching after sex <u>does not</u> prevent STDs, including syphilis. Any unusual discharge, sore, or rash, especially in the groin area, should be a signal to stop having sex and to see a doctor at once.

TRICHOMONAS INFECTION

Trichomonas vaginalis is a microscopic parasite found worldwide. Infection with trichomonas is called trichomoniasis (trick-oh-moe-nye-uh-sis). Trichomoniasis is one of the most common sexually transmitted diseases, mainly affecting 16-to-35-year old women. In the United States, it is estimated that 2 million women become infected each year.

Trichomoniasis is spread through sexual activity. Infection is more common in women who have had multiple sexual partners.

A common misbelief is that infection can be spread by a toilet seat; this isn't likely, since the parasite cannot live long in the environment or on objects.

In women the signs and symptoms of infection range from having no symptoms (asymptomatic) to very symptomatic. Typical symptoms include foul smelling or frothy green discharge from the vagina, vaginal itching or redness. Other symptoms can include painful sexual intercourse, lower abdominal discomfort, and the urge to urinate. Most women who develop symptoms do so within 6 months of being infected.

Most men with this infection do not have symptoms. When symptoms are present, they most commonly are discharge from the urethra, the urge to urinate, and a burning sensation with urination.

Trichomonas infection is treatable. Your doctor will prescribe an antibiotic for you and all sexual partners you have had since becoming infected. If all current sexual partners are not treated, it is possible to become reinfected. Infants and children who are infected should be treated.

Trichomonas infection can be prevented by following these guidelines:

- ✓ Abstain from sexual intercourse; or,
- ✓ Use a latex condom properly, every time you have sexual intercourse, with every partner.

✓ Limit your sexual partners. The more sex partners you have, the greater your risk of encountering someone who has this or other STDs.

✓ If you are infected, your sexual partner(s) should be treated. This will prevent you from getting reinfected.

Once you are infected, you are not immune. You can get infected again.

HIV AND AIDS: ARE YOU AT RISK?

What is HIV and how can I get it?

HIV—the human immunodeficiency virus—is a virus that kills your body's "CD4 cells." CD4 cells (also called T-helper cells) help your body fight off infection and disease. HIV can be passed from person to person if someone with HIV infection has sex with or shares drug injection needles with another person. It also can be passed from a mother to her baby when she is pregnant, when she delivers the baby, or if she breast-feeds her baby.

You can get HIV:

✓ By having unprotected sex—sex without a condom—with someone who has HIV. The virus can be in an infected person's blood, semen, or vaginal secretions and can enter your body through tiny cuts or sores in your skin, or in the lining of your vagina, penis, rectum, or mouth.

✓ By sharing a needle and syringe to inject drugs or sharing drug equipment used to prepare drugs for injection with someone who has HIV.

✓ From a blood transfusion or blood clotting factor that you got before 1985. (But today it is unlikely you could get infected that way because all blood in the United States has been tested for HIV since 1985.)

Babies born to women with HIV also can become infected during pregnancy, birth, or breast-feeding.

You cannot get HIV:
- ✓ By working with or being around someone who has HIV.
- ✓ From sweat, spit, tears, clothes, drinking fountains, phones, toilet seats, or through everyday things like sharing a meal.
- ✓ From insect bites or stings.
- ✓ From donating blood.
- ✓ From a closed-mouth kiss (but there is a very small chance of getting it from open-mouthed or "French" kissing with an infected person because of possible blood contact).

How can I protect myself?
- ✓ Don't share needles and syringes used to inject drugs, steroids, vitamins, or for tattooing or body piercing. Also, don't share equipment ("works") used to prepare drugs to be injected. Many people have been infected with HIV, hepatitis, and other germs this way. Germs from an infected person can stay in a needle and then be injected directly into the next person who uses the needle.
- ✓ The surest way to avoid transmission of sexually transmitted diseases is to abstain from sexual intercourse, or to be in a longterm mutually monogamous relationship with a partner who has been tested and you know is uninfected.
- ✓ For persons whose sexual behaviors place them at risk for STDs, correct and consistent use of the male latex condom can reduce the risk of STD transmission. However, no protective method is 100 percent effective, and condom use cannot guarantee absolute protection against any STD. The more sex partners you have, the greater your chances are of getting HIV or other diseases passed through sex.
- ✓ Condoms lubricated with spermicides are no more effective than other lubricated condoms in protecting against the transmission of HIV and other STDs. In order to achieve the protective effect of condoms, they must be used correctly and consistently. Incorrect use can lead to condom slippage or breakage, thus diminishing their protective effect. Inconsistent use, e.g., failure to use condoms with every act of intercourse, can lead to STD transmission because transmission can occur with a single act of intercourse.

✓ Don't share razors or toothbrushes because of the possibility of contact with blood.
✓ If you are pregnant or think you might be soon, talk to a doctor or your local health department about being tested for HIV. Drug treatments are available to help you and reduce the chance of passing HIV to your baby if you have it.

Effectiveness of Condoms

Condoms are classified as medical devices and are regulated by the Food and Drug Administration (FDA). Condom manufacturers in the United States test each latex condom for defects, including holes, before it is packaged. The proper and consistent use of latex or polyurethane (a type of plastic) condoms when engaging in sexual intercourse—vaginal, anal, or oral—can greatly reduce a person's risk of acquiring or transmitting sexually transmitted diseases, including HIV infection.

There are many different types and brands of condoms available—however, only latex or polyurethane condoms provide a highly effective mechanical barrier to HIV. In laboratories, viruses occasionally have been shown to pass through natural membrane ("skin" or lambskin) condoms, which may contain natural pores and are therefore not recommended for disease prevention (they are documented to be effective for contraception). Women may wish to consider using the female condom when a male condom cannot be used.

For condoms to provide maximum protection, they must be used *consistently* (every time) and *correctly*. Several studies of correct and consistent condom use clearly show that latex condom breakage rates in this country are less than 2 percent. Even when condoms do break, one study showed that more than half of such breaks occurred prior to ejaculation.

When condoms are used reliably, they have been shown to prevent pregnancy up to 98 percent of the time among couples using them as their only method of contraception. Similarly, numerous studies among sexually active people have demonstrated that a properly used latex condom provides a high degree of protection against a variety of sexually transmitted diseases, including HIV infection.

WHAT IS AIDS?

AIDS–the acquired immunodeficiency syndrome - is a disease you get when HIV destroys your body's immune system. Normally, your immune system helps you fight off illness. When your immune system fails you can become very sick and can die.

How do I know if I have HIV or AIDS?

You might have HIV and still feel perfectly healthy. **The only way to know for sure if you are infected or not is to be tested.** Talk with a knowledgeable health care provider or counselor both before and after you are tested. You can go to your doctor or health department for testing or buy a home collection kit (for testing for HIV antibodies) at many pharmacies. To find out where to go in your area for HIV counseling and testing, call your local health department or the CDC National AIDS Hotline, at 1-800-342-AIDS (2437).

Your doctor or health care provider can give you a confidential HIV test. The information on your HIV test and test results are confidential, just as your other medical information. This means it can be shared only with people authorized to see your medical records. You can ask your doctor, health care provider, or HIV counselor at the place you are tested to explain who can obtain this information. For example, you may want to ask whether your insurance company could find out your HIV status if you make a claim for health insurance benefits or apply for life insurance or disability insurance.

In many states, you can be tested anonymously. These tests are usually given at special places known as anonymous testing sites. When you get an anonymous HIV test, the testing site records only a number or code with the test result, not your name. A counselor gives you this number at the time your blood, saliva, or urine is taken for the test, then you return to the testing site (or perhaps call the testing site, for example with home collection kits) and give them your number or code to learn the results of your test.

You are more likely to test positive for (be infected with) HIV if you:

- ✓ Have ever shared injection drug needles and syringes or "works."
- ✓ Have ever had sex without a condom with someone who had HIV.
- ✓ Have ever had a sexually transmitted disease, like chlamydia or gonorrhea.
- ✓ Received a blood transfusion or a blood clotting factor between 1978 and 1985.
- ✓ Have ever had sex with someone who has done any of those things

The only way to determine for sure whether you are infected is to be tested for HIV infection. You cannot rely on symptoms to know whether or not you are infected with HIV. Many people who are infected with HIV do not have any symptoms at all for many years.

(Author's note: The Web MD website offers this additional information with regard to HIV symptoms:

Many people have a flulike illness 3 to 6 weeks after they are first exposed to HIV. These symptoms may develop only a few days after exposure. This first stage of infection with HIV is called acute retroviral syndrome. Symptoms of acute retroviral syndrome, which are often mistaken for symptoms of another viral infection such as influenza or mononucleosis, include:

- ✓ Fever.
- ✓ Sore throat.
- ✓ Headache.
- ✓ Muscle aches and joint pain.
- ✓ Enlarged lymph nodes in the neck, armpits, and groin.
- ✓ Skin rash.
- ✓ Abdominal cramps, nausea, or vomiting.
- ✓ Diarrhea.

The symptoms of acute retroviral syndrome usually disappear on their own after 2 to 3 weeks. After the initial infection with HIV, a person may go many years without any sign of illness. When symptoms do occur, they may change a lot and be hard to describe.)

The CDC website continues:

The following <u>may be</u> warning signs of infection with HIV:

- ✓ rapid weight loss
- ✓ dry cough
- ✓ recurring fever or profuse night sweats
- ✓ profound and unexplained fatigue
- ✓ swollen lymph glands in the armpits, groin, or neck
- ✓ diarrhea that lasts for more than a week
- ✓ white spots or unusual blemishes on the tongue, in the mouth, or in the throat
- ✓ pneumonia
- ✓ red, brown, pink, or purplish blotches on or under the skin or inside the mouth, nose, or eyelids
- ✓ memory loss, depression, and other neurological disorders

However, no one should assume they are infected if they have any of these symptoms. Each of these symptoms can be related to other illnesses. Again, **the only way to determine whether you are infected is to be tested for HIV infection.**

What can I do if the test shows I have HIV?

Although HIV is a very serious infection, many people with HIV and AIDS are living longer, healthier lives today, thanks to new and effective treatments. It is very important to make sure you have a doctor who knows how to treat HIV. If you don't know which doctor to use, talk with a health care professional or trained HIV counselor. If you are pregnant or are planning to become pregnant, this is especially important.

There also are other things you can do for yourself to stay healthy. Here are a few:

- ✓ Follow your doctor's instructions. Keep your appointments. Your doctor may prescribe medicine for you. Take the medicine just

the way he or she tells you to because taking only some of your medicine gives your HIV infection more chance to grow.
- ✓ Get immunizations (shots) to prevent infections such as pneumonia and flu. Your doctor will tell you when to get these shots.
- ✓ If you smoke or if you use drugs not prescribed by your doctor, quit.
- ✓ Eat healthy foods. This will help keep you strong, keep your energy and weight up, and help your body protect itself.
- ✓ Exercise regularly to stay strong and fit.
- ✓ Get enough sleep and rest.

How can I find out more about HIV and AIDS?

You can call the CDC National AIDS Hotline at **1-800-342-2437** (Spanish/ Español: **1-800-344-7432**; TTY access: **1-800-243-7889**). The Hotline is staffed with people trained to answer your questions about HIV and AIDS in a prompt and confidential manner. Staff at the Hotline can offer you a wide variety of written materials and put you in touch with organizations in your area that deal with HIV and AIDS.

On the Internet, you can get information on HIV and AIDS from the CDC Division of HIV/ AIDS Prevention at http://www.cdc.gov/hiv/dhap.htm. Other sources of information are the CDC National Prevention Information Network, http://www.cdcnpin.org/ or AIDSinfo, http://www.aidsinfo.nih.gov/.

For more information
DSTD—http://www.cdc.gov/std//

CDC National STD Hotline
(800) 227-8922 or (800) 342-2437
En Espanol (800) 344-7432
TTY for the Deaf and Hard of Hearing (800) 243-7889
**National HPV and Cervical Cancer
Hotline** (919) 361-4848
Resource Center www.ashastd.org/hpvccrc/

National Herpes Hotline
(919) 361-8488

CDC NPIN
P.O. Box 6003
Rockville, MD 20849-6003
1-800-458-5231
1-888-282-7681 Fax
1-800-243-7012 TTY
www.cdcnpin.org
info@cdcnpin.org

American Social Health Association
P. O. Box 13827
Research Triangle Park, NC 27709-3827
1-800-783-9877
http://www.ashastd.org

APPENDIX 5

SEXUAL FANTASY STORIES

Condensed from *My Secret Garden* and *Men In Love*
By Nancy Friday

Although I devote Chapter 11 to a discussion of fantasies, it is not to redo Nancy Friday's great work. It is to build on her work for the benefit of helping people improve their quality love relationships. She has done the research and collected the stories. I have described the importance of fantasies in enhancing emotional closeness, and also the considerations that factor into the decision to share or not share sexual fantasies with your partner.

In this appendix I include a variety of condensed fantasies from Nancy Friday's two pioneering books, *My Secret Garden* (women's fantasies) and *Men in Love* (men's fantasies). I include them to encourage readers to expand their limits, increase their opportunity for emotional closeness, and enhance their chances of success in the search for a quality love relationship. As William Blake says: "The road of excess leads to the palace of wisdom."

> Hopefully the messages here are clear:
> Fantasies are crazy
> Enjoy them
> They are OK

Along with the condensed stories I have included condensed explanatory comments from Nancy Friday. I encourage all readers to purchase the referenced books by Nancy Friday and read them to develop an even better understanding of sexual fantasies.

Read these fantasies with an open mind, listening to Nancy Friday's explanations. Keep in mind what you have learned in *Love Is Not A Game (But You Should Know The Odds)* about sexual deprivation, chemical connection, emotional closeness, and emotional maturity.

True soulmates ( ) can enjoy these fantasies without judgmental inhibitions.

Enjoy!

Here are the stories:

Anonymity (Linda). *"I'm at this very posh hair store. I've just had a facial, so I've got this mask on, and there are cool cotton pads on my eyes. I can't see a thing. On the other side of a curtain is a row of young men—big strapping types—half nude. They are there to service us. The guy in charge strides up and down with a whip making sure none of them misses a stroke—so to speak. That first moment is wildly exciting: I'm lying there, my legs in a big V, waiting for my particular guy. I can't see him approach, I don't know he's near, until his tongue suddenly flicks me with the most excruciating Zing! To him I'm just another cunt. But suddenly, with me, it's different. I'm special. The life he's aroused in my cunt communicates to him, this incredible sexuality I have...His cock is enormous now as he brings me closer. The whipmaster gives him a terrible blow, but the guy is lost to everything but me...We're getting closer and closer, together now, and we reach the most glorious climax of our lives!"*

NF comment: *Anonymity is fantasy's best friend. It heightens romance and adds drama; it increases pleasure and eliminates guilt, fantasy's enemy. ... No matter how it's achieved, a woman will strive for anonymity in her fantasies for its known sure-fire power of release and lift.*

<u>Oral Sex (Walter)</u>. "There is this beautiful girl sitting next to me. She slowly unbuttons my shirt and runs her fingers through the hair on my chest, then slowly goes down further and unzips my pants and sucks my cock. Pulling my pants down further, she inserts two fingers up my ass. By this time I've got my fingers up her. She stands in front of me nude. She then starts kissing and licking me all over. I shove her head down to my cock. She sucks it 'til I come. She takes my cum in her mouth, and then we are kissing and I am tasting my own cum. Then we just lay there together holding each other."

NF comment: *Though I wince when men fantasize about shooting sperm all over the woman's face, is this really a notion of aggression? He isn't covering her with acid. It is the essence of himself, the stuff he loves most. How exhilarating if, when a woman who stands at least in part for that no-saying figure of long ago drinks the man's semen, it turns out that she loves it! Approval of his hidden self—at last!*

<u>The Audience (Caroline).</u> "Ever since I had to do a love scene in a play, I've needed to feel that the same audience is there when I'm making love at home or anywhere else. In the beginning I tried to keep a little "distance" between the personal me, and me, the actress, making love in front of all those people. But I couldn't. My nipples would become tight and erect. I began wearing tighter, more see-through blouses. Now even if I'm with the man I love, somehow in my mind behind his back is the audience, and they're applauding him for making love to me and applauding me for responding to him in such a loving way. And as my own excitement mounts and mounts, the applause gets louder and louder..."

NF comment: *We spend most of our fucking lives trying to be alone, trying to improve the privacy of our fucking. But fantasy goes in the opposite direction: more often than not there are other people present. Anyone who has ever fucked in the warm sunlight of a (seemingly) secluded beach must admit the added excitement which the imminence of an audience brings to an already fine fuck...or she's a liar.*

<u>Cunt Worship (Dan)</u>. "*My fantasies revolve around that most delightful of creations, the Glorious Female Cunt. I love to look at my partner's body, and tell her what a beautiful cunt she has and how much I want to kiss it and taste it and caress it with my tongue, and how much I want to tease and caress her clit and bring it to a thunderous, star-bursting exploding release. The climax is when I enter my partner, but the most exquisite and enjoyable part is my adoration of the Glorious Female Cunt.*"

NF Comment: *I love these fantasies. They fill me with hope. It has long been my conviction that oral sex is the key: If women could be made to feel heart and soul that what is between their legs is lovable, it would be an enormous step toward feminine self-esteem.*

RLH note: It is interesting to me that the "Windows 2000" spell check dictionary in my computer contains the words "cock" and "prick" and "cunt" but does not contain the word "soulmate"!

<u>Rape (Julietta)</u>. "*While I enjoy going to bed with some guy I dig almost any time, I especially like it if there's something in the air that lets me think I'm doing it against my will. That I'm being forced by the man's overwhelming physical strength. So when I'm in bed with someone, when I get to a certain point, when I really become excited, I close my eyes and I imagine that I've been brought to some warehouse, or place like that, against my will. I'm stripped naked*

and the only thing I'm allowed to wear is a black silk mask. I can imagine the men, all big and powerfully built. They're naked too, while they wait their turn with me. Meanwhile, the guy who is really with me, every time he tries a different position, I pretend to myself that it's the next man in line. So it's always exciting because I have an endless supply of men fucking me... That picture in my mind makes me come every time."

NF comment: Rape does for a woman's sexual fantasy what the first martini does for her in reality: both relieve her of responsibility and guilt. It's worth repeating my conviction that fantasy need have nothing to do with suppressed wish-fulfillment. These women would run a mile from anyone who raised a finger against them. The message isn't in the plot—the old hackneyed rape story—but in the emotions that story releases.

<u>Visual Gratification (Josh).</u> *"I have often fantasized about making love to women who model in magazines, nude and semi-nude. I see one in a magazine and I fantasize seeing her walking down the street. We go to my apartment. I say: "It's hard to believe your breasts are size forty-four, you being five-three," and she takes her blouse and bra off and out pop two big breasts. I stare at them, and I touch, lick, kiss, and suck them. Then she says, "Have you got a camera?" and I say, "Yes." So she strips nude and says, "Take your own picture," and I do. We fuck and fuck, and later when she leaves she says, "I enjoyed my day."*

NF comment: We speak of "feasting the eyes," a metaphor that tells us there is a primitive, even somatic pleasure to be derived from something supposedly so intangible as looking. Satisfying food is being offered, a hunger is being fed. A walk through a rose garden shows these needs are felt equally by both sexes, even thought there is no socially acceptable way to say "Feast your eyes on me."

Humiliation (Nathalie). *"My fantasy is that of being spanked: I have always provoked the spanking, it's never unjustified. My lover says, very quietly, "All right, that's enough!" I say "Don't order me around." He says, "You're asking for a good spanking." I say, "I'd like to see you try it," in a very taunting manner. At which point he grabs me, pulls down my panties, and turns me over on his knee. I am embarrassed and scared. He usually uses his hand, spanking me maybe two dozen times, very hard. I am sobbing and enraged. The rage turns to humiliation, which turns to submission. At the end he forces me back on the bed and enters me, at which point I am eager to do whatever he asks."*

NF comment: *Nathalie may get spanked into submission, but we don't need Nathalie to tell us that it isn't the spanking itself that turns her on. It's the state to which that humiliating act reduces her that matters.*

Anal Sex (Jackie). *"We first tongue kiss, then I kiss her face, forehead, lips, neck. I begin sucking her titties and she takes my prick in her hand asking me all along the way if I want certain things done. I lick and tongue kiss her big glorious, juicy ass, rubbing my face and my nose in the lovely crack, doing analingus. (A beautiful ass on a woman automatically turns the heads of we men who can kiss a woman's ass in our minds forty times a day!). She says "Tell me what you want me to do. I want to be your very own whore. My pussy belongs to you alone and it always will." I pull her up and lay her on the bed and start fucking her madly but sensitively. Then she screams and tells me how good I am. I then wet my finger and stick it up her sweet asshole gently. She takes off, screaming and sobbing and demanding: "Fuck me, fuck me, oh fuck me!" Meanwhile she gives me the finger in return up the ass. We both see stars together."*

NF comment: *My own disinterest in anal sex, even aversion to it, speaks of my particular lifelong fears and prejudices. As one psycho-*

analyst said to me, "Considering that both sexes begin by taking pleasure in anal activities early in life, and that our earliest experiences cut the deepest, you might say that to stop *being interested is more unnatural, more repressed, than the reverse. The love affair on the part of both sexes with the breast never ends, but women turn off all their interest in the anus." Why?* Because mother passes on her own repressions to her daughter far more successfully than to her son.

<u>The Thrill of the Forbidden (Emma).</u> *"I am hiding from the others. We are playing a game of 'hide-and-seek' and I have been given a head start to find a hiding place. At the top of the house I have found an empty room. Quickly, in the dark, I slide under the bed. The others are far away, except for one pair of footsteps that is getting closer and closer. I catch my breath, my heart pounding, because I know it is the one person in the group I want to have find me. He slides under the bed beside me in the darkness. I hardly dare breath as I listen for the others' voices. My skin is alive, the excitement running all through me. His mouth caresses me all over. My hands find his erection like a rock. The voices on the floor below are calling to one another, "Have you found them?" The louder their approaching voices get, the more urgent our bodies grow. Among the others I hear my boyfriend's voice, and the fear and anxiety I feel make me hotter. "More!" I demand. "More!" Our fucking is paced in double time to the steps coming closer and closer. And we get closer and closer, out of control, until I come."*

NF comment: At full strength, the sensation of guilt contains the possibility of being discovered. My own fantasies often ride high on the risk of doing the forbidden. I am by nature, like a lot of other women, the "faithful type." For us, fantasies involving this or that sexually attractive man give us the desired sexual kick without the real guilt. In fact, guilt, the deterrent in reality, has been transformed into guilt, the exciter. We win both ways.

<u>Water Sports (Fitz)</u>. *"My fantasies are an outgrowth of an incident that occurred during my adolescence. I was in the midst of a heavy petting session with a girl in a secluded wooded area when she suddenly said, "I gotta pee." She then yanked down her panties and peed right there in front of me. I was fascinated, watching her thick, copious yellow stream rush to the ground. I was sexually aroused by this incident. My sexual fantasies thus always revolve around a woman who desperately needs to relieve herself. I come to climax when she pees."*

NF comment: *"Nothing human is alien to me." "The proper study of man is man." I nod assent to these tag ends of philosophy right along with the best of you. But the eroticization of pissing? How can that be? It seems to me that it is not the urine which excites, but the act. In short, "being very naughty," a deep-rooted need to rebel against our normal everyday restraints. There are obviously many people who, "normal" in all other respects, need an escape which is different.*

<u>I Am Beautiful (Betty).</u> *"During the last phase of intercourse is when I fantasize. I pretend I have turned into a very glamorous woman (in real life I know I'm somewhat plain). When I begin feeling myself to be this other woman, I mount my husband and give myself a good working out on his gorgeous cock. I close my eyes and seem to be watching this other beautiful woman who is me from some other place, outside myself. I can see her so vividly that I want to shout encouragement to her...she loves it so much. I want to say to her, 'Go on, go on! Enjoy it, you deserve it.'"*

NF comment: *Women respond so directly to the promise of more beauty that even factories have discovered that better mirrors in the ladies' room means higher production from the women workers. So no matter what her beauty in reality, every woman who enters the "House of Fantasy" will want a reassuring moment in the "Transformation*

Room." *Illusions of greater beauty, even fantasy illusions, heighten sex by heightening the woman's own awareness of her desirability.*

<u>S&M (Eliot)</u>. *"I act out my fantasies with submissive females. This actually happened. She came to my studio and I soon had her on her knees, her hands tied behind her, naked but for a dog collar and leash. I sat on the bed, the leash in one hand and a whip in the other, and told her what I was going to do to her. At first she was terrified. But I told her it is because you don't dare do it that you must do it. This is the ultimate fascination. I calmed her fears, tied her spread-eagle on the bed, and whipped her, gently at first, then building from there. As soon as she realized that it wasn't really going to hurt and that nothing terrible was going to happen to her, she became more sexually excited; and the experience blew her mind."*

NF comment: *To begin, I had to move from the point of view of the shocked judgmental observer; get rid of the relentlessly egocentric picture of myself as possible victim. I was to enter a make-believe world of mirrors, contradictions, and opposites. Fantasies like this illustrate men's ultimate love/rage polarization.* Beneath their wildly differing and exotic details, the common denominator is fury at the loss of authority and control to women. *The man is taking revenge for hurts he has felt ever since he was a boy. S&M fantasies provide a safe outlet.*

<u>Earth Mother (Vivian)</u>. *"Jimmy put me into this position that inspired the idea that I was being planted. I mean, you can't have the feeling that you're being planted unless your cunt is pointed straight up at the sky, can you? I remember looking up and seeing him boring straight down into me. I felt very wide and open, waiting for him to fill me up with his thrust. Waiting for him to plant seed like I was a large, warm, fertile hole in the earth. In fact I was all hole. I was all the holes, I was the earth. I was planted again and again. It was so*

exciting...and so right. Lying there with my legs up in the air, it seemed, at last, the most natural position in the world."

NF comment: *Many women live the earth mother fantasy. Of all women's sexual fantasies, those that depend on the idea of woman as the symbol of fertility are probably the least threatening to both men and women. Even the fantasy of a matriarchal society where men are fed to satisfy women's sexual appetites is close enough to mythology and to "nature" to be acceptable. But for all its Mother's Oats cycle-of-life connotations, the image of fertility is potent to some women.*

<u>Two Women (Clive).</u> *"My ex-girlfriend (Anne) and my wife (Jane) were friends long before I knew either of them. I am constantly being excited by seeing Anne in very skimpy clothing. One Saturday, Jane tells me that she and Anne had started discussing sex and even got so horny that they played with each other a little bit. She says that she would like to have a threesome with Anne. She tells me that she will go to the store; and while she is gone, I am to try to seduce Anne. I am successful and am eating Anne's juicy pussy on Jane's return. Jane comes into the room and tells me that it's not nice to screw without her. She undresses and starts kissing Anne's breasts. It is not long before Anne comes. Anne swings around and starts eating Jane's pussy, while I am screwing Anne from behind. We all have orgasms and I hold both of these women while we rest."*

NF comment: *In the end, the image of women making love to women grips the male imagination because it expresses one of the dominant themes of male fantasy: sexually insatiable women.* Women who would not dream of saying no. *In reality, this is not easily accomplished. Jealousy rarely sleeps. The man who dares suggest multiple sex to his lover is usually met with tears or anger. In these fantasies it is important to note that the women are described as not being jealous of one another.*

REFERENCES/RECOMMENDED READINGS

This is a list of the books that I have quoted and/or condensed in the text of my story. I highly recommend reading each one as they have much to say and I could only touch the surface, bringing forth what seemed particularly relevant to the soulmate search.

Bach, Richard. *The Bridge Across Forever—a lovestory.* New York: William Morrow & Co., 1984.

Bach, Richard. *Illusions.* New York: Dell Publishing Co., Inc., 1977.

Bessell, Harold. *The Love Test.* New York: Warner Books, 1984.

Blake, William. *The Essential Blake.* Selected by Stanley Kunitz. Hopewell, N. J. The Ecco Press, 1987.

Brilliant, Ashleigh. *I Have Abandoned My Search for Truth, and Am Now Looking for a Good Fantasy.* Santa Barbara, CA: Woodbridge Press Publishing, 1980.

Casteneda, Carlos. *The Teachings of Don Juan: A Yaqui Way of Knowledge.* New York: Washington Square Press, 1968.

Eichenlaub, John E. *The Marriage Art.* New York: Lyle Stuart, 1961.

Friday, Nancy. *Men in Love—Men's Sexual Fantasies: The Triumph of Love Over Rage.* New York: Dell Publishing, 1980.

Friday, Nancy. *My Secret Garden—Women's Sexual Fantasies.* New York: Simon & Schuster, 1973.

Gibran, Kahlil. *The Prophet.* New York: Alfred A. Knopf, 1923.

Horney, Karen. *Neurosis and Human Growth–the struggle toward self-realization.* New York: W. W. Norton & Company, 1950.

Moore, Thomas. *SoulMates—Honoring the Mysteries of Love and Relationship.* New York: HarperCollins Publishers, 1994.

Peck, M. Scott. *The Road Less Traveled—A New Psychology of Love, Traditional Values, and Spiritual Growth.* New York: Simon & Schuster, 1978.

Robinson, Marie. *The Power of Sexual Surrender.* New York: Signet Books, 1959.

ABOUT THE AUTHORS

Randy Hurlburt, B.S.E., M.S.E., M.P.A.

Relationship expert Randy Hurlburt has advanced degrees from Princeton University and the University of Southern California, graduating with highest honors and Phi Beta Kappa.

Randy has 20 years experience evaluating love relationships. He has been around the world in his own search for a soulmate. In collaboration with world-renowned psychologist and therapist Harold Bessell, Ph.D., he has blended his own experiences and the experiences of others to form a new strategy for romantic life.

Randy has devoted his life to understanding what love is all about. Observing from his own personal experience that most self-help relationship books sadly miss the mark, Randy has hit the bull's eye with *Love Is Not A Game (But You Should Know The Odds)*. This is a life-changing book that brings logic and love together in a practical, reader-friendly story.

Randy lives in San Diego, California. He is blessed with two children from a first marriage and, using the system described in this book, is now engaged to be married in a new love relationship, one that is not a game.

Harold Bessell, Ph.D.

Dr. Bessell received his Ph.D. from Purdue University and practiced clinical psychology for over 30 years in La Jolla, California. He researched and developed the famous Bessell Measurement of Emotional Maturity Scale. He is also author of highly acclaimed books including *Romance With The Right Person, The Parent Book,* and *The Love Test,* a book explaining how you can predict the future chances for success in your love relationship.

Recognized as an authority in the development of emotional maturity in children, Dr. Bessell was co-creator of The Magic Circle, part of the Human Development Program.

Dr. Bessell taught at Wichita University, University of California at San Diego, San Diego State University, and National University. He was chairman of the Theory Department of the California School of Psychology in San Diego, and he was past president of the San Diego Psychological Association.

Dr. Bessell appeared on top national television and radio programs, and his articles have appeared in many periodicals including Psychology Today, The American Journal of Psychotherapy, McCalls, and Redbook.

Books by Harold Bessell, Ph.D.

The Love Test

Romance With The Right Partner

The Parent Book

If you are interested in receiving more information about any of these books, direct your inquiry to:

Insights of Io
5519 Clairemont Mesa Blvd. #140
San Diego, CA 92117

Or you may visit our Web site at **www.loveisnotagame.com**

Jim Judy

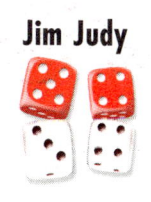

DISCOVER WHAT IT TAKES
TO FIND SPECIAL LOVE
AND EXCITING SEX

Meet Jim and Judy. They have a typical American love relationship. When they rolled the dice and fell in love they thought it would last forever.

It lasted through marriage and kids, until chronic unfulfillment, disappointment, and discouragement resulted in divorce.

They are out kissing frogs again…

Love relationships are not for the fainthearted.

Using the unique "Love Dice," *Love Is Not A Game (But You Should Know The Odds)* realistically portrays the obstacles to finding special love and exciting sex. Chapters such as "Kissing Frogs" and "Sex is like Water" create memorable images showing how to overcome these obstacles once you know the secrets of the Love Dice.

Love Is Not A Game offers strategies to deal with the sexual and emotional deprivations that cause couples to jump into relationships that are not good love. And true-life stories openly deal with the confusion that often causes divorce.

Controversial and compelling,

**Love Is Not A Game
(But You Should Know The Odds)**

will challenge you to learn more about life and love.

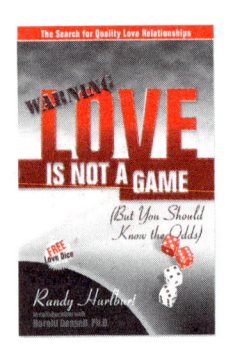

Books Make Great Gifts

Order Form

Love Is Not A Game
(But You Should Know The Odds)

☐ YES. Please send____copies of *Love Is Not A Game (But You Should Know The Odds)* at $16.95 each. (Please also send a **FREE** set of Love Dice with each book ordered.)

My check or money order for $_____is enclosed and includes $3.00 shipping for one book and $1.00 for each additional book.

Name   _____
Organization _____
Address   _____
City/State/Zip _____
Phone   _____
Email   _____

Payment must accompany orders. Please allow 3 weeks for delivery. Make your check payable and return to:

Insights of Io
**5519 Clairemont Mesa Blvd. #140
San Diego, CA 92117**

☐ YES. I am interested in having Randy Hurlburt speak or give a seminar about quality love relationships. Please send me information.

**You can also call toll free: 1-877-MAGIC-04
or visit our Web site: www.loveisnotagame.com**

DO YOU KNOW THE ODDS OF LOVE?

Whether it's Valentine's Day or any other day, lovers everywhere are wondering—"What are the chances that our love will succeed?"

The answer is "Not very good, unless you know what you are doing."

If you are looking for something special in a love relationship, then you need to know the "Secrets of the Love Dice." From romantic chemistry to sex, fantasies, emotional maturity, and fear, the Love Dice explain it all with memorable clarity and simplicity.

Love Is Not A Game (But You Should Know The Odds) clearly lays out what you need to know to find good love, very good love, or best of all, a soulmate relationship. The specially designed Love Dice tell you the odds of finding the quality love relationship that you want. These unique Love Dice make it easy to remember the twelve relationship secrets contained in the book.

Receive your **FREE** set of Love Dice when you purchase this book. You can enjoy experimenting at home with the Love Dice. Just return the coupon on the reverse side of this page.

Insights of Io distributes the free Love Dice as a part of our dedication to revealing hidden truths about quality love relationships. One-half of all net proceeds from book sales is donated to organizations that assist victims of bad love.

FREE
Love Dice

For use with the book

Love Is Not A Game
(But You Should Know The Odds)

We want everyone to know and understand the secrets of the Love Dice. So **FREE DICE** are offered with every copy of the book *Love Is Not A Game (But You Should Know The Odds)*.

☐ YES. Please send me a **FREE** set of Love Dice.

Name _____
Organization _____
Address _____
City/State/Zip _____
Phone _____
Email _____

Photocopies of this form are not accepted. Please allow 3 weeks for delivery. Include $1.00 for postage, and return this form to

Insights of Io
**5519 Clairemont Mesa Blvd. #140
San Diego, CA 92117**

Remember: **Love Is Not A Game!**